FELIPE REY DE CASTRO
and the Agrupación Católica Universitaria

BIOGRAPHICAL ESSAY

FÉLIX VARELA COLLECTION # 67

ENGLISH EDITION

EDICIONES UNIVERSAL, Miami, Florida, 2024

Roberto Méndez Martínez

FELIPE REY DE CASTRO
and the Agrupación Católica Universitaria

BIOGRAPHICAL ESSAY

Copyright © 2023 by Roberto Méndez Martínez &
Agrupación Católica Universitaria (ACU)

First English edition, 2024

EDICIONES UNIVERSAL
P.O. Box 450353 (Shenandoah Station)
Miami, FL 33245-0353 USA
(Founded 1965)

e-mail: ediciones@ediciones.com
http://www.ediciones.com

Library of Congress Catalog No.: 2024931271
ISBN (paperback edition): 978-1-59388-349-2
ISBN (e-book edition): 978-1-59388-352-2

Composition of text: María Cristina Zarraluqui

Cover design: Efraín Zabala
Final cover design: Luis García Fresquet

On the cover portrait of Fr. Felipe Rey de Castro, SJ.

All rights
are reserved. No part of
this book may be reproduced or transmitted
in any form or by any electronic or mechanical form,
including photocopiers, recorders or computerized systems, without the written
consent of the author, except for brief excerpts incorporated in book reviews
or in magazines. For additional information contact
Ediciones Universal.

To the memory of my mother Josefina Martínez Álvarez, formed since infancy in Ignatian spirituality in the shadow of the temple of Sacred Heart Church on Reina Street.

Truly, truly, I say to you, unless a grain of wheat falls into the earth and dies, it remains alone; but if it dies, it bears much fruit.
                    John 12, 24

Table of Contents

Prologue 11
By way of introduction 13
I   Seed that fell on good soil 15
II   Origins of a vocation 25
III   Promise fulfilled 39
IV   Formation of the select 45
V   First steps 51
VI   Dangers of politics 71
VII   Character of a founder 85
VIII   The social apostolate 91
IX   Evangelization and social work in Las Yaguas 97
X   Conquest of the university 115
XI   Consecration and surrender 127
XII   Politics as service 133
XIII   Catholic Action and Agrupación Católica 151
XIV   The female world: toward Mystic Rose 163
XV   Times of consolation 175
XVI   Fr. Rey and the Agrupación in the world 191
XVII   Crusade of love of Fr. Lombardi and Fr. Rey 197

| XVIII | The road to the Father | 207 |

| XIX | The harvest | 219 |

Bibliography 231

Index 239

Appendix
Consecrated to Jesus through Mary in the
Agrupación Católica Universitaria 245

Editor's translation of the original Spanish letter
included in November 1952 issue of *Esto-Vir* 253

Reproduction of original letter included
in November 1952 issue of *Esto-Vir* 255

Editor's translation of the Cardinal García's prayer
for beatification of Felipe Rey de Castro 256

Cardinal Garcia's prayer for beatification
of Felipe Rey de Castro 257

Prologue

Fear of the truth

I hope that no one will rush to say, influenced by Terence, that I am afraid of telling the truth in order not to break the sortilege of all that Roberto Méndez, Ph.D., delights us with, once I am done rambling, in this sketch, excuse me, History with capital "h," on the life and work of the always endearing Fr. Felipe Rey de Castro, S.J.

It is because of an inseparable pairing between biographer and biographed that the author of this prologue is weary of the sentence of Tunisian playwright Publius Terence, that about "Veritas odiumparit," which in common Castilian becomes the title of this essay, fear of the truth.

It is a contagious fear, because I dare say that such fear is shared and even contagious. It is shared by writer and, needless to say, more so historian. And since that fear does not paralyze, it is best that the good historian feel it. And that fear, which I dare say was experienced by Méndez Martínez, Ph.D., because in the face of such a personage as that affectionate Galician, that ingratiated and identified with Havana and very quickly with its people, that was unafraid to look after the 400 officers, many of them injured, that took refuge in the National Hotel on September 8, 1933.

It also goes to show that Rey de Castro, "forger of the select," as full-throated Spanish precursors cackled, was no elitist, and was always ready to serve at a moment's notice wherever his presence was fruitful. Certainly, a forger of high-flying professionals who knew how to toil at lower levels when necessary. That anecdote I so admired since I first came across it, redacted by expert hands in the Diary of the House and Temple of Reina, in the archives of said House portrays him better than the glossies and obituaries published in *Esto Vir* at the time of his untimely death.

The historian does and should indeed have fear of the truth. Only in that way does he pass from compiler or simple redactor of facts to the category that we all wish to attain. Not out of fear, embarrassment or timidity, but rather out of plain righteousness. And that is the category, the only fitting one for Dr. Roberto Méndez resulting from his historical biography which you will enjoy. I promise it.

José Luis Sáez, S.J.
Santo Domingo, D.R.

By way of Introduction

One of the most difficult tasks I have had to face in my life as a writer and researcher has been the entrustment of this book by the Agrupación Católica Universitaria in Miami. For starters, because authoring of it brings great responsibility, as it will be the first biography of Father Felipe Rey de Castro, SJ. Although there are earlier writings on his founding and direction of that Marian sodality, there is no book prior to this one that takes a biographical approach to the study of its protagonist and, additionally, because it will be used to support a process of canonization that got underway recently and that calls for very careful discernment of a life's trajectory and must show not only his human merits, but also his heroic virtues. More than once I have had to pause and consider if I might be incapable of bringing this charge to safe harbor, yet persistence and prayer have helped me overcome weaknesses.

As often happens with first biographies of great personages, one must break ground others will later tread in laboring to draft evermore exact images of a priest and of a sodality. It may be best to start with a modest summary of what has been available to be researched, so that others may uncover that they hold missing pieces of the mosaic. Hence, if this firstling book is to be worth anything, may it be to announce where additional research is needed to complete, in full color, the image I was able to sketch here.

A number of difficulties besieged my work at first, starting with the rather wide dispersion of archives to research, the loss of a great many documents that might have facilitated the work, and the nearly absolute absence of witnesses within Cuba. And this was compounded by the impossibility of traveling to places where the biographed was born and formed, as well the inability to consult other relevant collections. These shortcomings were countered thanks to the assistance of Mr. Efraín Zabala, who has not only been my contact with the ACU in Miami, but also a regular provider of electronic files to nurture my study. Similarly, I must thank the Society of Jesus in Cuba, especially Fr. Román Espadas, SJ, for his counsel and assistance in getting access to other sources. I do not wish to overlook *Palabra Nueva* [*New Word*] magazine and its chief editor Yarelis Rico that so generously offered online and print editions to disseminate the article that first shared some of the initial fruits.

Also essential was the support of my wife that sacrificed herself for over two years so I might conclude this work. Under very difficult conditions she assumed lone responsibility for day-to-day affairs while I, at my workstation, strived to unravel fragmentary information, compared data, filled gaps and gave these pages final form.

We all know that God's time is not identical to that of his greatly limited human creatures. Perhaps my remaining life will not be long enough to offer an opportunity to be present at Father Rey's beatification, but I thank Our Lord for calling on me to serve humbly on this cause, so I, like Moses, may see the Promised Land with my eye from afar, but probably not arrive on it. One sows and another reaps. I hope that the Lord of History might look compassionately on this modest offering that I place before his altar.

The Author

I
Seed that fell on good soil

The new campus of the Society of Jesus' Colegio de Belen [Bethlehem School] in Mariano opened its door in September 1925. A modern, spacious and well-equipped facility meant to replace its initial location in the oldest sector of Havana: the Convent of Our Lady of Belen, where the institution was born in 1954 under the name of Real Colegio de La Habana, although it would soon be known simply as Colegio de Belen, name that would take root for the rest of its time there.

The center had garnered prestige during its more than seventy years of existence. It was not only the most prestigious among the island's religious schools for boys, but it quickly becomes the preferred school for the country's well-off classes. Prominent intellectuals such as distinguished doctors Pedro and Joaquín Albarrán Domínguez, poet and journalist Julián del Casal de la Lastra and, until 1925, one of its alumni had become president of the Republic: General José Miguel Gómez, veteran of the War for Independence and founder of the Liberal Party. During the balance of its history until 1961 there were four additional heads of state formed in this or another Jesuit center on the Island: Carlos Mendieta Montefur, Miguel Mariano Gómez Arias, Carlos Prío Socarrás and Fidel Castro Ruz.

The new edifice also showcased a brand-new directorate. Fr. Antonio Galán Arias was named Rector on July 31, who came to replace Fr. Camilo García. This Spanish religious, born in 1883, would stay in that position until October of 1930. Next to him was a Spaniard from Galicia, of below average height and smiling countenance that had just completed his tertianship in the

15

Cave of St. Ignatius in Manresa and was destined for Cuba to fill the position of Vice-Rector of Discipline and Secretary. He was Fr. Felipe Rey de Castro (Brión, Galicia, 1889 - Havana, Cuba, 1952).

Belén Jesuit, Havana, Cuba (primary and secondary education)

The first impression made on the student body by that young administrator has been preserved thanks to the testimony of one of the upperclassmen of the center that would soon become one of Father Rey's most important collaborators in the founding of the Agrupación Católica Universitaria, future Doctor of Medicine Juan Antonio Rubio Padilla:

> "Among its novelties was found its Prefect: Fr. Felipe Rey de Castro. His affable countenance and forthright manner won us over from the start. But a question came to our lips at once: Could such a young, smiley, and simple man make a good Prefect?
>
> Accustomed to confusing coercive rigor for discipline, brought up in an environment of distrustful vigilance and hard and fast rules, we could not imagine authority as

anything other than quick and firm reproaches and punishments dispensed upon us.

That little Galician priest, charismatic, joyful, and simple, was the antithesis of the classical Prefect.[1]

Community of Jesuit Fathers and Brothers, inaugural teachers of the new Belén of 1925, honored the night prior to the school opening. They are Fathers. Rey de Castro, Bonefacio Alonso, Franganillo, L. Estefanía, Tadeo, Hurtado, Goberna, Barbeito; and Brothers Peláez, Mandalena, Espeso, Arregui, García and Oribe.

The reaction of the outstanding student was perfectly understandable. The cloister of the school was made up of very competent teachers in their subject matter, it is enough to cite Fr. Pelegrín Franganillo Balboa (León, 1873 - Havana, 1955) one of the greatest specialists in the study of arachnids, first in Spain and later in Cuba and Fr. Rafael Goberna Costas (Pontevedra, 1903 - La Paz, 1985), distinguished scientist in the nation's meteorological studies, in addition to very competent others such as Fr. Bonifacio Alonso, Emilio Hurtado Ruiz and Francisco Barbeito Ramos. They, along with the excellent and expensive installations, seemed

---

[1] Dr. Juan A. Rubio Padilla: "Genesis of the ACU". Preface to M. Figueroa: History of the Agrupación Católica Universitaria, p. 19.

to guarantee a first-class education; nevertheless, educational methods were not forefront.

Discipline was exerted with utmost rigor. Instead of collaborating with students they were threatened with punishments and past century teaching was the rule: rote memorization of material, repetitive learning and the predominance of coercion above creativity. It was so pronounced that a large number of families deemed the school to be akin to a military institution that was supposed to submit their sons to the discipline that they were incapable of inculcating. Even through my own infancy I heard the fallback common phase: "I wish I could send you to Belen, so the Jesuits might straighten you out." Religious piety was the order of the day. That explains why a good share of students would practice just the required religious duties and many would turn their back on the practice of the faith after graduation.

This was worsened by social circumstances. At the start of the twentieth century the Church in the Island was continuously accused in the public square for having been unconditionally Spanish and against independence. Predominant among the intellectuals and politicians of the time were masonry, agnosticism and anticlericalism. At the "Christian regime" family level there was a widely accepted notion that one went to the temples to enter marriage, to baptize the offspring and to attend funeral Masses. Only a tiny percent of professed Catholics attended Sunday Mass. Moreover, devout men were considered "weak" and "less than masculine," as religion was deemed a "woman's thing." Very few males dared to receive the Eucharist in public, to pray the Rosary or engage in other forms of devotion.

Said situation began to turn around very slowly in select Catholic sectors, thanks to initiatives like the foundation of the Knights of Columbus by Augustine priest Fr. Edward Moynihan OSA in 1909 in the parish of Holy Christ of the Good Voyage, with the intention of countering the growth of Masonic Lodges through its own rites and ceremonies. In Sagua la Grande, some months prior to the arrival of Father Rey in Cuba on the fourth of January 1925, attorney Valentín Arenas and Frs. Esteban Rivas, SJ and Cástor Apráiz, OFM founded the Asociación de Caballeros Católicos [Catholic Knights Association] that only four years later would become the National Catholic Knights Association.

In that same year of 1925 the National Congress of Students takes place at the University of Havana. Among the participants, in addition to university and high-school students, were others coming from religious institutions, including a delegation send by Colegio de Belén. The event was difficult for Catholics, which had to defend themselves against open attacks opposing private education, particularly Catholic, from that portion of the youth with communist ideas like Julio Antonio Mella and Alfonso Bernal del Riesgo.

This not only forced them to publicly defend their faith and the rights of religious institutions, but also, following the event, those representatives of Catholic schools began to meet and nurture the idea of forming a federation. The catalyst of the idea was Brother Victorino, of the Brothers of Christian Schools — better known as La Salle Brothers — who also founded the Cuban Catholic Youth Federation on February 11, 1928, in the school that the congregation had in Vedado.

To this we should add another, much older, sodality and also closer to the context within which the religious young Galician exercised his educational trade: the Marian Sodality of the Anunciata, described this way in the *Introduction to the history of the Catholic Church in Cuba*:

> Founded in 1875 by Father Manuel Piñán, SJ, in the older Colegio de Belen. The sodality promoted Jesuit spirituality, and also nurtured formational and apostolic dimensions. It was probably in that environment where the 1891 encyclical *Rerum novarum* was first studied in Cuba. The "anunciatos" relied on assistance from teachers at Belen.

One of the fruits of it was the birth of "Workers of Charity and St. Joseph Marian Sodality," one of the first Catholic attempts at a workers' union in Cuba, at the time when these groups were heavily influenced by anarchistic Spanish immigrants.[2]

The sodality had only 40 members, among them 25 students or alumni of Belen and 8 businessmen. After the construction of the new temple on Calzada de [Causeway of] Reina in 1923, a new three-story building for the sodalists was erected around the back, on Estrella [Star] Street, with a large assembly hall, chapel, classrooms and other facilities. During the oversight of its last director, Fr. Esteban Rivas Serna, SJ (Santander, Spain, 1878 - Cali, Colombia, 1962)[3], the sodality multiplied its rolls and reach of activities, including conferences, movie screenings, religious instruction and promotion of periodic publications. At the time of its closure in 1961, the Anunciata had 2,952 sodalists or partners on its rolls.

While the new teacher at Belen was aware of the workings of these associations, he aspired to something novel: a select group of students whose spirituality would be nurtured in a demanding way, side by side with their human formation. That explains why, shortly after the start of classes, he conducted a series of interviews to handpick those with the wherewithal to be part of an innovative formational experience. His purpose was admirably summarized by Rubio Padilla, one in the first group of selects, as: Strengthening willpower, with the assistance of Grace, so as to

---

[2] Rivas y Méndez: Introducción a la historia de la Iglesia Católica en Cuba, p. 79.

[3] Cf. Sáez: Presencia de los jesuitas en el quehacer de Cuba [Presence of Jesuits in their doings in Cuba], pg. 109. Although the sodality as such disappeared, the Society of Jesus was able to preserve, miraculously, its campus, which today houses de Loyola Center for Faith and Culture.

voluntarily meet our personal duties[4]." Duties for said students pertained to the ideals of chastity and study.

First session of Ignatian Exercises for high school seniors and university students of the Island

That memorable senior class of 1925 to 1926 was a trial run for the plan that is essentially the same plan of the ACU in all important respects: educate our free will following St. Ignatius, teach us to study as men, place in our hearts the heroic ideal of chastity, train us in the Spiritual Exercises, the ascetic norms and the techniques of spirit that best conditioned us to succeed. What Exercises those, the first in Cuba! How we must have been earnestly envied by those who did not have the privilege, the grace from that Apostle of God! This was the second great cornerstone of the Agrupación's foundation: the Spiritual Exercises[5].

As the faithful close to the Society of Jesus know, the Exercises, created by its founder, St. Ignatius of Loyola, are the backbone of

---

[4] Dr. Juan A. Rubio Padilla: "The Genesis of the ACU," p. 22.
[5] Ibidem.

his spirituality. The association of the old tradition of the retreat and monastic solitude with an ordered guide for meditation grounded in concrete plans to transform the life of the exercitant and to show a love for Christ through works, was one of the great gifts to post Tridentine religious life.

Those Exercises with handpicked students made the difference for some of them. They sowed a seed in their souls that became the germ for the future Agrupación.

And that explains why the initial group that graduated and went on to the University stayed true to the faith and continued to follow the nascent Agrupación:

> During that first term, our first at the University, we continued to go to Mass with Fr. Rey every Sunday at 9 a.m. in the Chapel at Belen. [José] Rouco and I helped out. Almost all of us from the famous senior year that graduated in prior months attended. We received Communion and later shared breakfast in the same spirit as in ACU's Sunday breakfasts. And on Holy Week of 1927 we had the first public miracle: we cloistered ourselves in Belen for three days to do the first Exercises for university students ever done in Cuba[6].

Of the expected 25 exercitants, 22 attended, contradicting the skepticism of various members of the Society of Jesus that considered young Rey de Castro a dreamer, whose pursuits were destined to fail. Those Exercises sowed the evangelical seed on good soil. There the future ACU would take root. The small group of university students that attended Mass in Belen on Sundays and were committed to do the Exercises every year, were already a small sodality, not yet settled in, but alive, as Rubio affirms:

> "The daily efforts for a year-and-a-half full of difficulties and stumbles were turning into reality. The ACU had

---

[6] Dr. Juan A. Rubio Padilla: "The Genesis of the ACU," p. 25.

ceased being a pipe-dream, a project, an ideal. Like a poor newborn, we had neither name, nor home, nor properties, nor visits from a social chronicler, but we were alive and all else would come in due time."

"The basic and the essential had been attained. The house close to the University of Havana, by then already planned, the hymn, the banner, the bylaws and everything else were important, but not essential. The essential had been accomplished. Fr. Rey had his Catholic university student sodality"[7].

But, when that handful of young men most needed their zealous pedagogue and spiritual guide, an apparently unsurmountable obstacle appeared. A few months after that retreat in the summer of 1927 the young Father Felipe received an order from his superior to return immediately to Spain where he is destined to the Colegio La Inmaculada [Immaculate School in Gijon], again as Prefect and Secretary[8].

Some of his sodalists shed bitter tears over his departure. They, like the disciples from Emmaus, think that all is lost. Even Rubio Padilla, whom the founder appoints as guard over his harvest, does not feel up to the task when he accompanies the priest to the San Francisco docks, where the ship is about to cast off. Nevertheless, the spirit of that pastor leaves no room for doubts, because his faith in Christ is unharmed:

Fr. Rey, with the evangelic simplicity so proper to those who befriend Jesus Christ, told me: I will continue to be your Director from Spain, and my prayers will only be for

---

[7] Dr. Juan A. Rubio Padilla: "The Genesis of the ACU", pg. 27.

[8] In the yearbook of the Colegio La Inmaculada in Gijón, corresponding to the 1927-1928 academic year, he appears with these duties. It has not been possible to verify his continuation of said duties until 1931, because the records of the School have been mutilated or destroyed due to the enormous damage incurred by the institution during the Civil War.

you all, but the true Director and Master remains among you all, and will not fail. Don't you fail, don't you all fail and He will not fail you![9]

These words served as a lenitive to that young man who from that moment on and for nearly four years, propelled him "in hope against hope"[10] to do the most incredible negotiations to insure the return of the priest to Cuba.

Jesuit school in Gijon, Spain, The Immaculate

---

[9] Rubio Padilla: "The Genesis...", p. 36.
[10] Rom 4, 18

II
Origins of a Vocation

Parenthetically, while Father Rey settles in at the school in Gijon, exercises his prefecture and offers mathematics and religion classes to students in fifth and sixth grades, always filled with hope in Divine Providence, we will devote a few pages to a most important subject: the story of the vocation of that pious Jesuit, so as to better understand his personality and his pursuits.

Felipe Rey de Castro had been born in Brión, province of La Coruña, Galicia, on November 8, 1889. He was the son of Apolinar Rey and Juana de Castro. He was baptized in the local parish of San Félix that same afternoon by chaplain Gerardo de Castro. His godparents were Fr. José María de Castro, uncle to his mother and pastor of that church, and María Ventura Castro, Juana's sister.

St. Felix Church, La Coruña, Galicia, Spain

We have little information about the first decade of his life, but that which we do have is eloquent. He was born to a fervently Catholic family, not only was he the nephew of the pastor of Brión, but one of his mother's sisters, Benita Castro, was a nun in the Monastery of the Benedictine Sisters in Cunis, Pontevedra, where she later became Abbess.

Just twelve days after birth, his father Apolinar died. His mother brought him up with the assistance of his godfather, although she possessed some financial resources. As some members of his family recall, the pastor would welcome "Felipito" to the rectory frequently: "he was a regular on Thursday afternoons, would stay over Saturdays in order to spend Sundays there, as he would on other school-less days"[11], and trips to the monastery with his mother were not rare, in fact, Sor Benita wrote years later that Felipito was "always very caring, docile and inclined to piety since little, and was widely loved by all who dealt with him"[12] and that the religious community "adored and venerated him". Nevertheless, these affections did not turn him into a spoiled child: "His mother reared him with both tenderness and severity, but in spite of being a single child, she never condoned whims, and God, our Lord, endowed him with such good nature that he never gave his mother any trouble."[13]

Thanks to this very testimony we know that the boy's initial schooling was in the Jesuit La Guardia School in Pontevedra. Where, according to his religious aunt, "he was a model of virtue, hard work and dutifulness"[14].

---

[11] Letter of Sor Benita Castro to Dr. Jorge Casteleiro, Abril 2, 1952, p. 2.
[12] Ibidem.
[13] Ibid, p.3.
[14] Ibidem.

We have more information regarding his secondary education at the Jesuit *Colegio Apóstol Santiago* [St. James Apostle School] in Vigo. These years were decisive with regard to Felipe's vocation for it is there that he has his first contact with Ignatian Exercises. As Jesuit historian Evaristo Rivera tells us:

> The importance of a good Spiritual Father was evidenced in 1907 when, thanks to the initiative of he who had that post then (Fr. Maximiliano Sanmartín), a new practice that was common elsewhere was introduced at the School, namely, that secondary education students do Spiritual Exercises during the summer and decide on their vocation in their light, as St. Ignatius intended.[15]

Onetime Jesuit school "de la Guardia," Pontevedra, Spain.

While this spiritual practice visibly influenced Rey's religious vocation, it was perfectly complemented by another that would

---

[15] Evaristo Rivera: *Colegio Apóstol Santiago*, p.218.

accompany him throughout his life: being part of the school's Marian Sodality. Rivera contends:

> Devotion to the Virgin continued to be a decisive lever catalyzing religious enthusiasm and promoting yearnings for mystical purity in those juvenile souls [...] The 50th anniversary of the Dogma of the Immaculate was celebrated in 1904. It was a Marian year par excellence, marked by endless events and commemorative practices. The Marian Sodality flourished and was leaven in the dough of the 115 students that made up the School.[16]

It is not hard to imagine that while calling on Belen's students for that novel spiritual experience he evoked earlier experiences as sodalist when he was about fifteen years old.

Through the Book of Minutes of the Sodality we know that he was accepted as member of Immaculate Conception and St. Louis Gonzaga on March 19, 1903, on the celebration of St. Joseph.[17] A little more than a year later, on the 20th of November, 1904, he is named *"capillero"* [churchwarden] in the meeting of the Sodality, and so served during the celebrations of the Marian year, as Rivera alluded. In the pamphlet entitled *"Año Mariano en el Colegio Apóstol Santiago"* are listed the "Gifts collected by the Marian League from the *Colegio* students and offered to the Immaculate Virgin on her jubilee year," one that stands out among them is the one penned by student Felipe Rey de Castro: "Without your love I am as a bird without a nest."[18]

It might be said that the phrase reflects the sensibility and language of an adolescent, that it does not amount to more than rudimentary poetry. Nevertheless, I believe that in that simple line

---

[16] Ibidem.

[17] *Actas de la Congregación Mariana de la Inmaculada Concepción y de S. Luis Gonzaga*, p.179.

[18] *Año Mariano en el Colegio del Apóstol Santiago*, p. 47.

one finds some of the virtues the future Jesuit will possess: conciseness, beauty of expression when addressing matters of the spirit, and the expressive vigor of the truly strong, unafraid of compromising their masculinity because of sincerely expressing their devotion.

It is not surprising that this pious, sensitive high-schooler of strong physical and moral constitution would discover in himself, toward the end of his studies, a religious vocation to which he would surrender unconditionally for the rest of his existence. It surely came as no surprise to his teachers, nor his fellow sodalists, and much less to his pious mother or aunt Sor Benita. One or another relative or acquaintance may possibly have thought of it as just one more among that large number of members of the family dedicated to the Church, but could not imagine that, from among them, he would be one exceptional in fidelity, coherence, and exercise of heroic virtues within his ministry.

On September 7, 1908, the young Galician entered the Novitiate of the Society of Jesus at Carrión de los Condes, Palencia. That was, quite possibly, his first journey outside the immediate boundaries of his birthplace, but that house, located amidst Castilian plains and far from sea, though it would look strange at first sight, would soon become familiar, not just because it amassed novitiates from the most diverse ends of the Spanish realm, but rather because they were united in the desire to be formed "for the greater glory of God." While observant of the strict discipline of such a place, it is not hard to imagine him roaming the beautiful plateresque cloistered monastery of San Zoilo, or praying in the church of Santiago, a devotion very much alive among those born on Jacobean soil.

His juvenile imagination must have been much impressed by the traditions and legends about Sor Luisa de la Ascensión, nun that lived during the end of the XVI and beginning of the XVII centuries, twice Abbess of the Convent of Saint Clare, defender of the Immaculate Conception before it was declared dogma, pursued by the Inquisition for more than 14 years for her notoriety as miracle worker, liberated from all suspicion only after her death. Perhaps one of his professors pointed out Sor Luisa's sepulcher in the convent and relayed to him that during the years that she wielded the crosier in that house, she equaled all the other religious in dutifulness, even those from noble families and enforced the vow of poverty with such rigor that she won the spite of some nuns and of their influential families. Not neglecting, surely, to also mention that the bold Abbess adorned her devotions with songs and couplets, for she was versed in music, scandalizing some by "divinizing" well known profane love poems, as she also did with some texts of Lope de Vega.

We know that Felipe professed his first vows in 1910 and that his master of novices was Father Camilo García (Orense, 1863 - Havana, 1942), a personage that would make more than one appearance in his life. We have yet to uncover information regarding the relationship between master and novice, but knowing formation practices at the time we can intuit that the former was generally harsh and demanding towards the student, sometimes to the extreme, because it was supposed that this strengthened character and respect for obedience, as the novice would exhibit patience, fidelity, and devotion that we know would accompany him until the end of his days.

Years later, when Rey arrived in Cuba in 1925, Fr. García had completed his very brief assignment as Vice-Rector (1924-1925). We know, from Fr. Sáez book *Presencia de los jesuitas en el quehacer de Cuba [The presence of Jesuits in their doings in Cuba]*, that he not only remained in Cuba, but that between 1931 and 1933 he was Vice-Provincial of Cuba, from which position he was very critical of the recently founded *Agrupación Católica Universitaria*, the pretext being the disgust high levels of Gerardo Machado's government showed towards that university association that they characterized as conspiratorial. Moreover, considering that he remained in the community of Reina until his death in

1942, community to which his past disciple also belonged since returning in 1931, we can imagine the encounters that the fervent Jesuit had to endure with charity and patience towards his brothers in the Society of Jesus. Just as recorded in the lives of so many saints, founders of sodalities or other pastoral initiatives, some of his worse critics and even opposers can be found among those around him, calling for much integrity in the suffering of their wrongs, until God puts things back in place.

Following profession of first vows in 1910, at the end of two years of novitiate, the young Felipe must stay for two additional years in Carrión de los Condes to complete the "juniorate," which included Humanities, Rhetoric and other subjects. Afterward, he shall continue for two more years in *Colegio la Merced* in Burgos.

As the *ratio studiorum* of the Society of Jesus is long and demanding of its seminarians, he must do three years of Philosophy in Oña, Burgos, before starting the cycle labeled "magisterium," for which he is destined to the Colegio de Orduña in Vizcaya, where he will remain from 1917 to 1920.

There remains, from this very period, a basic document that allows us to know the spiritual disposition of this young man in training. It is a letter penned by him to Fr. Modesto Armisén, dated August 1, 1918, in which he refers to the piety of students in Orduña, very particularly to the works done by a Marian Sodality there to generously help those in need.

In that lengthy epistle, redacted by him at the request of peers undergoing formation, he points out the intense devotion to the Sacred Heart of Jesus, promoted by the Apostolate of Prayer; first Fridays of the month Masses with general Communion; the work of the Missions, particularly collections to support the mission of China; but what especially stands out is the students' fervor for their Marian Sodality. Because the extensive missive ran the risk of being judged as wholly apologetic in nature, its author allows himself a touch of humor towards the end: "Having read this far you, V. R., might say: So?, haven't you considered the canonization of the schoolmen of Orduña? — Perhaps some, in time; but not all, no Father."[19]

Some lines later, his tone gives advance notice of the good judgement of the forger of young men in him: "the most edifying thing about our schoolmen, the most intimate, is not included in these pages, yet balancing their virtues with their defects, do justly deserve the moniker of edifying and are well deserving of the letter dedicated to them."[20] Although not yet 29 years-old and far from completing his Jesuit formation, there is something in his discernment and vigor of expressions that presages the founder of the *Agrupación Católica Universitaria* and great spiritual director of Cuban youth to come.

Towards the end of the summer of 1920, Felipe leaves the territory of Spain for the first time. He has been destined to the prestigious "Ignatius Colleg" of Valkenburg-Limburg (Holland) where he shall do the four-year cycle of theology. The institution is one of the jewels of the Society of Jesus. It is an international center of formation where Jesuits from different areas of Europe are educated. In its classrooms there are Spaniards, Dutch, Germans, and men from other nations. It was a large center where, according to still preserved statistics, there were usually some 300 persons, counting professors, students, and brother coadjutors. They were all united by the Ignatian charism but, at the same time, a diversity of languages and cultures prevailed, something that helped all seminarians prepare to serve anywhere in the world where they might be sent.

---

[19] "ORDUÑA. Fructuosa labor con los alumnos. Letter of Br. Rey to Fr. Armisén". *Cartas Edificantes de la Provincia de Castilla*, book VII, no. 1°, March, 1919. Bilbao, La Editorial Vizcaína, 1919, p. 20.
[20] Ibidem.

The safest way to convey the formational rigor at the institute is through the qualifications of some of its professors and students. Fr. Agustín Bea, professor of Sacred Scripture, future Cardinal and influential figure in the development of the Council of Vatican II was the academics prefect while Rey was there. Other notable professors were Joseph Fröbes, professor of Psychology and Agustín Merk who taught New Testament.

The records of the institution show that among fellow students of our autographed, are other religious men that would turn out to be exceptional figures in various fields, among them noted author Erich Przywara in the area of spiritual theology, who had decisive influence on the thinking of Saint John Paul II; Karl Rahner, innovative theologian, also notable for his influence on Vatican II; as well as Gustav Gundlach, who would become known for his texts on social philosophy.

We lack evidence of the Galician religious young man having close friendship with some of these professors and students, but it is evident that he enjoyed the privilege of completing his formation in a center free of any kind of provincialism or narrow thinking. Nevertheless, there is an anecdote, not "scientifically" validated, that may give an idea of the prestige that the student was able to garner in Valkemburg, even after concluding his studies there. Here is how Doctor of Theology Sixto García, professor at various prestigious North American educational centers, as well as researcher and consultant to the Jesuit "Pedro Arrupe Institute" in Miami, where he became an ACU congregant in 1967, puts it:

> Some years back, Dr. Antonio López[21], my colleague at St. Vincent de Paul Seminary where I taught for 30 years, shared with me the following anecdote: his years of

---

[21] Dr. Antonio López Villalba González (Toni). ACU sodalist. His consecration took place in New York in 1971.

doctoral studies at the University of Fordham, in New York, coincided with a visit by Rahner to that city. The Fordham professors asked Tony to show Rahner around that great metropolis. During the tour, Rahner shared with Tony that in his years of basic theology in Valkenburg, Holland, he heard talk about Fr. Felipe Rey de Castro, a Jesuit that had studied basic theology at that same institution. Fr. Rey was later director of the *Agrupación Católica Universitaria* in Cuba. Rahner was so impressed with the renown of Father Rey, his spirituality, his intelligence, his discernment, that, as he shared with Tony, it occurred to him to ask his superiors to send him to Cuba as a missionary. We leave to the imagination of the readers, that know the history of the ACU so well, to ponder on the impact of Rahner on the Church and on theological development, on the history of the Church in Cuba — of the Universal Church! — and on the future of theology if his initial wish had reached fruition.[22]

At the end of the third year, as was the custom, Rey de Castro was ordained priest in the Coleg, on August 24, 1923, and he celebrated his first Mass the following day. It was evident among those that knew him that the Holy Spirit had showered his gifts generously on the new presbyter, as Sor. Benita Castro witnesses in a letter previously cited:

> Fr. Rey was highly esteemed here by all who knew him. Once ordained priest he came to Spain and spent a few months in the Santiago residence. He offered Exercises to various communities in the city and preached in the main

---

[22] Ph. D. Sixto García Sánchez: "Karl Rahner y la identidad cubana. Reflexiones sobre un amor improbable". Instituto de Política Internacional UFV, Madrid. Apuntes 14, 9, October 9, 2020. Source https://ipi-ufv.com/wp-content/uploads/2020/10/Apunte-2020-14-Karl-Rahner-y-la-identidad-cubana.pdf, September 14, 2022, pgs. 1-2.

churches, and if memory serves us, also in the cathedral; his preaching was so admired that he was invited from different locations. The Archbishop of Santiago de Compostela at the time showed his favor many times and also, on his own initiative, authorized him to offer confession to all nuns in the Archdiocese. But, as he stayed only a short while in Galicia that concession has only been taken advantage of by those from this Monastery, and then only a few times.[23]

An additional testimonial of that very time involves one of his visits to Brión during which he served as mediator between the local church and some neighbors, regarding the ownership of some land. His mediation was so successful for all involved, that he was called "true king of peace." It was clear that someone like this would not constrain himself to be a famous preacher or a remarkable confessor, because he could involve himself in social issues and in seeking truly Christian solutions to them.

Once his studies in Holland came to an end, the religious young man was destined to the Cave of St. Ignatius, Manresa, Catalonia, to spend what is called "tertianship" there. The institution had its origin in the grotto where St. Ignatius of Loyola found refuge in 1522, after his pilgrimage from Montserrat, and where he prayed and fasted for ten months, and where tradition says he also redacted his *Spiritual Exercises*. In the XVII century a temple had been erected as a portico to the cave and in 1896 a Jesuit convent and a spirituality center were added on. To spend his "tertianship" there meant to unite spiritually with the founder of the Society of Jesus and to prepare for receipt of his principal charisms.

---

[23] Letter of Sor Benita Castro to Dr. Jorge Casteleiro, p. 2.

It is not difficult to imagine Rey praying there for a time in the silence of that refuge and reviewing the vigorous pages of the *Exercises*. It is not hard to imagine him, in the penumbra of the afternoon, once the day's obligations have been satisfied, kneeling, and sprouting from his lips the prayer of total surrender that the saint placed at the epigraph of the "Contemplation to attain the love of God": "Take, Lord, and receive all my liberty, my memory, my understanding, and my entire will— all that I have and call my own. You have given it all to me. To you, Lord, I return it. Everything is yours; do with it what you will. Give me only your love and your grace. That is enough for me."[24]

Just as some fruit matures better in the shade, so the spirit of the young man became fully formed in that tertianship. One proof of it were the journeys that ensued after its conclusion, and back in Galicia, when he preached the Exercises full of apostolic fervor, as this note from the "Noticias de la Provincia de León" [News from the Province of León] from May 1925:

> Ministering of Fr. Felipe Rey [in Vigo]. Doctrinal Exercises from 23rd to 29th, day of general communion; some 350 attended. Exercises of five days for the town of Bayona, well attended and numerous confessions; and lastly, Exercises in Vigo to some 250 gentlemen during Holy Week; confessions on Maundy Thursday.[25]

A young religious man with his spirit could have been destined to one of the centers of spirituality on the peninsula and he would have guided souls there in a very promising way. But the Spirit destined him, as the Apostles after Pentecost, to a different

---

[24] San Ignacio de Loyola: *Ejercicios espirituales*. Texto autógrafo. Biblioteca Digital Universal, Editorial del Cardo, 2003, epígrafe 234.

[25] "Noticias de la Provincia de León" (mayo 1925). Taken from: P. Manuel Cabada: *Sobre el P. Felipe Rey de Castro. Datos sueltos o complementarios*, 2018.

mission in another part of the world. And a mere three months after having fulfilled those ministries, he will have to cross the ocean and disembark for the first time in Havana.

III
Promise fulfilled

Just as promised when he bade goodbye to Fr. Rey at San Francisco Pier, Juan Antonio Rubio Padilla, medical student and first among those that welcomed the call to a new sodality, he took charge of keeping lit the flame of that renewal movement. Indeed, he succeeded, at least, in keeping the promise of doing the Exercises as a group once a year.

> During the three and a half years that Fr. Rey was away, my shoulders and my sleep bore the weight of the command received on San Francisco Pier. The group stayed united. Humans after all, and given the Apostle's absence, many faltered, but others from incoming classes came to occupy their places. The first Exercises, in his absence, were done not with 22, as we had in the first session, but with 35, and we never missed a year.[26]

Nevertheless, obstacles abound, and his letters to the founder during those years make reference to the presence of "opponents to university students getting close to Colegio de Belen", no doubt influenced by the state of political activism at the university, where a group of students was in open opposition to the government, including Rubio Padilla himself.

Separately, Juan Antonio as well as various other faithful followers of that first spiritual nucleus, made various appeals to Fr. Enrique Carvajal, Vice-provincial of Cuba between June 1929 and April 1931. At first he assured the young men that it was impossible to remove Fr. Felipe from his prefecture at the Colegio de

---

[26] Dr. Juan A. Rubio Padilla: "The Genesis of the ACU", p. 14.

Gijón and much less at midyear. But the insistence of the young men was such that when Fr. Carvajal travelled to Spain in 1930 he arranged for the return of the religious priest back to Cuba to lead his young men's sodality at once.[27]

It is clear that Fr. Rey was not a man given to haste, but rather to thoughtful conduct. That explains why, in spite of his great joy, he did not opt for the first ship back to the Island, but rather for a three-month tour through various European cities, among them France and Germany, to visit institutions that might serve as model and example in the perfection of his own.

As Miguel Figueroa recounts:

> He could not arrive in Havana until the 3rd of March. By then he had the Agrupación perfectly ideated, down to its most minute details, from the name it would carry to the type of influence it should exert on our society in the future. The project was so thought out, that in his parting visit to the Abbess aunt prior to shipping off, he described his future work with the precision it would have if it were already in existence.
>
> That explains how so shortly after its foundation it projected a sense of maturity, and how by the end of 1931, when it had barely 10 months of existence, it was much like it is today, poorer, smaller, still without its own house, but already active and complete in all its forms, because like Minerva burst from the head of Jupiter, the Agrupación was born in the mind of Fr. Rey, fully armed.[28]

---

[27] For these reasons Figueroa, in his already cited history of the ACU calls him "initiator." He was also known as "sodalist number one."
[28] M. Figueroa: History of the Agrupación Católica Universitaria, p. 23.

Upon disembarking on the roadstead of Havana the religious priest decided to meet with the group of founders that had remained faithful. In fact, he did so the following day, March 4. His first unpleasant surprise was the absence of Rubio Padilla who was in hiding due to persecution by the police for political opposition to the sitting government from within the ranks of the *Directorio Estudiantil Universitario* [University Student Directorate]. They were disquieting days, until the "forces of order" were able to apprehend him on the 19th and confined him to the Castillo del Príncipe [Prince Fortress]. The priest went to the fortress to comfort him. He was released the ensuing 5th of May following multiple efforts to free him and the next day, the 6th, he celebrated his wedding with Dania Padilla at the Colegio de Belen's chapel and went into exile immediately, for his life, while on the Island, was in danger.

It was not difficult for the priest to discover that the city and country he had returned to were not exactly the same ones he left a little over three years ago.

The president of the Republic since 1925 was Gerardo Machado. He had earned the rank of general during the War for Independence of 1895 and his ascension to the first magistracy, following a campaign that promised "Water, roads and schools," led him to be acclaimed by a good portion of the people. Since the price of sugar in the international market was unstable, poverty reached out not only to the less favored classes, but also to small and medium businesses and unemployment indexes had risen alarmingly.

Machado delivered on his electoral motto via a vast plan of public works that included the building of the Carretera Central [Central Highway], diverse educational institutions, among them Secondary Education Institutes in each province, as well as aqueducts, sewers and a building that would become emblematic, the Capitol, majestic seat of the Nation's Legislative Body. These increased job opportunities.

The politician, according to the Constitution, should vacate power after a four-year term but, following poor advice from his followers, he decided to finagle an "extension of powers" based on reform of the Magna Carta. Even though he was supported in his endeavor by numerous politicians, landowners and American investors, many sectors of society stood in opposition: veterans, students, intellectuals, workers' unions from different ideological orientations, and citizens from all classes. Strikes, clandestine propaganda, demonstrations and even terrorism broke out. The government answered with censure and violent repression. Jails filled up with the opposition. The North American Great Depression of 1929 impacted Cuba, a privileged commercial partner, and generated extreme misery that stoked the worsening situation.

Rubio Padilla had been one of the founders of the *Directorio Estudiantil Universitario* in 1930 and his opposition was well known, thus nothing could impede his persecution and that of many others. It was a heartache that Rey had to endure, and that was made worse by the fact that the political issues also permeated the Church in Cuba right from the top, for Monsignor Ruiz, Archbishop of Havana, was an unconditional admirer of Machado when another group of clerics were frankly oppositional.

In the very residence where he was lodged, abutting Sacred Heart church on Reina street, political opinions were divided, but the greatest sensitivity was that, since April 1931, the new Vice-provincial was Fr. Camilo García, who lined up with the "party of order" and saw Rubio and other students as dangerous for the Society of Jesus. Since he was apparently close to the presidential circle, the problems to "Palacio [Presidential Palace]" instigated by certain young men echoed there as well and he demanded that the "rabble-rousers" in the sodality be expelled, or else that it be dissolved, because to the authorities the mere mention of the upper-level formation center was an allusion to an oppositional stronghold.

Nevertheless, none of this delayed the official declaration founding the sodality that, as of yet, lacked a definitive name, when he got together on the 4th of March with some of the young men that remained faithful to his initiative. According to Fr. Sáez, a year later some would still call it the "Asociación de Jóvenes Católicos del P. Rey de Castro [Young Catholic Men's Association of Fr. Felipe Rey de Castro]" and the founder himself used the moniker of "Congregación de Jóvenes de la Anunciata [Young Men's Anunciata Sodality]"[29] for a time, since their interim facility was the new house of that sodality, next to the community of Reina, yet, ultimately, the name that defined its identity would reign: "Agrupación Católica Universitaria."

As Figueroa asserts, it was a quixotic endeavor:

> From a merely human point of view, a worse historical moment could not have been picked to start that work. It was a year of exacerbated passions, of tough struggle, of a political and economic situation unlike any other before in Cuba, the university closed, the authorities on the lookout for any student action, the attention of all polarized towards violent resolution: it seemed impossible to find anyone interested in spiritual renewal, nor with sufficient serenity to consider a slow process of formation with long-term benefits, nor possibility to attract new candidates, nor fields for apostolic work of any kind.[30]

We have already mentioned the misgivings that anything coming from the university awoke in Fr. Camilo García and other religious priests, to the extent that for them, as for the government, the upper house of formation was a dangerous place, full of conspirators and violent people. The fact that the most notorious of its members, Rubio Padilla, was being pursued by repressive forces reinforced that idea, and the insistence of the founder to

---

[29] Sáez: *Presencia de los jesuitas...* p.116.
[30] M. Figueroa: *History of the Agrupación...* p. 24.

highlight the commitment of *Agrupados* to the public square rather than to a merely pious organization did not reassure skeptics. Moreover, if we consider that the police distrusted any type of gathering, it is possible to understand why various residents of the Reina community did not see that idea kindly and seemed to them impossible to bring together those young men, even for Spiritual Exercises, without taking great precautions.

Yet the vigor of Fr. Felipe did not allow him to cower in the face of obstacles and, indeed, the first session of Exercises commenced on the 29th of March and soon thereafter subsequent ones were announced for the 2nd of April, 9th of October and 4th of December. The Galician priest was convinced that for God nothing is impossible.

IV
Formation of the select

More than a few —including very committed laypeople— misinterpreted from the start Fr. Rey's decision to seek members of his Agrupación from among well-formed young men, culturally and religious speaking, from an already selective school like Belen — something he would later expand to others at similar levels — specially because it had to do, in most cases, with sons of well to do families. At first sight it seemed that he was seeking to build a sort of exclusive religious club and left behind the work of evangelizing in a society in which the poor held the majority.

The history of the ACU has shown that it has never been far from the needs of the less fortunate, among which it exercised its apostolate of assisting the sick and handicapped, educating those on the margin, including the spiritual healing of the imprisoned. Yet the objective of the founder was not to bring about other charitable association, nor an institute dedicated to catechism but rather, following the charisms of the Society of Jesus, to form a select group of young men sufficiently trained in cultural matters, with spiritual solidity in order that they might influence society decisively. It was a Christian militia in a country where politics, the press, entertainment and even family life seemed to dechristianize under the approving gaze of secularist governments.

This sort of initiative was not new within the Society of Jesus. Very visible precursors like the apostolate of Fr. Ángel Ayala, SJ (Ciudad Real, 1867 - Madrid, 1960) who, while working with the Marian Sodality "Los Luises" of Madrid, initiated the Catholic Association of Propagandists in 1909. Its first objective was to support a powerful and influential Catholic press in Spain, as well as to create a Catholic Association of young university students, a great labor organization with identical goals, so that from these initiatives charismatic political leaders might emerge. It was all about an authentic social apostolate that would disprove the popular opinion that "los Luises of Madrid were devout, entertaining and useless young guys."[31]

Fr. Felipe Rey de Castro, SJ, with twelve select apostles. Among them, to his right, future Auxiliary Bishop of Havana, Fr. Fernando Azcárate Freyre de Andrade; to his left, the future doctor and intellectual José Ignacio Lasaga Travieso.

---

[31] Ayala: *Antología de formación de selectos, p. 33.*

Even though propagandists had to battle greatly in public square from the start, it was during the religious persecution that it had to test its valor. It was precisely during those years that Ayala writes and makes known his *Formación de Selectos* [*Formation of the Select*] where he defines his objectives and goals, albeit the circumstances surrounding the Civil War delayed first publication until 1941. It is there that he makes known what he considers the "select:" "A select, social director, must be a man of good judgment, enterprising, energetic, enduring, in love with the ideal of the Church, a fighter, high-sighted, selfless, modest, open to counsel."[32] According to him, their formation required sacrifice, penitence, chastity, docility and humanity, as well as spiritual education based on the Exercises, retreats, mediation and daily communion.

The fruits of the Association were multiple: the Catholic newspaper *El Debate*, The Federation of Catholic Students, the Instituto Social Obrero [Workers Social Institute] and the Library of Christian Authors (BAC, in its Spanish acronym), founded in 1943 by his collaborator Ángel Herrera Oria —later cardinal of the Church in 1965— and it has become one of the principal publishers of classic Christian authors in the world.

Seen in this light, it would seem that Rey de Castro simply retraced the experience of Ayala, but we are obliged to consider that when he placed his foundation's cornerstone in 1925 he most probably had knowledge of the work of the Propagandists, but by the time the *Formation of the Select* saw the light of day the ACU was already using methods akin to those found in the book. More than thinking of an imitation or direct influence, it must be realized that both men drew from the Ignatian charism and educational tradition and, faced with similar circumstances found like solutions.

---

[32] Ibid, p. 39.

Indeed, Fr. Felipe takes advantage of the experience found in the Marian Sodality to which he belonged since his youth. Here, again, he does not exactly retrace them, but rather his privileged mind and his discernment ability allow him to leapfrog routines, the various devotions separate from apostolic works, and applies time-proven guidelines within the Society of Jesus to the particular needs of the country where he is ministering. It is surprising that when, three decades later, His Holiness Pope Pius XII issued the apostolic constitution *Bis saeculari die* on the Sodality of our Lady, we seem to find in its pages the image and apostolic works of the ACU:

> Among the primary ends of the Sodalities, one must consider every form of apostolate, particularly the social apostolate, since the apostolic work of propagating the Kingdom of Christ and defending the rights of the Church have been mandated to Sodalities by the ecclesiastical hierarchy itself. "In order to ensure real and complete cooperation of Sodalities with the hierarchical apostolate, it is not at all necessary to alter or innovate Sodality Rules regarding means to achieve it."[33]

Long before that pontifical document was penned, the Cuban sodality was worthy of being considered among those that, in exemplary fashion, was already brilliantly executing what the Pope describes:

> In our confused times violently disturbed by so many calamities, we are greatly consoled by the Sodalists of Our Lady who all over the whole world work so strenuously and effectively in every field of the apostolate.
>
> By getting men of every class to do the Spiritual Exercises, Sodalists of Our Lady have aroused them – particularly youth and workingmen – to become men of real

---

[33] Pius XII: *Bis* saeculari *die*, (37) XI

virtue who ardently long to live a more Christian life. In their private lives, Sodalists have been quick to come generously and constantly to the relief of those in grave spiritual and material need. In civic legislatures and in positions of supreme power, many have used their influence to promote laws that are in keeping with the principles of the Gospel and social justice.[34]

In a previous document, the speech of the Holy Father to Marian Sodalities on January 21, 1945, one finds words of acknowledgment for the heroic work of these around the world, they exude the experience of the Primate within the European political landscape of those complex years, but regarding the ACU they had a prophetic flavor:

> Sodalists have fought in the front lines in all battles to defend Christian Europe and to keep the tyranny of heresy from spreading with the spoken word, with pen and the printing press, they have defended Catholic truth in discussions, controversies, and learned treatises. Thus, they sustained the courage of the faithful and came to the aid of those professing the Faith. They worked with Catholic priests by assisting and supporting these priests as they carried out their difficult tasks in the face of great opposition. Sodalists relentlessly attacked public immorality with means that were always dynamic and effective and even at times novel. On the frontiers of Christianity, they sometimes also wielded the sword to defend civilization: Sobieski, Charles of Lorraine, Eugene of Savoy, and other great leaders, together with many thousands of their soldiers, were all Sodalists.[35]

---

[34] Ibid I (10)
[35] Ideals and Norms for Sodalities (Sodality Golden Jubilee Address of Pope Pius XII, January 21, 1945, p. 2.

Although for some members of the Society of Jesus in Cuba the foundation of the ACU was a bold idea doomed to failure, and enemies of Christianity looked upon the labors of Rey de Castro as a futile effort to counteract many of the endemic ills of the island, from the moral laxity of its people to the scourges of corruption in most of the social spheres, guided by sound ecclesial doctrine, his stalwart confidence in God and ingrained devotion to Mary, he took charge of summoning and grouping that elite, convinced that his preparation and sending on into the world would bring innumerable good works to that homeland that he had already adopted as his own.

V
First steps

In his book *Agrupación Católica Universitaria. The first fifty years*, José Manuel Hernández attests that by the end of 1931, through sessions of Exercises offered for *Agrupados* "the spiritual concrete set so splendidly that we find the Agrupación, then, essentially as it is today, fifty years later."[36]

Such an affirmation may seem an exaggeration, but the author is referring, above all, to the spiritual climate, the enthusiasm of the small group of followers of Rey. The author himself, some lines later, points out that *"Agrupados*, as a whole, barely fill one pew of the Church on Reina on Sunday mornings. Yet, not even the classic ping-pong table is missing from the locale that is, naturally, on loan to the Agrupación.[37]

Following the definitive foundation of the university sodality, Fr. Felipe —cognizant of the pressing need for its own locale, but lacking the resources, for the moment, to lease one— had moved it from Colegio de Belén to the new headquarters of the Anunciata, part of the temple consecrated to the Sacred Heart and residence of the community in the centrically located Reina Street.

The director of that centenarian sodality, Fr. Estevan Ribas lent out one the halls in spite of the reticence of some of the Jesuits residing in the community on Reina Street for whom the words university students was indicative of political disorder and conflict.

---

[36] José M. Hernández: ACU: Los primeros 50 años, pgs. 12-13.
[37] Ibid. p. 13.

Thus, the Sunday Masses and breakfasts shared by the small group of *Agrupados* shifted from the school in Marianao to the institution's new headquarters, where they could also make use of a hall for meetings and recreation. In fact, they begin to be called "the sodality of young men of the Anunciata." The founder, however, although appreciative of the high caliber of that centennial congregation, does not want to sacrifice the baptismal name that he has finally settled on: "Agrupación Católica Universitaria."

Figueroa makes reference to the first prayerful notice that the priest placed on the bulletin board in 1931: The A.C.U. is an institution of practical and apostolic Catholicism founded for the more complete moral and intellectual formation of its members."[38] An idea that he will elaborate on that very same year in another of his writings: "His objective is to congregate Cuba's Catholic students for their more complete religious and social formation, and for the propagation of Catholicism."[39]

In contrast to other new organizations that pursue, at all cost, to grow in short order the number of members, that illuminated priest thought of it as an elite, a group of selects, educated for, and committed to a social apostolate. In that sense he followed, to the letter, Jesus' parable: "The kingdom of heaven is like leaven which a woman took and hid in three measures of meal, till it was all leavened."[40] The members of the ACU were that pinch of leaven, able to make the volume of the mass grow much beyond themselves. His work was spiritual fermentation. That is why he was never interested in "massiveness" nor statistical success.

---

[38] Figueroa, History of the Agrupación...p. 30.
[39] Ibidem.
[40] Mt 13, 33.

Felipe Rey de Castro and the Agrupación Católica Universitaria

Founding members of the Agrupación Católica Universitaria — not all represented.

Juan Antonio Rubio Padilla
P. Ricardo Chisholm Fernández, Sj
Ataulfo Fernández Llano
Angelberto Coro Del Pozo
César Incera Soriano
Roberto Incera Soriano
César Rey Rodríguez
Julio Andino Pella
Eduardo Chisholm Fernández
Rafael Díaz Masvidal
Cecilio González Vallejo
Alfonso Gutiérrez de la Cantera
Ernesto Gutiérrez Sanabria
Ovidio de Laosa Capote
José Ignacio Lasaga Travieso
P. René León Lemus
Oscar Lombardo Valladares
Alberto Petit Hernández
José Mario Mariña Esquirol
Carlos Martínez Arango
Ismael Orta Lemus
Enrique Oslé Tur, Sj
Hno. Miguel Pichardo Peñalver
Juan Simón Gutierrez
P. Juan Suárez Pérez

Armando Trelles Reyes
Pedro H. Cruz Nogués
Mario Alcoz Gómez
Enrique Amorín de Armas
Luis Delgado Gardel
Mons. Calixto García Rayneri
Alfonso Ledo Rodríquez
Aurelio Montes Medina
Luis Morse Delgado
Manuel Otero Ruisánchez
Antonio Solllinde Gómez
P. Juan Suárez Pino
Pompirio De La Vega Gandón
Alfredo Vidal Pérez
Julio Alfara Cárdenas
José Álvarez Díaz
Sergio Álvarez Mena
P. Alberto De Castro Rojas
Francisco Cuadra Aguirre
René Font Canto
Francisco Gómez Hernández
Juan José Gómez Hernández
Eugenio Jiménez Fumagalli
José M. Lázaro García
Manuel Mesa Santo Domingo

Francisco Pérez Vich
Andrés Del Pino Santua
Anibal De Los Reyes Noreña
Osvaldo Rodríguez Rodrígues
José María Rouco Aja
Luis Felipe Salazar
Manuel Suárez Carreño
Andrés Triny Rodés
Juan José Varela Álvarez
Luis De Velasco Castellanos
Ramón Barcia Conejo
Emilio Fernández García
Antonio De Goicoechea Cosculluela
Manuel Maza Páez
José Ramón Miquel Franca
Marino Pérez Duran
Aureliano Rodríguez Hernández
Rafael Talavera Gastón
Alfredo Alexander Riva
P. Fernando Azcárate Freyre de Andrade
Enrique de Cárdenas Aguilera
Felix Chediak Ahuayda
Santiago Choca Garganta
Armando Ruiz Leiro
Héctor Trelles Reyes

His work was firmly built on careful selection of candidates, intense spiritual and intellectual formational efforts, personalized tracking of progress, until they were ready to be sent out into the world.

He selected university students for his work insightfully, because he surmised that it was the phase within which young men were malleable and completed formation of their character, for adult professionals, immersed in other interests and obligations, found it difficult to adapt to the duties of the Agrupación.

The founder chose to distinguish in the Book of the Sodality in a special way the first *Agrupados*, those that were part of the first seven *"pases"* [consecrations] from 1931 to 1934. Firstly, he named those congregated in the initial session of March 4, 1931 the "Class of the Anunciata": the first was Juan Antonio Rubio —even thought he was not able to attend, as we have already explained—, Ricardo Chisholm Fernández, Ataulfo Fernández Llano, Angelberto Coro del Pozo, César Incera Soriano, Roberto Injera Soriano and César Rey Rodríguez.

In his *History of the Agrupación Católica Universitaria*, Figueroa clarifies that the purpose for bringing them together on that date was essentially symbolic:

> But this "Promoción de la Anunciata" is a tradition and was recreated by Fr. Rey years later when he inscribed all the names of the consecrated in the Book of the Agrupación. Those that formed the initial nucleus were not seven, but six, and not all met on the 4th, as the others joined in the course of the month of March. Chisholm was not a member of the Anunciata but, finding himself abroad when Fr. Rey inscribed his name, he was not able to correct the error. Luis Blanco is not listed among them even though he was part of the initial group, but the omission is understandable, as he was an Agrupado for merely a month — he died on April 5, 1931. On the other hand, in

just recognition of the work done during his absence, he added the name of Rubio at the top of the list, rightfully first among peers, even though he was not at the initial meeting and did not participate in some subsequent activities. He also placed Ataulfo Fernández Llano amidst the famous "Promoción," one of his most valuable aides in the Agrupación from day one, who at the time was President of the University Youth of the Anunciata and did not come over to the new institution until some time later.[41]

The first formal consecration of *Agrupados* took place on January 3, 1932 in the Church of the Sacred Heart (Reina), when 19 new sodalists were added to the initial nucleus. Some would make history in the Agrupación, like José Ignacio Lasaga Travieso, Enrique Oslé Tour and Juan Suárez Pérez.

The second one took place on the 4th of September of that very year and contributed an additional 13 sodalists. The third, on May 6, 1933, 21; the one on June 3, 1934 contributed 8 and then 7 more on the 8th of December of that year, Solemnity of the Immaculate Conception —adopted as the official date from then on— very distinguished consecrated sodalists merged from it, such as Fernando Azcárate Freyre de Andrade and Armando Ruiz Leiro. This rounded out the roster of those Fr. Rey considered founders.

The decree of the General of the Society of Jesus dated 19th of July was read out loud in the latter ceremony, wherein the Agrupación was separated from the Anunciata and erected as the Immaculate and St. Peter Canisius University Sodality, and part of Rome's Prima Primaria.

The application sent from Havana proposed St. Ignatius of Loyola as co-patron to the Immaculate, but the Jesuit General's

---

[41] Figueroa: *History*... p. 54

decision, very probably based on the common use of that name in numerous sodalities around the globe, was to substitute it with that of one of his first followers, Holland's St. Peter Canisius (1521-1597), eminent theologian, author of a *Catechism* used for several centuries and considered the main apostle of Catholicism in Germany during the days the Lutheran Reformation and proclaimed Father of the Church in 1925 by Pius XI. His great devotion to Mary was likely also taken into account, as well as his preoccupation for education of the young and for being considered one of the fathers of the Catholic press.

It appears that this amended attribution was welcomed approvingly by Fr. Rey and his disciples. Nevertheless, in the booklet *What is the ACU* penned by Dr. José I. Lasaga and published by the Bureau of Information and Outreach in the year following his death we find: "The A.C.U. has the Most Holy Virgin under her Immaculate invocation and St. Ignatius of Loyola as patrons."[42] Could it be that the co-patronage of Loyola was implanted in the collective memory or that by that time the Society of Jesus had authorized a return to the original formula? To date, we have not been able to turn up a confirmatory document.

To fully understand the reach of said decree it is important to explain that Fr. Jean Leunis, Belgian Jesuit, founded in Rome the Marian Sodality of the Roman College in 1563, with the consecration phrase *Ad Jesus per Mariam* (To Jesus through Mary). It was recognized by Pope Gregory XIII —great benefactor of the College and the Society of Jesus in general— in the Bull *Omnipotentis Dei*, promulgated on December 5, 1584. His successor, Sixtus V, in the Bull *Superna Dispositione* granted to the Society of Jesus' Superior the right to add other sodalities to the first one (*Prima Primaria*) in order to enjoy the same privileges and indulgences, *tamquam membra* (as members of it).

---

[42] Dr. José I. Lasaga: *Qué es la ACU*, p. 5.

Other similar sodalities began to appear, first around Europe —Paris (1567), Douai, Belgium (1573)— followed by America —Lima (1571), Mexico (1574)— later in Asia and Oceania. Since they adopted the norms and spirit of the first one, even if they differed according to the circumstances and culture of each country and dioceses, they commence to "add on," that is to say, to join spiritually with the Roman College, designated and honored as the Prima Primaria.

Benedict XIV, in the Bull *Praeclaris Romanorum*, succeeded in increasing the vigor of the sodalities, which until that time had kept alive the practice of Marian piety, but had lost fervor towards the social apostolate. When the Society of Jesus was suspended in 1773 they kept the Ignatian charism alive through catechetical, Catholic publications, and works of mercy in favor of those in need.

In the 20th century Pius XII update earlier work with the already mentioned Bull *Bis Secular Die* (1948) that promoted creation of the World Federation of Our Lady's Sodalities in 1953.

The structure of the ACU followed the usual model of other Marian sodalities. But it developed gradually, starting in 1931. At first its Board of Directors had a Secretary General, a Treasurer, a Prefect for Liturgy, a Head of hospital visits, and a Delegate assigned to the game room.

Towards the end of November, the need to select a President and a Vice-President, recommended by the Board of Directors and approved by the founder, becomes evident and is approved, although *Agrupados* could propose other candidates to the Board. The leadership was appointed for a single term. In the occasion, Ricardo Chisholm Fernández became President and Rafael Buigas, Vice-President.

The organization ended up this way:

On the appointed date and after Fr. Rey's proclamation of the duties of members of the board, the new directors were consecrated before the image of the Immaculate Conception. In addition to Chisholm and Buigas, Juan Suárez was appointed Secretary General; Julio Andino, Treasurer; Head of Catechisms, Enrique Oslé; Angelberto Coro, Liturgy; José M. Mariñas, school for laborers; José Ignacio Lasaga, *Esto Vir*; Enrique Rodríguez, social events; Esteban Beltrán Cuesta, hospital visits.[43]

The supreme authority was embodied in the figure of Father Director and he was advised by the Board of Directors, composed of President, Vice-President, Secretary and Treasurer. As the Agrupación developed, the organization would become more complex as the Board grew to include presidents of groups by profession: Engineering, Medicine, Liberal Arts, as well assistants to assure the proper working of more generalized tasks: Apostolates, Liturgies, Culture, External Affairs.

Years later, as sodalists began to graduate from the University to commence their professional life, it was necessary to form two separate sections: the Professional Section, under the Board of Directors, and the Student Board of Directors in charge of the Student Section, under the Professional Section. This Board had its Student President, member of said Board, and also: Secretary, Treasurer, Aspirants' Instructor, Prefect of liturgy and apostolate, presidents of each specialty, Sciences, Medicine and Liberal Arts. Once a permanent location was established, it was necessary to appoint a President for the student residence and a Delegate for the Library, thus adding one more member to the Board.

The organization might appear to have been somewhat complex, but in fact it should be understood as an extension of the arms of the Father Director. The Board of Directors assessed him with

---

[43] Figueroa: *History of the ACU*...p. 100.

respect to decision making and assumed responsibility for activities of the Professional Section, while also supervising and assisting with matters of the Student Board of Directors.

Fr. Rey was not given to excessive bureaucratic formalities, but did appreciate dearly the role of the Board of Directors in important matters having to do with significant investments toward the proper functioning of the sodality, as well as planning tasks related to educational or apostolic pursuits.

He often heard the advice of its members on matters of economics or politics and heeded it, without imposing his authority arbitrarily, for he considered them bona fide specialists.

The one thing the founder had the last word on was spiritual matters. If his experience indicated that a sodalist was not up to the standards of the sodality, he did not hesitate in expelling him from the ranks, for he was not concerned about the number of sodalists. He preferred a smaller number, upstanding and well formed, rather than a large crowd of laidback and uncommitted ones.

Even though the origin of the ACU was with upperclassmen at the Colegio de Belén, the decision from the start was to accept aspirants when they began their university years, so that professional and spiritual formation could proceed hand in hand. Those entering as postulants had to be endorsed by at least one sodalist and received five weeks of basic instruction, during which time inquiries were made about his conduct in Church and in the world.

Those deemed worthy became aspirants and received special formation that nurtured them with the ideals of the Agrupación for at least nine months, roughly the length of a school year, to be then judged if apt to become a sodalist.

It became traditional for the *"pase"* (pass from aspirant to sodalist) to take place during the vigil of the Solemnity of the Immaculate

Conception of the Blessed Virgin Mary, which improved with each successive year, starting with a talk, followed by a Holy Hour with Exposition of the Sacred Sacrament, and ending with a Solemn Mass, during which aspirants received the sodalists' medal and professed their consecration vow, while those already in the ranks renewed their consecration.

Book of Life

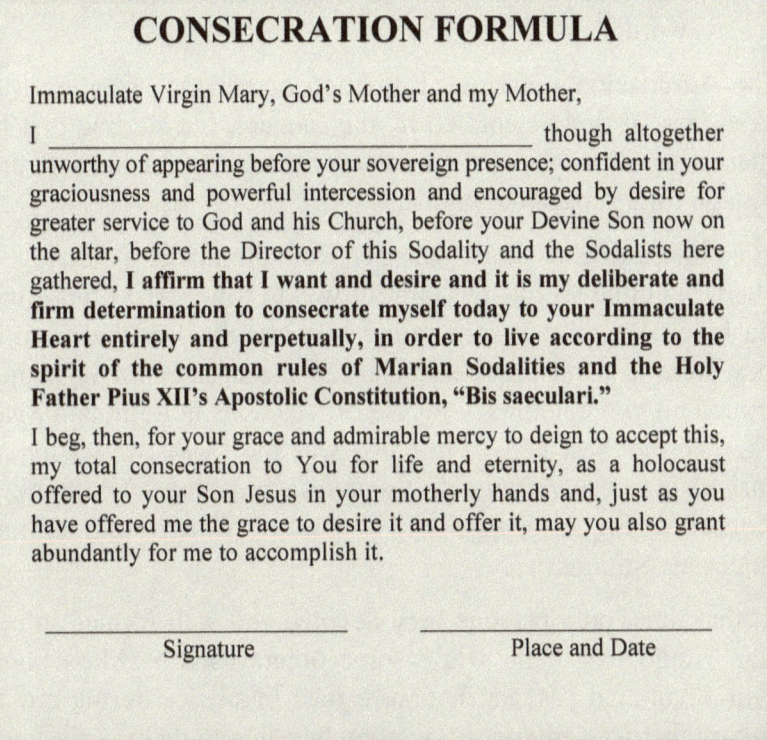

CONSECRATION FORMULA

Immaculate Virgin Mary, God's Mother and my Mother,

I _____ though altogether unworthy of appearing before your sovereign presence; confident in your graciousness and powerful intercession and encouraged by desire for greater service to God and his Church, before your Devine Son now on the altar, before the Director of this Sodality and the Sodalists here gathered, **I affirm that I want and desire and it is my deliberate and firm determination to consecrate myself today to your Immaculate Heart entirely and perpetually, in order to live according to the spirit of the common rules of Marian Sodalities and the Holy Father Pius XII's Apostolic Constitution, "Bis saeculari."**

I beg, then, for your grace and admirable mercy to deign to accept this, my total consecration to You for life and eternity, as a holocaust offered to your Son Jesus in your motherly hands and, just as you have offered me the grace to desire it and offer it, may you also grant abundantly for me to accomplish it.

_____ _____
Signature Place and Date

Starting in 1950, Fr. Rey decided upon a stricter measure. "New sodalists" would spend a two-year period in the, so called, "Junior (Study) Circle" at the end of which, with Board of Director approval, their names were entered in the Book (of Life) of the Sodality. In the memorandum that laid this out, the Director added this reflection:

> In the A.C.U., perhaps unlike any other society, not only is the individual tested and given sufficient time to think on and come to grips with what he is doing and pledging; such that the aspirant is constantly made aware that each step he takes is voluntary; but once the definitive step is taken it is final, it is lifelong, vowing his "word of honor;" leaving to each the responsibility of assessing

and acknowledging the worth and meaning of his word.[44]

The Agrupación's spiritual formation cornerstone was the Sunday Mass, at first celebrated by the founder, but starting in 1934 alternating with other priests, always reserving for himself time enough for a substantial homily.

It is interesting to note that Fr. Rey promoted a "dialogued Mass," in other words, the faithful was to follow the liturgy with the help of a missal, responding accordingly. For that purpose they were to avail themselves one of the missals for laypeople, printed on two columns, with the offices texts in Latin and Spanish. The one best known in Cuba was the *Daily Missal for the faithful (Misal cotidiano de los fieles)*, redacted by a monk of Monserrat, Fr. Alfonso María Gubianas, which went through numerous editions.

At that time, only persons very devoted and well formed in religion would use them, while some others used a "Mass book" with devotional prayers that were read in silence during a celebration that was otherwise incomprehensible to them. This active presence by sodalists that soon thereafter would be complemented with courses dedicated to explaining the Liturgy, was anticipating reforms that would come with the Second Vatican Council, contributions for which the founder has not been sufficiently credited.

To this was added the annual practice of Exercises, which Rey called the "main source of our spiritual wellbeing."[45] In those early years they were segregated into those doing them for the first time, and those being done by more experienced sodalists. They were later further specialized by profession: doctors, lawyers, professors.

---

[44] Figueroa: *History of the Agrupación* ...p. 37.
[45] Ibid. p. 49.

By means of the ACU, Rey de Castro developed in Cuba a charism that had been initiated in Spain, namely, sessions of Exercises. Since they did not have their own facilities, they used Colegio de Belén.

It was an apostolate that reached much beyond the Agrupación and that began to be ingrained among the Catholic men of Cuba. In only two years, between May 1931 and 1933, the institution offered 16 sessions, not including those that the priest directed in the city of Camagüey in an old house the community had on Martí Street, close to the diocese, dedicated for years towards that end.

In the board meeting of January 28, 1932 it was agreed to: "Establish Saturday Guards of Honor to the Mother of God, to implore for her intercession, special graces for the moral and material needs of sodalists."[46]

This Marian devotional practice commenced with just eight sodalists, taking turns during Saturday afternoon, in groups of four, for thirty minutes, in silent prayer, before the exposed Blessed Sacrament.

At the start of 1933, given the number of participants, mental prayer was substituted by prayer of the Holy Rosary, followed by a fifteen-minute spiritual talk offered by the Director, format which was used for many years. In 1936, at the request of some sodalists, alternative guards were established starting at seven in the morning for those that due to work reasons could not attend in the evenings. Although certain historical situations in the country affected the number of participants and the time of day of the guards, the practice has been, from then until now, one of the backbones of the Agrupación.

The other spiritual formation practices grounded in the Ignatian tradition are: personal meditation and examination of conscience,

---

[46] Ibid, p. 48.

as preparation for frequent reception of the Sacrament of Reconciliation and daily prayer of the Rosary.

It is important to properly value this path of religious education because it was not at all common in Cuba nor any other countries. These strict rules were and are associated with the life of the religious or with the regimen of some seminaries strict in the formation of the clergy. In this Caribbean island it seemed almost scandalous given how seldom one found such truly devoted men, and much less so publicly, visible and unabashed.

This was complemented by intellectual formation. From the very first year of the foundation Fr. Felipe began to offer classes to his sodalists, starting with a cycle on socialism and communism, timely topic, for both in the agitated Spain of the Second Republic that he left behind, as among some of those that made up the opposition to Machado in Cuba, these ideologies have gained strength and prestige, such that, supported by the ecclesial magisterium, particularly in the then recent teachings by Popes Pius XI and XII, show their dangers for society and specially for the Church.

At the end of that same year, he taught them Apologetics, for his young men would have to learn how to defend their faith in the public square and should have solid arguments at their disposal. The ensuing year his subject matter would be Rational Psychology.

As time passes and the Agrupación grows, some of these same basic courses are delivered to new recruits, and other teachers are added to present new disciplines: Fr. Román Galán SJ to teach Liturgy, while Fr. Francisco Javier Asensio SJ takes on Ethics.

Courses multiply just a few years later: Metaphysics, History of the Church, Sacred Scripture. Particularly important are the classes by Cuban Jesuit Manuel Foyaca de la Concha on the Social Teachings of the Church —a subject in which this religious becomes an authority at a global level— and conferences by one of the most distinguished sodalists at an intellectual level, Dr. José Ignacio Lasaga, on topics related to Psychology.

This intellectual formation begins to be systematized and integrated to structures that today we call "continuing education." The Study Circles are founded in 1932, and topics are presented and debated by members. In the early years they were led by intellectually relevant sodalists: Ataulfo Fernández Llano and José M. Lázaro. Subject matter related to Psychology, Politics, Social Doctrine, even reflexions on the history of thought in Cuba and its most relevant figures" Félix Varela, José Antonio Saco, Gaspar Betancourt Cisneros.

Moreover, to the extent that the Agrupación developed, this Circle had to be divided and specialized. That is how circles on Law, Medicine and Engineering were born, the careers that were most common among its members, as well as, later, Philosophy particularly for those that studied Liberal Arts.

The Ascetic Circle was a special case, for those members that wished to deepen their spiritual life and become "leaven for the leaven." It was very small at first, but it later had to be divided in two: one for students and another for professionals. The intent was to find in ascetics the engine for the apostolic work of sodalists. Fr. Rey wrote: "Consequently, the principal aim of the Circle is the attainment of intimate friendship, generous and active, with Jesus Christ, sincerely seeking practical means best suited to take us to it."[47]

These formational paths converge in a different kind of Christian, very well captured by Miguel Figueroa in his *"Ideario de la ACU:"*

> The two objectives of the peculiar trajectory followed by the Agrupación, within Marian Sodalities, converge in the creation of a new kind of human being, upon which it proposes to build that new man, created for Christ and for society, able to bring to fruition the ideals

---

[47] Figueroa: *History of the Agrupación*...p. 47.

of the institution, a sodalist that should be natural, open, sincere, honest, loyal, upstanding, generous, valiant, active, giving, genuine, spiritual and abnegated, good friend and normal, but not mediocre, in whom piety, study and action are in perfect equilibrium."[48]

It is not by chance that the founder should adopt the Latin phrase, *Confortare et esto vir*, as the motto for the Agrupación. The Latin verbal form c*onfortare* from which English verb "to comfort" comes from, has a double meaning, on the one hand it means to console and animate, on the other hand it makes clear that strength and energy are being transmitted. And *esto vir* can be simply translated "be a man," but to understand its reach it is important to know that Rey de Castro took it from the Vulgate, the Latin translation of the Bible, where the admonition appears at least three time in the Old Testament that can be translated as "be a man."

The first in the first book of Samuel: *Dixit autem Saul ad David:* «*Ecce filia mea maior Merob, ipsam dabo tibi uxorem; tantummodo* **esto mihi vir fortis** *et proeliare bella Domini*». *Saul autem reputabat dicens:* «*Non sit manus mea in eo, sed sit super illum manus Philisthinorum*» (I Samuel 18,17) [Saul said to David: "Here is my elder daughter Merab, I will give her to you for a wife; only be valiant for me and fight the LORD's battles." For Saul thought, "Let not my hand be upon him, but let the hand of the Philistines be upon him."]

The second one is in the second book of Samuel, now on the lips of Joab, head of David's army: «***Esto vir fortis****, et fortiter agamus pro populo nostro et civitatibus Dei nostri; Dominus autem faciet, quod bonum est in conspectus suo*». (II Samuel 10,12) [Be of good courage, and let us play the man for our people, and for the cities of God; and may the LORD do what seems good to him."]

---

[48] Figueroa: *Ideario of the Agrupación*...p. 2.

In both cases the state of being male is not a simple identification of gender, but rather is associated with characteristics like valor, strength, disposition to volunteer in combat in favor of God and his people, which is in perfect agreement with the definition of "sodalist" that we just transcribed.

Nevertheless, it is in the third of these passages that Fr. Rey seems to have focused on: *Adpropinquaverant autem dies David ut moreretur praecepitque Salomoni filio suo dicens ego ingredior viam universae terrae confortare et* ***esto vir*** (I Kings 2,2) [When David's time to die drew near, he charged Solomon his son, saying: "*I am about to go the way of all earth. Be strong, and* ***show yourself a man***"]. It is paternal advice, as one can see, although in the imperative, reaffirming masculinity as bearer of valor and personal integrity.

Surely, in our time, when feminist narratives and gender studies have gained space, it might seem that what the founder of the ACU wanted to exacerbate was Cuban "machismo," amidst all social levels to reinforce their supposed superiority over women.

Firstly, it is important to recall that in his time, in Spain as in Cuba, public life in general and intellectual and political circles in particular, were spaces almost exclusively masculine and that in shaping his Agrupación he chose precisely a part of that elite that could have influence on society.

But the sagacious priest knew how to march with the times and when it became evident that women on the Island were in ascent intellectually and ever more present among the professions, writers, social activists, he will be the driver behind the creation of a feminine association, *Rosa Mística*, to which we will return later.

On the other hand, note that due to biblical roots, as much as a seal brandished on sodalists through formation, common faults of Cuban "machismo" were not reinforced: rudeness, boastfulness, mistreatment of women, but rather exactly the opposite, those virtues that should abound in good husbands, fathers and friends.

As Figueroa points out:

> This individual, which should be a man deeply committed to being "consecrated" to the renewal of society, to transform it and lead it to reason and to a Christian education, is the leaven yeast that will ferment society in order to catalyze its institutions and restore the environment undone by enemies of the Church, the one appointed to orient the thinking of his contemporaries to the point of directing it and thus turning it back to Christ.[49]

These reflexions about the educational endeavor of that illumined founder could be summed up with the testimony of a sodalist, Luis Fernández Caubí, penned nineteen years after the passing of Fr. Rey de Castro to the Lord's House:

> He wanted his sodalists, the *"Agrupados,"* to be deep in piety, privileged in their formation, joyful, audacious, with a vocation for disinterested service that sets apart the apostles of the bourgeois. He also wanted them to be lords and not slaves of their environment.
>
> He was a true teacher and as such did not settle, but rather demanded stalwartness.[50]

Not all the projects of Fr. Rey developed according to his expectations. The ways of the Lord are mysterious. And so, in 1932 three of the most valuable sodalists on the Board of Directors of the Agrupación that took their positions in December 1931: Ricardo Chisholm, Enrique Oslé and Esteban Beltrán, requested enrollment in the Society of Jesus. It was hard to lose them when the sodality was still small and so much work laid ahead. The founder considered the possibility for them to do their novitiate in Cuba, but it was not a possibility at the time and he had to bid them goodbye on November 15 when they shipped out to Belgium.

---

[49] Ibidem.
[50] Luis Fernández Caubí: La muerte es ganancia, p.3.

As if that were not enough, that very same day it was made known that Father Rey was to be transferred to Camagüey as superior of the residence in that city. It did not seem like the sodality could survive that shock.

Yet, even that test was passed. Juan Suárez, the General Secretary, decided, against wind and tide, to orchestrate the Director's return. He wrote to the Bishop of Camagüey, Msgr. Enrique Pérez Serantes, asking for his assistance in the return of the Jesuit. He did not receive a response, so he reached out to the Vice-Provincial Camilo García for him to weigh in on the issue. The latter answered that he would try to reduce Rey's absence "to a minimum," though it seems he did nothing, which is understandable given, as we have said above, that he was uneasy with the existence of the Agrupación and that, perhaps, the reassignment had been his own idea. Suárez was persistent and alerted Chisholm who, in turn, contacted Father Provincial Enrique Carvajal in Hendaya and updated him on the situation. The Provincial send a cablegram to the Vice-Provincial immediately alerting him if he did not want Fr. Rey de Castro in Havana assigned to the ACU, to let him know so he could send him back to Europe to found another one just like it.

Fr. Camilo García succumbed to obedience and Fr. Felipe was back in Havana on September 26, although he went back to Camagüey briefly in October to offer a session of Exercises that were previously committed. No one ever again would try to separate him from his primary work, although he would not be totally free from setbacks and obstacles with respect to some of his brothers in the community.

Juan Suárez continued to be one of the most diligent collaborators of the Agrupación. Some years later he found his priestly vocation. He became a diocesan priest without ever forgetting the ACU. He was pastor of Madruga. He remained in Cuba following the 1959 revolution and served his ministry during very difficult years, occasionally amidst indescribable poverty. Because of the grave shortage of clergy he had to take charge of the Parish of

Bejucal starting in 1961, as well as the associated San Felipe and La Salud, and be Chaplain of the Santa Susana home for the elderly run by the Sisters of Charity. He did not have private means of transportation, so he had to make use of those infrequent and deficient buses available in that simple town. The ACU was no longer operating in Cuba, but he maintained the vigor and ascetic spirit of an exemplary sodalist.

Monsignor Antonio Rodríguez remembers him this way:

> During his years as pastor of Bejucal he slept on the floor atop the area-rug underneath the main altar and often fed himself at the end of his pastoral workday, thanks to the canteen sent by the Sisters of Charity, when the food was already cold.[…] And this was accompanied by derision, shouts, loudspeakers and demonstrations accosting the temples. […] He never said that he could not live in Cuba." Only partly retired, he died on March 26, 1977 in La Covadonga Hospital. He was pastor of Havana's "Santo Ángel Custodio (Guardian Angel Church)."[51]

---

[51] Mons. Antonio Rodríguez: «Los que se quedaron». Palabra Nueva, La Habana, no.299, abril-junio, 2022, p.29.

VI
Dangers of politics

It is obvious, for he who studies the life of Fr. Felipe, that he was someone strongly committed to his apostolic work and undisposed to being deterred because circumstances presented obstacles to his initiatives. Yet, during the times of his return to Cuba, the political situations in both Spain and the Island were alarming.

A mere month after his return to the Island the Second Republic of Spain was proclaimed on April 14, 1931 and Alfonso XIII had to go into exile. Although some Catholic Prelates like the Archbishop of Tarragona, Francisco Vidal y Balaguer, and publications like *El Debate*, guided by Fr. Ayala and led by Ángel Herrera Oria succeed in striking a respectful and dialogical attitude with the new regime, the greater part of the clergy, religious and faithful show in favor of the monarchy.

The inauguration of the Monarchic Circle in Madrid the following 10th of May was seen as provocative by radical republican elements and exalted mobs and led to a lack of order in the city and to the burning of the Casa Profesa of the Jesuits on Flor Street.

Although it was presupposed that President Alcalá Zamora and governmental Minister Miguel Maura were Catholic, they did not know how or chose not to impose their will on other members of the Provisional Government that did not want to alienate the goodwill of the people and acted with irresponsible indifference.

The Convent of the Bernadas in Vallecas and the church of Santa Teresa next to the Discalced Carmelites on the Plaza de España burned as well soon thereafter. Followed by the burning of

Catholic schools and seats of pious associations, not only in the Capital but also in Málaga and other cities on the Peninsula.

Contradictions exacerbated when the Republican Constitution of December 1931 was approved. Separation of Church and State was decreed, declaring it a "public right corporation," and freedom of religion was established. This was the general rule in secular republics of Europe, but it went further, by including Article 26, which stated that no religious association could receive State assistance of any kind and that congregations with a fourth vow of obedience to other than the Government, would be suppressed, their schools closed and assets seized.

It was a strike directed specifically at the Jesuits. In fact, the Society of Jesus was suppressed in Spain in 1932, a new chapter in the persecutions it had suffered in that land since 1767 when Carlos III expelled them from his dominions.

Even though the Order was restored in Spain in 1815, it was suppressed anew by the constitutional government in 1820 until 1823, even before the approval of the Constitution. The Provincials of the Society of Jesus submitted a document of protest before the Constituent Courts on October 12, because they were on to the suppression plan. It was unsuccessful, as the Jesuits were suppressed on January 23, 1932 by II Republic and all assets seized. Two thousand six-hundred Jesuits had to leave the country and find refuge in Marquain and Marneffe, Belgium.

These events, encouraged by leftist politicians, mostly laypersons, anticlerical and socialist-leaning, promoted a fracture between their followers and another large portion of people that still somewhat sympathetic to the Republic and its reforms saw their personal beliefs under attack. This was a breeding ground for rising polarization through 1936 that brought on the Civil War, wherein the republican side increased religious persecution, specially from the anarchic and communist ranks, that promoted the martyrdom of very many Christians and of the "national" ranks of military personnel that revolted, the use of Catholicism as a means of support and cohesion, justified by a good portion of the hierarchy. That allowed for setting the foundation of National-Catholicism promoted by *"caudillo"* (leader)" Francisco Franco, supported by the Spanish Falange of José Antonio Primo de Rivera.

Thanks to Divine Providence, Fr. Rey de Castro was spared these vicissitudes. Indeed, Immaculate School of Gijón was designated as barracks and was completely destroyed during the Civil War. It wasn't rebuilt until 1946. He did not have to live to join his brothers in exile nor suffer martyrdom. God kept him for other tasks.

The Spanish conflicts extended to Cuba due to the abundant presence of Spanish clerics and great number of Catholic emigrants. Support of the National Side was visible in the large regional societies like Centro Gallego (Galician Center), as well as the role of [newspaper] *Diario de la Marina* against the Republic and in favor of military subversion. It was known that the Exterior Service of the Falange had sponsored the creation of a subsidiary in Cuba that expanded its actions between 1936 and 1941, although it was not supported by the country's governments in that time and suffered pressure from the American embassy which accused it of collaborating with the Gestapo and hastened its end as soon as Cuba added itself to the antifascist bloc.

Fr. Felipe, opposed to the excesses of the politicians from the left and in solidarity with his persecuted brothers, did not opt for political action, in contrast to Spanish priests like Fr. Fernández Gayol y Lobato. He did not support the National side, even though it counted with well-known sympathizers like the president of Caballeros Católicos [Catholic Knights], Valentín Arenas Armiñán.

He knew that those clashes tended to divide the Christians in Cuba, just as they did in Spain. His response was educational and hence, very early on he started to offer courses in which he engaged in critical analysis of socialist, communist, and anarchical ideologies. This effort would be extended later in the Social Teaching conferences of Fr. Manuel Foyaca de la Concha SJ.

The more pressing circumstances of Cuban politics were also of concern. President Gerardo Machado intended to remain in power, following the "extension of powers" brought about unconstitutionally. The repression of opponents of the regime created an environment of terror in the country.

Students, workers, intellectuals, politicians of various tendencies were, at best, imprisoned, while those considered more dangerous were kidnapped and tortured in police stations or in the feared Castillo [Castle] de Atarés. Many disappeared in mysterious ways. The intimidating approach of the paramilitary group known as "La Porra [Club]" and denunciations to the secret police by the "*apapipios*" [untouchables]" completed the lugubrious panorama.

Since mechanisms of democratic opposition proved impractical, Machado's adversaries started to also avail themselves of terrorist methods that included attacks with deadly force against politicians and collaborators of officialism: bombings in public places, military expeditions to oust the president and numerous acts of vengeance and retaliation based on the law of "an eye for an eye." The government and its opposition coincided on just one thing, the use of violence to attain their objectives.

Even within the Church it was impossible to think serenely. We have already noted that the Archbishop of Havana admired and friended the President and that Fr. Camilo García kept up to date with the opinions of the "*Palacio*" [presidential office]" and was guided by them. That did not inhibit too many young Catholics to join the ranks of the opposition and, consequently, the ACU ended up in the crossfire, on one side it was considered by official spheres as a nest of rabble rousers, just because they were university students at a time when the higher centers of learning were bulwarks of antigovernment conspiracies and, on the other side, moderate members or those simply at the margin of politics within the sodality, were looked upon suspiciously by the active opposition that saw in them accomplices of the dictator.

Even the meetings of The Anunciata could raise suspicion at the police, and the Jesuit community on Reina Street looked upon the ACU too dangerous to tranquility and started to insist that it move to its own quarters in order not to endanger the priests living there.

Violence increased in the ensuing years until 1933 when the country was practically paralyzed by a general strike. On August 12 Machado and some of his collaborators left the country. The United States government dispatched a functionary from the Department of State to serve as mediator and keep the social situation under control and to coordinate among the different groups in the opposition. However, it was not possible to immediately achieve political stability nor public order.

The provisional government, led by Carlos Manuel de Céspedes y Quesada, was intransigent, unpopular, and fragile. On September 4 of that year a group of sergeants, led by Fulgencio Batista, and supported by representatives of the University Student Directorate, among them Juan Antonio Rubio Padilla, just back from exile, pronounced themselves from the barracks of Columbia and decided on the overthrow of the brand-new president.

It was resolved to form a collegiate government —the Pentarchy— that only lasted six weeks, failing to get the support of some of the most important political forces nor of the American government. It would be replaced by a head of state, doctor, and professor Ramón Grau San Martín, who was only able to hold on to power less than 100 days.

Although the new government took some positive social measures, it was boobytrapped by internal divisions. The minister of Governing was Antonio Guiteras, a socialist thinking man, but distant from the traditional communists with Stalinist tendencies. The head of the Army was Batista, who despised Grau, feared

Guiteras and conspired to undermine this restoring but fragile government.

The military man used limitless violence to eliminate his opponents. Some 400 ex-officers of the Army took refuge in the National Hotel on September 8 in protest over the coup d'etat perpetrated 4 days earlier and called on ambassador Welles for support in restoring the government of Céspedes, but Welles abandoned them to their own luck.

On October 2, the new Army chief led an operation in which the hotel was attacked by armed forces, with support from the Caribbean Army, composed of university students. They took shots at the hotel, not only with rifles but also with artillery, until the officers raised a white flag. Yet, when they started coming out to the garden, defeated, many of them were massacred en-masse. There were 11 dead and 122 injured. The anonymous redactor of *Diario de la Residencia Jesuita de Reina* [Diary of the Jesuit Residence in Reina] reports for that day:

> As a result of the tragic news that have just been received, Frs. [Antonio] Arias and Rey [de Castro] leave now for two hospitals: Emergency, and Calixto García to offer spiritual first-aid to the injured there. They return at 9:30, after tending to some 30 of the injured at Emergency Hospital and another 20 in Calixto García Hospital. The great majority of soldiers were hospitalized in Columbia.[52]

It is important to also consider the events that occurred a little earlier, on September 29, 1933, that indirectly implicated the Society of Jesus itself. Members of the Communist Party had agreed to bring the mortal remains of Julio Antonio Mella from Mexico to render funeral honors in a place located on Reina Street, just a few feet from Sacred Heart Church. The intent was to inter

---

[52] APA (Habana) Diary of the Residence of Reina II (1930-1934), folio 253. Cited by Sáez: Presencia de los jesuitas...p.244.

him later in Parque de Fraternidad [Fraternity Park], under a small and quickly made obelisk. The heads of the Party knew full well that there would not be consensus regarding this act from either the government nor the armed forces, but decided to push the issue and re-vindicate its presence in the political field.

Guiteras gave permission for the funeral proceedings at first, but cancelled them at the last minute when he realized that Batista would resort to violence against them. The communists ignored the prohibition and took to the street. The brand-new Coronel Batista ordered guards to demolish the small obelisk with sledgehammers and they confronted the funeral procession as soon as it went outdoors. Both sides were armed and the exchange of fire that ensued caused the death of a child that was part of the Party's procession, along with various others injured and run over.

Some armed men —perhaps from the Army— had taken positions on the steps of the nearby temple, and a rumor was started that persons linked to the Society of Jesus had fired at members of the procession from there. Said malicious rumor motivated a document signed by representatives of Caballeros Católicos, ACU, and the so called "*Ejercito Estudiantil Pro Ley y Justicia*" [Student Pro Law and Justice Army]," that ran in Cuban newspapers *Información* and *La Mañana*[53], exculpating the Jesuits from that incident.

Tensions remained so high during the following months that with news of another manifestation in the neighborhood on December 21 of that very year, a head of the police patrol visited the Jesuit community's Superior and informed him that "a vigilance checkpoint would be stationed on the roofs and tower of the building."[54]

---

[53] Sáenz: *Presencia*...p.117.
[54] Ibidem.

A rebellion against the government from members of the ABC took place, after the aforementioned events, on November 1, which was put down by the head of the Army on the 9th in a massacre at the Castillo de Atarés where the last rebels concentrated themselves. Many of those rounded up by the military forces were killed right there by firing squad. One hundred dead and 200 injured were counted. On the following day the anonymous writer of the *Diario* notes:

> At 9:30 a.m. a large number of shots fired around our Residence, Reina-Belascoaín and Parque de Finlay, between soldiers patrolling city streets and unidentified people stalking their steps from rooftops, raise alarm among passersby that quickly seek refuge at the entrance hall of the church. In the end, with so many shots resounding, with such frequency, day and night, above and all around, there is fear that some residents' nerves will be frayed and it is miraculous that we are all still alive. We are only a day short of a full week of memorable horrors and tragedies.[55]

One needs to add to these happenings the months-long rumors that propagate around Havana about the possibility of attacks against certain convents. Although such a thing did not come about, the fear was not unfounded, since there were anticlericals, communists and anarchists among the contending groups and the Jesuits knew, based on the historical Spanish experience, that they were habitually considered the scapegoats for those elements, and they also knew about the violence unleashed against religious from the start of the Second Republic in the Peninsula, on top of the fact that some of the most senior remembered the events of the Tragic Week in Barcelona in the summer of 1909. The noted "frayed nerves" was not an exaggeration by the author of the *Diario*. But the residents of that house held on, including Fr. Rey.

---

[55] Diary...f.260, Sáez: *Presencia*...pgs. 245-246.

The end of Grau's government and his succession by the veteran Coronel Carlos Mendieta Montefur, under the protection of the chief of the Army, did not bring peace to the country. Strikes, confrontations between police and students, all sorts of conspiracies and the multiplication of imprisoned and maltreated created the impression that the epoch of Machado had not ended.

Only after the elections of January 1936, at first under the presidency of Miguel Mariano Gómez, brought to an end, after six months by Congress, at the initiative of Batista and later succeeded by Vice-President Federico Laredo Bru until the term's end, was a certain political stability obtained and parties were reorganized with a view towards the Constituent Assembly of 1940 that gave Cuban democracy a fresh start.

Nevertheless, those years of revolutionary effervescence, resting on violence and disorder took a toll on society. Old opponents of Machado turned into "professional revolutionaries" grouped into supposed parties which in reality were gangs expert in extortion, intimidation, and the struggle to dominate official positions and devour great quantities of the public treasure.

Sadly, the University turned into a privileged location to convene and serve the operations of these elements. There were armed students and professors, public clashes among factions and even assassinations in full public view. Amid all this, the ACU sodalists had to exercise a difficult apostolate, starting with witnessing themselves Christian in an environment where agnosticism, skepticism and even some Marxist orientation were the norm. On the other hand, they needed to behave as authentic students where others were only interested in "*tánganas*" [unruly behavior]" and disorder. The best grades in various Law, Medicine, Philosophy and Liberal Arts, and Civil Engineering courses during 1937 were earned by "*Agrupados*" [Sodalists].[56]

---

[56] Hernández: *Agrupación*...p. 22.

Amidst these agitations the Sodality had managed to grow. According to the minutes of the *"Consejo"* [Board]" meeting held on October 22, 1933 we find that at that time there were some 80 sodalists. It was at that meeting that it was agreed to adopt the Immaculate Conception as patroness and also, thanks to the rapid evolution of the Agrupación, to solicit from Rome recognition as a Marian Sodality added to the Prima Primaria.

This growth called for dedicated quarters. They needed a roof close to the University: "Close to the high center of learning. And far from the window-gazing Jesuits set on their ways." They spotted a century-old building of the Count of Lersundi, on the corner of San Miguel and Mazón streets, roomy and in good condition. It was not easy to come by the rent money. Thanks to Msgr. Ruiz, who offered the Agrupación a grant of fifty dollars per month, it was possible to move there on December 1, 1933, with a chapel blessed on January 15, 1934.

They received two important pieces of news that very year: a signed Papal decree that declared the ACU a Marian Sodality added unto the Prima Primaria and in October authorization to permanently install the Blessed Sacrament in the chapel, which took place on October 28's Feast of Christ the King. The sodalists' practice of visiting the tabernacle upon arriving and departing the ACU was born on that day.

The growth in sodalists, the gamut of their interests and the practical needs of the country led[57] to the increase in study circles and academies. Hence the founding in November 1931 of the Academy of Languages and Commerce that taught English, German, typing, bookkeeping and other subjects, although it quickly focused exclusively on the teaching of foreign languages.

---

[57] Ibid, p. 33.

The Literary Academy was formed in 1932, destined to forge Catholic writers and speakers, directed by Fr. José Rubinos, who had experience in journalism due to the pages of *Diario de la Marina* and led the Avellanada Academy in the Colegio de Belén.

Said institution promoted courses in theory like the one taught by the director in 1937 on "Oratory in Antiquity", as well as conferences delegated to prestigious intellectuals, with records of those offered by the diplomat and art critic, Guy Pérez Cisneros, on "Contents of Afro-Cuban poetry" in 1936. In a similar way a group of sodalists concentrated in a kind of literary workshop designed to exercise those wishing to become writers or journalists. The goal of the latter was to spur the foundation in 1935 of the Journalism Circle, also under the direction of Fr. Rubinos.

The work of the Social Circle also started in 1935, devoted to studies of a sociological character with a Christian viewpoint. That same year the Medical and Juridical Circle were started.

The former was of enormous importance within the ACU. It was possible, in its bosom, to complement and reinforce the formation of medical students through conferences or courses on the subjects of Physiology, Pathology, Biochemistry, Anatomy and Histology. It specialized in ever smaller groups, aimed at students of a given school year in order to reinforce the most important subjects of the academic curricula, yielding one for those in their final years dedicated to discussion of specific clinical cases.

And the work of this Circle was not exclusively internal, but rather as the social apostolate began to develop it expanded into talks on sanitary education, guidance and medical consultation, particularly the work undertaken in Las Yaguas neighborhood.

In time, the scope would increase even more via the Seminary of Historical Research (1936) and Science and Commercial Sciences Circles in 1938.

We must not overlook the development of the Agrupación's library in 1933, growing in subsequent years through donations, like that of Mrs. Rosalía Fernández Quevedo who donated the juridical library of her husband Cristóbal Bidegaray, augmented by frequent acquisition of texts in all the branches of knowledge. Over the years it was organized by sections, corresponding to the different university specialties, each in its own room with some dedicated to study, where sodalists could review their class material without disruptions.

Thus Fr. Rey posited his own pedagogical answer to the complex political circumstances of Cuba. He answered chaos with order. In view of a University that was frequently closed and in which few we consecrated to study, he opened classrooms to dig deeper into intellectual subjects and form competent professionals. He combined spiritual with intellectual learning. He sought well-formed doctors, lawyers, engineers, journalists that could excel in the realization of their social apostolates. It was a rare political proposition. What he wished to delay was direct work with the different political parties, exemplified in tribunals and communications media, with their compromises and corruptions, for which, he affirmed, it was necessary to be well formed.

Personally, he eschewed political parties and preferences of any kind. He completely rejected totalitarianism, anti-Christian propaganda, and violence enemy of democracy. He did not make the common error of the time of turning a public figure, pious as he/she might be, into a Christian leader role-model to be followed by the faithful and only belatedly —after 1948, as we shall see further on— did he listen to proposals of his disciple to form a party based on the principles of Christian Democracy, but at the time of his passing the effort had not gained acceptance, becoming unviable for Cuba in subsequent years. His life-lessons are still applicable for those Christians that desire to enter the political fray anywhere in the world.

VII
Character of a Founder

Those who have read the biography thus far, may have noticed that the life journey of Felipe Rey de Castro has a dearth of captivating or funny anecdotes. His existence, with the exception of a detail or two, follows a straight path, without dramatic passage. His own self-image lacks distinguishing traits.

On the other hand, I could argue that select virtues of the religious, perhaps those God most values, do not appear to be of great interest to man: fidelity, coherence, tenacity to sustain works previously created, modesty that eschews any particular attention to self, poverty assumed with discretion in day-to-day life, a regimented existence not only true to the Society of Jesus, but rather to exercise dutifulness without distractions. He was far from exhibiting what today might be considered a media personality.

When we analyze the extant photographs of him, we find a young bespectacled Jesuit, always donning his generally black cassock, as was the custom in Spain. If the image is from 1931 or shortly thereafter we find a slight smile on his face that portrays that affability that his first Belén students and later his ACU disciples discovered.

It is the appearance of the welcoming professor, devoted to his formational duties, in no possible way could one derive from it a distended, permissive, laidback, witty, much less comical individual. In photos from his final years the expression is more dour: he has discovered the brevity of human existence that demands good use of time granted in order to leave ongoing work in good stead.

85

Group pictures call attention to his short stature, what some superficial person might judge a limitation, yet buttressed by a character that cannot be measured with a ruler.

It could be inferred, based on what one reads about him, that many factors weighed-in on the formation of his personality: the premature death of his father; the exacting maternal concern with respect to education in all intellectual and spiritual matters, without concessions to whims; the familial example of consecrated persons like his priest uncle and abbess aunt; the rigor of years of formation in the Society of Jesus; the tenacity and integrity that he had to apply in order to found and protect the Agrupación and defend it even from some of his brothers in the Jesuit community; the acceptance of the requirement to be living witness amidst young men born in a society that propitiates a disregard for customs and the enjoyment of all sorts of pleasures, without overlooking another Cuban habit, the *"guapería"* [peacocking] that passed for manliness, even among well-educated persons, that he must have had to confront and channel among *Agrupados* towards an authentic Christian virility.

I believe that to many of his contemporaries, at first sight, he seemed brusque, shy, unsympathetic, not given to flattering superiors, brothers or the powerful, shortchanged, just as many saints prior to him or during his own lifetime were shortchanged, among them Ignatius of Loyola.

One of his *Agrupados*, Luis Fernández Caubí, described him as follows:

> Wide forehead, vivacious eyes and broad smile gave him a dignified, intelligent, welcoming look. He walked with the brisk pace given to proactive people, never sprawled-out on a chair, he typically stood like the friar holding a missal, one hand over the other. He was a very gentle man. A slight contraction of his lips denoted his disapproval.

> When something amused him, his hand would cover his mouth so as to contain any boisterous laugh.
>
> [...]
>
> With an elegant sense of humor he defused tensions, held in line exaggerators, and enjoyed the lighter side of things. He possessed that most rare gift of counsel. Good measure was the defining trait of his character.[58]

Well known Jesuit Fr. Sergio Figueredo, who met Rey de Castro in 1950 when the Jesuit visited the novitiate in Havana to relay his experiences at the Conference for Promoters of Marian Sodalities, summarized his personality this way:

> Fr. Rey de Castro, if I were asked for a synthesis of his spiritual profile or of his life, was, firstly, a man of God, very particularly for what he made his own from St. Ignatius: the practice of reflexion.
>
> I was impressed each time we saw him, even though he did not always talk with us and was a rather serious man. In the book [Miguel Figueroa's *History of the Agrupación Católica Universitaria 1931-1956*], it is mentioned how focused Fr. Rey de Castro was on self-control.[59]

Fr. Figueredo has also referred to the long association of Fr. Rey with the Reina [Sacred Heart Church] community of which he was part from his return to Cuba in 1931 to his passing in 1952, even though the greater part of that time he lived in the ACU house, thanks to the forbearance of the Vice-Provincial. He is perhaps among the Jesuits with the longest association with that religious house.

---

[58] Luis Fernández: *La muerte* *[The death]*...p. 2.

[59] *Testimony of Fr. Sergio Figueredo*, Gesu Church, Miami, January 2021. Spanish transcription, p. 7.

One of Frank Salas' most casual reminiscences of Fr. Rey, is what he offers when comparing the personal styles of the founder and of his successor at the ACU, Fr. Amando Llorente, SJ:

> Fr. Rey de Castro, SJ was practically devoid of a private life; he did not attend parties, did not go on field trips, he was either at the Agrupación or at the Sacred Heart Church on Reina Street. He lunched at Reina. [...] He walked from San Miguel and Mazón to Reina [...] He did not, did not have, how should I say it, a great sense of humor. He failed to get jokes [...] You could not kid around with Fr. Rey, no you couldn't. However, one characteristic that impressed me: in his office, in his room, on a rocking chair he was, truly, a most charming person: tender, loving, but take one step out of line and you were out on the street. I remember one weekend during my years there when I got there on Sunday 30 or 40 had been "cleaned out" in the previous week, because they did not take the Agrupación seriously.[60]

We can complement this observation with a related anecdote by another *Agrupado*, Pablo López, that serves to illustrate Fr. Rey de Castro's humility:

> Fr. Rey was sent to Puerto Padre, Oriente [Cuba], on a mission — I don't know to what end — and the Archbishop of Santiago de Cuba, Pérez Serantes that was also Galician and obviously knew him, knew him very well, decides to surprise him. It was on a Sunday at 3 a.m., totally dark, he hears noises, turns on the light, and they find each other ready to clean the church of Puerto Padre. Such humility![61]

---

[60] *Oral testimony #1*, pgs. 6-7 (Spanish).

[61] Ibid, p. 12.

This digression in our narrative simply to photograph with words our biographical subject can be topped off with some fragments from an article "The Fr. Rey I knew at the ACU," by René de la Huerta, published in the *Esto Vir* issue dedicated to him in March 1952, shortly after his death:

> I confess that it took me years to get to know Fr. Rey and that in my first meetings with him I barely perceived his great human quality. I suspect something similar occurred with most *Agrupados* and it is logical, in a way, since our Director was a perfect paradox between his exterior appearance and manner, and his interior, pure asceticism and unique spiritual delicacy. Two of his greatest virtues; charity and his extraordinarily psychological interaction, were hidden under a mantle of apparent rudeness that was only a strategic weapon he put away completely in the confessional or in his Spiritual Director's office. What exquisite care he took to avoid seeming sentimental; in helping the destitute or assisting the sinner without virtue boasting or offensive tears!
>
> [...] perhaps the most perfect synthesis of the character of Fr. Rey: absolute absence of any mundane ballast that might hinder his febrile constructive activity; limitless ambition when it came to God's and the Agrupación's work; military-style work regimen, like St. Ignatius. All of this in contraposition with extremely uncommon spiritual exquisiteness.[62]

---

[62] René de la Huerta: "The Fr. Rey I knew at the ACU." *Esto Vir*, March 1952, p. 14 (Spanish)

Change of Board-members (circa 1934)

Admission of new consecrates (circa 1936)

VIII
The Social Apostolate

The ACU founder's educational efforts were not meant to cloister sodalists inside temples and Catholic institutions, but rather destined to evangelize society, so that along with strict spiritual formation, a large program of courses, conferences and debates, to very quickly commence apostolic works, particularly in areas where the most vulnerable, the marginalized, imprisoned, and sick were to be found.

Even though Fr. Rey's main concern was a Catholic presence at the University, he conceived his idea in an irradiating fashion. Sodalists must not only stand out academically, but must also offer their services in various fields, humble as their labor might seem.

The first of those apostolic tasks started as early as 1931: the conversion of a school for poor children into a night school for laborers in La Anunciata. According to Figueroa:

> It started with forty students and grew to ninety that very first year, the mayor portion young men that worked during the day and took advantage of the evening hours to study.
>
> [...]
>
> Of course, the work of catechizing was not overlooked. Three nights each week they offered religion conferences, and they were prepared to fulfill the Paschal Precept by Sunday, June 28.[63]

---

[63] Figueroa: History of the Agrupación...p. 88

In spite of the political convulsions of those years, enrollment grew to around 130 students that received lessons from sodalists in mathematics, Spanish grammar, civics and other subjects.

In an undated, but very interesting document found in the archives of the community of Reina, Fr. Rey de Castro asks Rev. Fr. Provincial for permission to carry out this work, along with Brother Coadjutor, in secular clothing, because he knew that a portion of the student body —influenced by anticlerical ideas— would respect and communicate with professors more if they weren't led by "priests."

We do not know if the request was heard, yet it not only demonstrates the environment in which pastoral work took place at the time, but also shows how distant the founder was from any type of formalism and his lucidity in seeking more the fruits of work than the safekeeping of appearances.[64]

This became the seed in 1934 of the future Belén Electromechanical School. Indeed, this one and other new ones that arose later had the objectives of readying students to enroll in said school.

In 1938 the institution moved its quarters to the new ACU building and commenced to guide its students in such subjects as electrical assembly, radiotelephony, and other specialties.

The doors to Sacred Heart School in Balcón de la Lisa neighborhood were opened in 1942. The construction was work of the Alumnae of Sacred Heart School and other collaborators. In the modest but solid structure, poor children attended morning classes. Three times per week young married and unmarried women of the neighborhood attended a course on housekeeping offered by members of the female association and by women catechists.

---

[64] Fr. Felipe Rey de Castro: Letter to Rev. Fr. Vice-Provincial, undated, on letterhead of the Jesuit Residence of the Sacred Heart of Jesus. Archive of the Vice-Provincial of the Antilles, Havana (Spanish).

During the evening, enrolled laborers could receive reading and writing classes, primary education and preparation for enrollment in the Electromechanical School. For many years, the campus was led by a well respected *Agrupado*, Dr. Álvaro Ledón.

That same neighborhood of La Lisa ended up running a Workers' Cooperative. Each week the neighbors deposited their few savings in the treasury, destined for a bank account. They were used to assist families in dire circumstances, and to finance initiatives that favored the entire neighborhood. It was a way of complementing the religious and intellectual formation laborers received via practical application of the Social Teachings of the Church.

Another school that yielded significant results was the School-Dispensary "San Lorenzo" run by the Augustinian Order. Some fourteen *Agrupados* offered classes there to a large student body, via a program at par with other centers. It was known for the large percentage of students that were able to enter the Electromechanical School.

Monthly visits took place, in parallel, since 1931, to the Leper Hospital in Rincón. That old malady was still subject to a type of social-exclusion stigmatization. The Daughters of Charity cared for the sick with true abnegation, but that spiritual contribution turned into more than an act of charity, it became a labor of human advancement. Thanks to its example, by the end of the year, 19 young people took part in these visits. Although this work was impacted in the middle of 1933 due to political violence and worsening economic conditions, it recovered later and continued, even after the death of Fr. Rey as long as the ACU remained publicly in Cuba.

Soon thereafter, catechization would be added on. In the beginning *Agrupados* taught Christian doctrine in Sacred Heart Church and in the seniors' retirement home of the Chinese society "Chung Wah." This work was expanded to Beneficence House —on San Lázaro and Belascoaín—, as well as in Baldor, Las Américas and San Antonio schools.

They also made themselves present, starting that very year, in the Reformatory for Minors in Torrens. They were able to work there for a few years with support of the center's authorities and assisted by La Salle Brothers. However, starting in 1952 the direction of the institution started to place obstacles in the way, and the ACU had to end its catechization there.

An unfulfilled dream was to also evangelize to the imprisoned in Castillo del Principe [Prince's Castle]. It should not be forgotten that Juan Antonio Rubio was confined there in the days of revolution against Machado and, most likely, he implored Fr. Rey about the urgent need to offer a Christian word for those men deprived of liberty. But authorization was never granted. It must be recalled that not only was the facility under control of a secular state that precluded all ecclesial works by public institutions, but the police and the military had individuals with irreducible anticlerical stands who took pleasure in making decisions that led to greater marginalization of the Church in the public square. In contrast with other Latin American nations, Cuba did not have military nor penitentiary chaplains during its republican phase[65], although from time-to-time certain priests and religious orders were allowed to visit prisoners.

This missionary work par excellence would be complemented by the greatest and most enduring ACU project: its work of integral human development in the marginalized neighborhood of, so called, Las Yaguas, but this, due to its importance, deserves separate mention.

---

[65] Fr. Hilario Chaurrondo, CM, director of the "Obra del Preso [Imprisoned Work]" under the Pauline Fathers, was able to make some progress in this institution by refurbishing the chapel of the fortress with the support of painters, René Portocarrero and Mariano Rodríguez, celebrate the Eucharist, offer talks and spiritual support to the imprisoned. Yet this was not a duly granted right, but rather under the favor of penal administrators and political winds.

It is striking that some sodalists of the early years found their vocation to the priesthood rather quickly: three of them, Ricardo Chisholm, Enrique Oslé and Fernando Azcárate would become members of the Society of Jesus, just as Juan Suárez and Calixto García Rayneri became secular priests.

This number would multiply over the years, and by 1957 a total of 31 *Agrupados* were called by Christ, 25 of them to the Society of Jesus and the rest secular clergy, among them Eduardo Boza Masvidal, future auxiliary bishop of Havana and today in the process of beatification.

A detail that should not be overlooked is the wide net of relationships established by Fr. Rey in order to develop the work of social apostolates. In contrast with the customary practice of religious orders of deploying their initiatives exclusively through their members, the brother/sisterhoods or sodalities affiliated with them and some of the faithful, the ACU did not limit itself to its own human capital, not even the rather ample one of the Society of Jesus in Cuba, but instead was able to establish joint projects with other congregations like the Augustine Fathers, de la Salle Brothers, Sisters of Mary Reparatrix, Handmaidens of the Sacred Heart of Jesus, Women Catechists, as well as Catholic Knights, other branches of Catholic Action and other lay congregations. In addition to very many people of goodwill, professionals or not and even unbelievers with certain civic and moral principles.

Even though Fr. Felipe referred to the Marian Sodality he created with pride and did not tire to talk about its successes, he had the gift of reaching out to organizations and very diverse people and convert them into collaborators. One could think that he made use of his personality or purely social skills, but it was his daily laboriousness and witness that allowed him to attempt the apparently impossible to gain so many followers.

IX
Evangelization and social work in Las Yaguas

Starting in the early 20th century various doctors, architects and other public figures had decried the critical situation of housing destined for people of low income in Havana. Some authors described the promiscuity and penury of the so-called "casas de vecindad" or *cuarterias* [rooms-for-rent, low-cost neighborhood housing]. Nevertheless, commencing in the century's third decade the concern became more urgent due to economic crisis and rising rental rates. It led to eviction of tenants in arrears, concomitant with increasing migration of families from farms close to the capital or from nearby provinces, looking for work in order to subsist. Thus, indigent neighborhoods began to spring up in the outskirts of Havana, composed of improvised housing with unsanitary conditions.

Very quickly a ring of precarious settlements formed around Castillo de Atarés, such as Isle of Pines, Villanova and La Cueva del Humo, in addition other parts of the city also experienced similar types of people enclaves, for example Las Yaguas [type of palm; its fronds used to provide cover from sun and rain], adjacent to the neighborhood of Luyanó and close to Loma del Burro [Donkey Hill].

The latter was not far from the center of the enclaves, housing laborers, middle class persons, and possessing a basic infrastructure of commercial, educational, medical, and religious institutions. In fact, the main entrance to the neighborhood was at the end of Nuestra Señora de Regla Street, corner of Quiroga, just paces from the Hijas de [Daughters of] Galicia Hospital, Religiosas

97

Esclavas del Sagrado Corazón Convent and the temple dedicated to Nuestra Señora de Guardia.

In 1936 reporter Francisco Bedriñaga visited the neighborhood and interviewed Mayor Manuel Farra, and with what he and others related to him and what he observed directly, he published an impactful report on "Las Yaguas," the neighborhood of the disinherited, in *Avance* newspaper. As researcher María Victoria Zardoya summarizes:

> Farra informed her that it had approximately 500 houses, with some 8,000 residents — Cubans, Spanish, Polish, Jamaican, one Chinese and, once, a now deceased American. He offered some other facts — a house of some 20 square meters [66 ft^2] could be bought for around four to five dollars, in a neighborhood with a "commercial area" of five bodegas, and boasted that the Department of Health cleaned the streets daily. Using glum irony Bedriñaga noted that there were aristocratic sectors within those neighborhoods, where housing was constructed exclusively of wood and *yagua*, and those lacking sanitary facilities had a ditch nearby.[66]

In 1947, during the constitutional government of Ramón Grau San Martín, it was announced that the unsanitary neighborhood would disappear, thanks to the construction of the Workers' Neighborhood of Luyanó, completed the following year, last of the presidential term. Nevertheless, very few were able to take advantage of the new housing, given that a monthly rent of 23 dollars, was simply out of reach.

---

[66]Francisco Bedriñaga: "Las Yaguas, el barrio de los desheredados". *Avance*. 1936; Año II (52):5. Citado por M.V.Zardoya: «Entre crónicas y críticas. Los barrios de indigentes de La Habana vistos por la prensa», s/p. ["Las Yaguas, neighborhood of the disinherited." Avance. 1936; Year II (52):5. Cited by M. V. Zardoya: "Between chronicles and criticisms. Indigent neighborhoods of Havana as seen by the press," s/p.

Dr. Zardoya, with a certain caution, refers in her article: "In some of those neighborhoods "listening sessions" were organized by university students and local charitable institutions, and in addition, Mass was celebrated on Sundays."[67] It is an allusion to the work the ACU had been doing in that place since the middle of the 1930's, under the auspices of Archbishop of Havana Msgr. Ruiz.

The first thing that creates interest in the apostolate the ACU was conducting in that neighborhood is its modern scope and methods. It must be recalled that up until the 19th century it was customary for benefactors to send alms to the poor via a chosen intermediary, but rarely through personal contact with them.

Blessed Federico Ozanam founder of the Society of St. Vincent de Paul, was the first to call on its members to personally approach the less fortunate, in order to breach social distances and display a truly charitable attitude towards the needy. This organization was constituted in Spain in 1850 and in Cuba just 8 years later, an initiative of Castilian Jesuit Narciso Doyagüe (Palencia, 1800 – Cádiz, 1864), with the support of laymen Antonio Rodales and Narciso José de Peñalver y Peñalver, II Count of Peñalver. The groups that constituted it, called "conferences," had an important function in Havana and other places of Cuba for exactly 100 years.

In 1932 they established a medical service and apothecary for the needy. They got as far as founding their own school and between 1956-58 developed a campaign "A roof for the poor," destined to amass resources to build economical housing for families that lived in precarious conditions.[68]

---

[67] M. V. Zardoya: "Between chronicles...", s/p (Spanish)

[68] Cf. Manuel Fernández: Catholicism present in Cuba, pgs. 20-21 (Spanish)

And in the 20th century, other religious congregations and lay organizations of Cuba were used to visiting marginal or disadvantaged neighborhoods, habitually carrying out missions in them, preaching and celebrating collective baptisms and weddings. From time to time a dispensary would spring up, along with a school for children in the local area. However, the ACU went much further.

According to Miguel Figueroa, first historian of the ACU, the work at Las Yaguas came from a request by Archbishop Manuel Ruiz to Fr. Rey, and presented by the latter in a meeting of the Ascetic Study Circle, considered the *Agrupado* elite, so they would take charge of implementing it. It was "favorably received." Thus, the will of the Prelate, the Founder and of various sodalists committed to the work, was unified.

A research project was kicked-off almost immediately, starting with visits by *Agrupados*, with the aim of knowing better and characterizing the neighborhood and its primary challenges.

In the 1937 yearbook of the Agrupación one finds an extensive and well-founded report on the characteristics of Las Yaguas and the living conditions of its inhabitants. In contrast to journalists cited by Dr. Zardoya, it was not limited to recounting anecdotes, nor to compiling adjectives to rate the place, but rather to developing a sociological study in which they made us of observation protocols, interviews, and statistical analysis, eloquent in itself and helpful in guiding the work. It shows that, from the start, they knew how to capitalize on intellectual capital at the Agrupación and how to form teams of professionals trained in Social Sciences, Medicine, Economics, and other specialties.

In fact, the report to which we are referring was a precursor of research conducted later, in the 1950's, by the Catholic Institute of Cuban Studies, adjoint of the Social Study Circle, led by Fr. Salvador Cistierna, OFM Cap, and ACU's Bureau of Information of Propaganda [Outreach]. Dr. José Ignacio Lasaga y

Travieso was among the later relevant figures trained in the methodology of social research in that part of town next to Lawton.

According to the report, the census determined that the neighborhood had more than 2000 residents, a good portion of them people "of color" although "there are a good number of white Cubans and Spaniard and one or another Syrian."[69] The number of houses were estimated at around 500, made with palm *yaguas* —of the type used to form *tercios* [wrappings that used the lower third of the yagua] of tobacco leafs— that a nearby warehouse gifted, secondhand lumber and unusable tin cans found in dumps.

The area was divided in half by a ditch with water from the Pastrana brook and offered the only drainage for that location. The houses on either side had been baptized with such names as "Havana" and "Matanzas" and it is noted that "two inhabitants from this latter place are more careful and serious, and look upon "Havaneros" with a certain pride. It is also pointed out that there exists a stretch of rather regular streets, allowing the "mayor" to designate lots for construction and facilitate internal traffic. The street names varied based on political circumstances, initially named after public figures in the Machado administration, but once he was deposed they were baptized anew with names of other distinguished opposition such as [Ramiro] Valdés Daussá and [Félix] Alpízar, and Avenue [Hermanos/Brothers] Freyre de Andrade.

It was noted that there were only three water faucets in the entire neighborhood, or one per 700 residents. "The house interiors are rather desolate: some old furniture, a few boxes, one or another

---

[69] ACU: "Report on the work done in the Neighborhood of Las Yaguas." Catalog of the Agrupación Católica Universitaria. Havana, 1937, s/p. (Spanish)

table, and at most one or two beds (patched-up cots or useless boxsprings)."[70]

They also took an interest in the genesis of the place. Apparently the neighborhood arose when politician José Izquierdo — in charge of the Central District— authorized a group of indigents to build housing with *yaguas* in fields owned by "Bouza" [Antonio Bouso],"[71] that had been previously owned by journalist and caricaturist Ricardo de la Torriente (1869-1934) and by a man surnamed Guillén" that had been a City Hall councilman.

And they also make reference to social work precursors in the neighborhood: members of the Communist Party had taken the initiative, a little before, following an exhortation by *La Palabra* newspaper, led by Juan Marinello. He gathered a bunch of professors to offer classes at Las Yaguas, among them Dr. Rosa Pastora Leclere and Andrea Tudela. Instructions were offered outdoors, under some trees in the old La Purisima estate, but were suspended due to the general revolutionary strike in March."

This makes sense, since professor Leclere was among the leaders of the Sindicato Nacional de Trabajadores de la Enseñanza

---

[70] Ibidem.

[71] According to our research, businessman Antonio Bouso, from Riotorto, Galicia, settled in Havana, and was one of the founders of Emigrants of Riotorto Society and its president from 1934 to 1936. He was an executive of Centro Gallego [Galician Center] and headed the Daughters of Galicia Society for two terms (1942-1944 and 1946-1949). This latter society built Concepción Arenal Hospital in Luyanó in 1824, popularly know as Daughters of Galicia. Perhaps the near location of this institution to the fields of Bouso in Las Yaguas was not a coincidence, but rather due to the fact that the clinic was placed in a section of his fields. The area was known as New Galicia, not only because of its proximity to the Centro Gallego's La Benéfica healthcare facility, but rather because its residents were numerous Galician immigrants of low means. They were probably a majority of the "white Spaniards" living in Las Yaguas.

[National Syndicate of Education Workers] and participated in the occupation of the Escuela Normal [Normal School] of Havana since March 1, 1935, from which she was evicted, along with other strikers, on the 7th, having to emigrate to Mexico where she lived between 1936 and 1937. The persecution of communists by the army, led by Batista, especially between 1933 and 1936, may it impossible for them to sustain any project out in the open.

The description of the misery of the inhabitants of the neighborhood could not be any more vivid and dramatic. It is described as "a city in miniature, whose monetary unit is the penny," sign of widespread poverty. And they point to tricks employed to acquire goods at low prices in the market — probably the Mercado Único de Cuatro Caminos [Four Road's Sole Market] in order to survive— spoiled potatoes are pared down to edible parts that can be sold to the needy; others sell meat brought from butcher shops that is not in good state, fruits and vegetables in similar condition, matches, bottles. Sending neighborhood kids to nearby homes, to search for leftovers, is a common practice and the only option to round-out their meals.

The authors of the text cite examples of persons that have offered assistance in the area, though almost always tied to political interests, especially near election time, for example the doctor that called on some patients there in name of CND (Conjunto Nacional Democrático) [National Democratic Union][72] or the lady of AR (Acción Republicana)[73] that assisted some families with the inscription of births and other legal documents.

---

[72] Cuban political party, founded in 1935, offspring of the traditional Conservative Party, led by Mario García Menocal.

[73] Political Party, part of the Tripartite Coalition that led candidate Miguel Mariano Gómez to the presidency in the 1936 elections.

They don't overlook the politician that offered to bring Christmas dinner to families that handed over their voting cards, but because the majority of the residents were not registered voters he did not deliver on his promise.

With respect to religion, it is not surprising that the authors, formed in Catholic families and schools, express astonishment at the syncretic beliefs of the residents: home altars where popular Christianism, *Santeria* and Spiritism are intermixed. Religious prayer cards of Saints share space with pictures of deceased relatives. Glasses of water to placate the thirst of spirits are common, as are celebratory gatherings, such as the habitual one on December 17 to honor St. Lazarus, where astonished visitors saw how participants moved rhythmically, before an altar full of sweets and other offerings, to the beating of a drum until a woman *le dio el santo* ["got the spirit"], along with tremors and convulsions to an extent that she was taken to the adjoining room, and "did not stop making prophesies until the teacher moved away." All of this, today so well-known and popularized, was then unknown in the whereabouts of the parish on Reina or in Colegio de Belén.

The novice researchers recognized that some of the elders possessed rudimentary Christian formation because they attended Catechism classes for adults offered by religious Maidservants nearby and, in other cases, there were individuals that had received some religious instructions in their previous neighborhoods.

Although pastoral effort is just starting, educational work is evident. Figueroa, in his history of the Agrupación reminds us that the construction of the school took place early on:

> Funds for the classroom were collected little by little and the Chapel-School was inaugurated on October 18, 1936, under the patronage Holy Virgin of Charity in Cobre [Cuba]. The edifice's structure and materials were the same

as those of the houses in the neighborhood, just bigger, with a closed surrounding area large enough to allow construction of 5 more classrooms, along with adjoining fields for games or plantings, and it was raised by José Ignacio Lasaga and workers from this father's farm.[74]

The report divulges that it counted with 21 professors, counting both *Agrupados* and female collaborators, distributed over three work shifts: mornings were devoted to 8 and 9 year-old children, afternoons for children 10 to 14, separated by sex on different days, with three weekly sessions for each group. Nights were devoted to children that worked during the day and male and female adults. They report that the average attendance was some 200 persons, but in reality, enrollment was much greater but the students need to "find food" keeps them from regular participation.

Among the subjects taught were: Arithmetic, Writing, Reading, English for adults, and Sewing for young girls, while boys are taught their classes. They also make reference to the outdoor Catechism classes, away from the edifice's classroom, offered by teachers under the supervision of Fr. Rey.

Another interesting apostolic work was the visit to the infirm. This was assigned to the doctors and students from the Medicine Study Circle of the Agrupación, who not only looked after the physical health of the patients, but also the spiritual health, as well as facilitating acceptance of the Sacraments through personal witness.

All of this was also supervised by Fr. Rey de Castro, though the Sacraments depended on the parish of the neighborhood, Buen Pastor de Jesús [Good Pastor Jesus] del Monte, Fr. José Rodríguez Pérez SJ— he visited the sick, comforted them and

---

[74] Figueroa: *Historia*...p. 91

encouraged and administered the anointment of the sick if they needed it.

Even though home delivery of clothing was among the customary practices of support for those in need at the time and always in Cuba, there were some really audacious initiatives, such as was left to a friend and collaborator of the Agrupación since its birth, Fr. Maturino de Castro SJ[75], who transferred to the neighborhood a movie projection system, thus allowing the majority of residents to see for the first time a work of the Seventh Art.

Likewise, the missionaries shared Christmas with the people. Some cards were doled out the morning of December 24, provided by the Superior of the Jesuit community of Reina [Street], for distribution at City Hall. At the school that afternoon, they celebrated a party around manger and Christmas tree. One of the professors explained to kids the history of the Gospel about the "indigent from Belén."

They expressed their gratitude to Doña Manuela, the faithful collaborator in the neighborhood and offered her "a serenade with local Cuban music" on her birthday, December 30. Thanks to the book *Manuela la mexicana* by Aida García Alonso,[76] which saw the light of day three decades after this referenced report, where the researcher gathers her direct testimony, we know that she was born in Mexico, from which came Manuela "the Mexican," even

---

[75] Fr. Maturino de Castro SJ. Member of the Society of Jesus in Havana. Part of the Colegio de Belén community. Physics professor. Considered initiator of Belén's Electromechanical School, named after him, and leader also of the emergence of the Laborer's Night School. Sympathized with the ACU from its start and supported Juan Antonio Rubio Padilla in calling for and delivering the Exercises to the first nucleus of Agrupados prior to the return of Fr. Rey in 1931 and continued collaborating with him on various initiatives of the Sodality.

[76] Aida García Alonso: *Manuela la mexicana*. Essay Mention, 1968. Editorial Casa de las Américas, Havana, 1968. García Alonso's book made her famous beyond the frontiers of Cuba and paradigmatic for some feminists.

though her name was Manuela Ascanio, and that she arrived in Cuba in 1914, along with a large group of compatriots looking to improve their economic situation aggravated by the revolutionary convulsions in their nation.[77]

She worked as a maid in various houses, although she had to resort to prostitution on occasion, until she came across the North American, Mrs. Jeannette Ryder (Wisconsin, 1866 - Havana, 1931),[78] who had founded in 1906 the Society for the protection of children, animals, and plants, better known as "Bando de Piedad" [Band of Mercy]. The endeavors of this benefactor influenced here greatly.

---

[77] Cf. Luis Ángel Argüelles Espinosa: "Los refugiados mexicanos en Cuba", p.121-122. ["Mexican refugees in Cuba", pgs. 121-122 (Spanish)].

[78] J. Ryder desembarcó en La Habana en 1899 y allí se estableció hasta su muerte. Se empeñó en proteger a los niños callejeros, alimentar a gatos y perros que deambulaban por la vía pública, así como se enfrentó a cualquier forma del maltrato de animales. Se opuso públicamente a la celebración de corridas de toros. Según el investigador Jorge Domingo: "creó un dispensario gratuito para atender a los menores, estableció un sistema de repartición de pan y leche a los mendigos, combatió el proyecto de establecer en Cuba las corridas de toros, distribuyó desayuno gratuito a las mujeres detenidas en las estaciones de policía y abogó por la supresión de las academias de baile, que en realidad constituían centros velados de prostitución. En todas estas campañas del Bando de Piedad también tomó parte activa el doctor Clifford Ryder, esposo de la fundadora e igualmente ciudadano norteamericano". Falleció en La Habana el 11 de abril de 1931. Cf. Jorge Domingo: "En el centenario del Bando de Piedad". *Palabra Nueva*, noviembre, 2006, s/p. [J. Ryder disembarked in Havana in 1899, where she stayed until her death. She endeavored to protect street children, feed stray cats and dogs, as well as animal advocacy in general. She publicly opposed bullfighting. According to researcher Jorge Domingo: "she created complementary dispensary to treat minors, established a bread and milk delivery system for beggars, fought against the establishment of bullfighting in Cuba, distributed complimentary breakfast to women detained in police stations and advocated for the suppression of academies of dance that in reality were veiled centers of prostitution. Dr. Clifford Ryder, United States citizen and husband of the founder of these initiatives of Band of Mercy, also took an active part." J. Ryder died in Havana on April 11, 1931. Cf. Jorge Domingo: "On the centenary of Band of Mercy." *Palabra Nueva*, November 2006, s/p.]

Following the death of her protector, she settled in Las Yaguas in 1931 and became a natural leader that was able to relieve the neighborhoods misery and sordidness, using means at her disposal.

She shared the few pennies at her disposal with the neighborhood children most in need, in addition to feeding numerous dogs and cats in the area. It is affirmed that a well-to-do family of Havana for whom she had worked as maid called her back, but she decided not to leave the neighborhood in order not to abandon her position at the school. In fact, she stayed there even after the revolution of 1959, when authorities wanted to relocate her along with other residents out of the neighborhood.

It is probable, particularly at the outset, that this woman was a bit shocking to the moral standards and gentrification of *Agrupados*, the majority coming from refined families, but they soon discovered that her presence was providential and irreplaceable. We know, via *Agrupado* Pablo López' testimony, that she supported ACU's Las Yaguas project director of many years, Dr. Álvaro Ledón:

> Well, I knew Alvarito Ledón. Alvarito Ledón was, in fact, his [Rey de Castro] right hand in Las Yaguas; Alvarito León and, I think her name was, "Manuela de las Campesinas," who was... yet Alvarito, Sub-Secretary of Agriculture or something like that, or maybe Vice-Minister— was in charge of "Las Yaguas." He did extraordinary work, a dispensary, classes, and a series of social service apostolates...[79]

Among the projects announced in the final document of the ACU can be found the construction of a site to care for the needs of residents of other similar neighborhoods like "Isla de Pinos [Isle of Pines]" and "La Cueva del humo [Smoke Cave]." Likewise, it proposed to raise two small dispensaries for medi-

---

[79] Oral t*estimony #1*, p. 16 (Spanish).

cal personnel to care for the sick and to welcome those in a more delicate state. They also considered the possibility of amassing resources with which to purchase equipment and materials to start small factories in Las Yaguas: Spanish sandals, brooms and other product lines that could generate work for the many unemployed there.

It is impossible to ask for more from a two year old pastoral initiative.

It is unknown whether Fr. Rey had any previous experience in this kind of apostolate that widened his horizons and helped him understand the reach of the Agrupación in direct, society-transforming work. There is evidence that he was able to delegate to a number of different *Agrupados* the conduct of the various initiatives developed in the neighborhood. He basically supervised them and fulfilled his particular direct charge, Sacramental Ministry and Catechesis, operation of the school, allocation of resources and preservation of the spiritual foundation of the endeavor so it would not devolve into simple activism or a toy of political interests.

In this, as in other work, he demonstrated his charism for leadership, his ability as coach, his systematic and constant perseverance to overcome any work difficulty and his ability to share responsibility with other groups and persons of good will, even though the work at Las Yaguas was sustained by the Agrupación, the support of the Hijas de María Auxiliadora [Daughters of Mary Help of Christians], Religiosas Esclavas [Religious Maidservants], Damas Catequistas [Women Catechists], Corte de María Reparadora [Court of Mary Reparatrix], as well as laymen and laywomen that devoted time and resources to proclaim the Gospel there, not only with words and support services, but also promotion of the human person.

Even though distribution of clothing and food, or services to the infirm was laudable, Christian education was the first step to restore the dignity of God's children to persons degraded by misery and ignorance.

As happens with the work of great founders, the work at Las Yaguas took sufficient root to last not only to the end of Fr. Felipe's day, but to continue yielding plenty of fruit after his passage to eternal life. February 8, 1954 was the inauguration of the School-Dispensary Fr. Felipe Rey de Castro, a building with three wings built around a patio, where all the activities that the Agrupación developed for the neighborhood comfortably took place.[80] The systematic work yielded Círculos de Estudios Obreros [Study Circles for Laborers], una Hermandad de Trabajadores [Workers's Brotherhood], la Juventud Obrera Mariana [Young Marian Workers], as well as the operation of male and female Marian Sodalities founded by neighbors.

This work only came to a stop with the political changes starting in 1959. The new propaganda chose to ignore history and assure that nothing worthwhile existed prior to the new plans and the ACU itself was satanized due to its confrontation with the Marxist turn of the government and had to abandon, initially, its public work and, later, its own quarters and country. But no good works are lost to God and this social apostolate already holds a dignified place in the history of the Church in Cuba.

---

[80] Figueroa: *Historia*...p. 91

ACU's social works at Las Yaguas (one of Havana's poorest neighborhoods)
Photos: Supplement of *Diario de la Marina*, Cuba's national newspaper

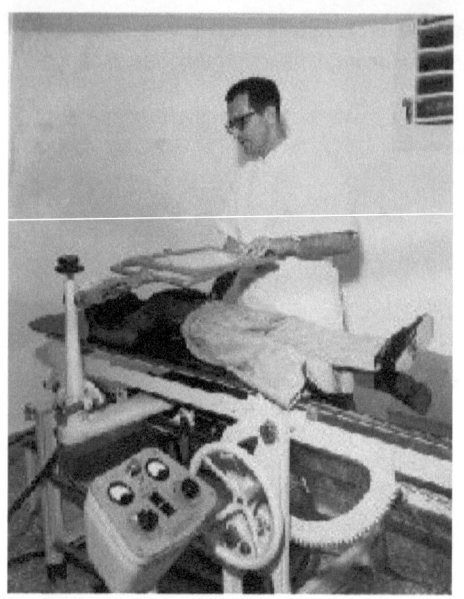

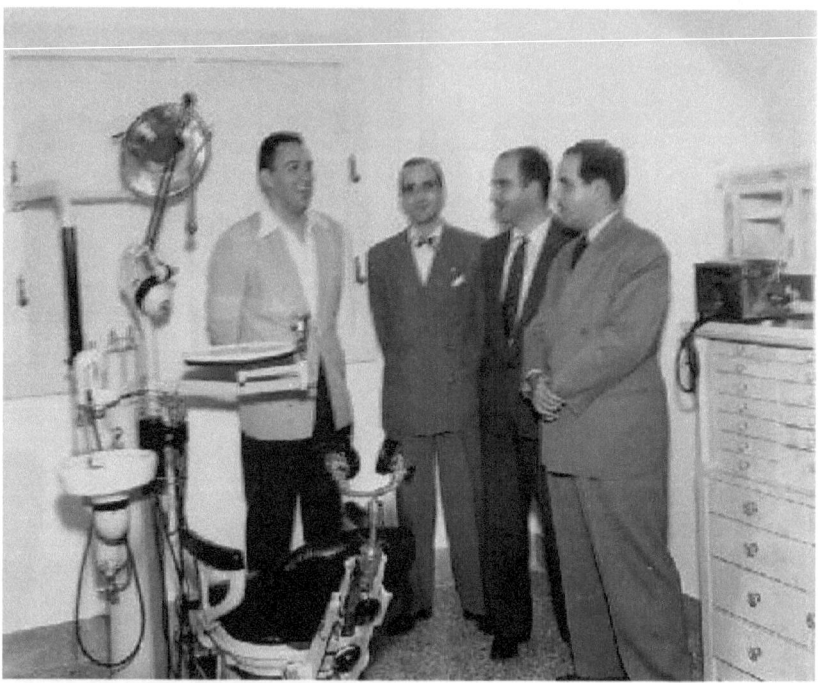

Felipe Rey de Castro and the Agrupación Católica Universitaria

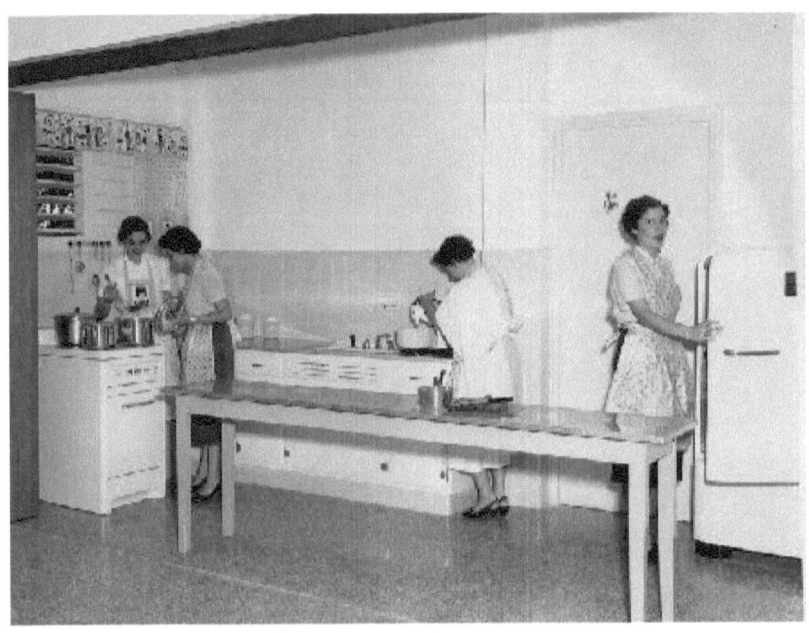

X
Conquest of the university

In previous pages we mentioned the dream of Fr. Rey, described by him as the "conquest of the university." His longing for the "formation of the select" allowed him to plausibly consider the possibility that the university [of Havana], only one in the country, with a marked secular attitude and agitated by frequent political and ideological clashes at its very core, might be influenceable by the Agrupación, firstly by the growing number of Agrupados pursuing studies in different fields but, above all, by occupying an appreciable number of deanships in the institution, to the point of changing the orientation of the campus from the inside.

In parallel, sodalists of the recently founded Agrupación were influencing the chaotic environment of the teaching institution after its reopening. As affirmed by a witness of the time, the Catholic jurist Leonel de la Cuesta:

> Given the participation of professors and students in the struggle against the dictatorship of Machado, he closed the university between 1930 and 1933. The provisional government of Dr. Ramón Grau San Martín granted it autonomy on October 6, 1933, though that did not keep it from being closed again between 1935 and 1937. Following its second reopening and particularly during the governments of Grau and Prío, the university's autonomy indirectly enabled the emergence and growth of political groups reliant on violence, which in the end turned to gangsterism. Students of the Orthodox Party and of Catholic congregations were opposed to this situation and

organized the relatively successful Student Pro-Dignity Movement.[81]

The author completes the image of the situation in another article:

> Gangs rise up around the country, especially in the capital [Havana] and particularly at the university. Among the many groups I will point out various ones at the University of Havana: UIR (Unión Insurreccional Universitaria/ University Student Insurrectional Union), led by Emilio Tro; MSR (Movimiento Social Revolucionario/ Revolutionary Social Movement), commanded by Rolando Masferrer and ARG (Acción Revolucionaria Guiteras/ Guiteras Revolutionary Action). The communists were also among the fomenters of violence, who maintained an intelligent policy of constant and effective penetration, not based on quantity (communists have always been in the minority), but rather on discipline and persistency. They went under the name of AIE (Ala Izquierda Estudiantil/Student Left Wing) and ORCA (Organización Revolucionaria Cubana Antiimperialista/Cuban Anti-Imperialist Organization), among others. In general, it was made up of violent young men that turned to guns at the smallest provocation.[82]

At first, the Agrupados matriculated on university hill were able to resist said environment civilly. They organized "Student Pro-Dignity Movement" through diverse forms of propaganda that combated the chaos and violence in the institution, as well as the

---

[81] Leonel de la Cuesta: "Vilanova's Evocation." *Another Monday*, HispanoAmerican Culture Magazine. Read on http://otrolunes.com/archivos/16-20/?sumario/este-lunes/evocacion-de-villanueva.html, November 21, 2022.

[82] Leonel de la Cuesta: "I, Fidel, at 65 years of age". *Another Monday*, Hispanic-American Magazine of Culture. Read in http://otrolunes.com/archivos/16-20/?hemeroteca/numero-18/sumario/este-lunes/yo-fidel-a-los-65-anos.html, November 21, 2022.

ideologies that fed those groups: anarchism, communism. And they defended Christian ethics publicly.

They were immediately rejected by their adversaries in the middle and even by some "leftist" press that labeled them as reactionaries, divisive, Falangist and even fascists. In spite of the rejection, they garnered some public opinion support and declared against the wish of such groups to appropriate for themselves student organizations. Towards that end they participated in violent physical confrontations among factions on university grounds. The confrontations were of such extent that many students were injured but then, once the opposing bands pulled back, a period of academic normalcy ensued. "Student Pro-Dignity" was dissolved, but the student uproar was defeated.

In this environment, many within the Church in Havana welcomed the founding of the Catholic University of Villanova on October 4, 1946, an initiative of the United States Augustinians in which various Agrupados would attain deanships. It seemed wiser, for those of Christ's faithful that could, to leave behind the official university and find a peaceful backwater elsewhere, illumined by the ecclesial magisterium and far from civil disturbances, but Fr. Felipe Rey de Castro was not one of them.

He did not turn his back on Villanova, but did not believe that the general formula should be to only rely on proper Catholic universities, believing that they were expensive and difficult to manage. Indeed, it seemed that in this he was in disagreement with other brothers in his own Jesuit community, who promptly began to think of the feasibility of a superior educational center next to Belén, that only materialized through the evolution of the Electromechanical School, some months after the death of Rey.

The dreams of the founder were realized in another way. The first semester yielded not only numerical, but also qualitative growth in the ACU, that called for the move to a new location, close to the University, on Mazón and San Miguel [streets], on December 1,

1933. It was a very old palace built by the Count of Lersundi. It was big enough for the different, required functions: chapel, offices, library, meeting space. This place, beyond being remodeled for religious devotion, was also remodeled for something equally urgent: for study.

First home of the ACU, once away from the meeting rooms of the Anunciata in the church on Reina Street, a short block from the University of Havana.

In years of instability at the university, ACU became a substitute. Agrupados that had graduated, or invitees, started to offer classes to their friends according to the specialty of their choice. Study circles by specialty came into being, in addition to initiatives designed to favor formation of university students during a time in which the work of some professors left much to be desired pedagogically.

The most relevant initiative was the Medical Studies Academy, founded around 1941 by doctors Juan A. Simón Gutiérrez and Armando Ruiz Leiro, both Agrupados.[83] It was not part of the

---

[83] Juan Simón was consecrated January 3, 1932 and Armando Ruiz Leiro December 8, 1934. Hence they were both part of the group that Fr. Rey considered «Founding Agrupados».

ACU at first, but it was inspired by its spirit. It was a private institution of learning, aimed at enlarging students' scientific knowledge and going more in depth into the subjects covered in the School of Medicine. It strengthened with time, following a slow start, and after a few years it grew to 565 students. It had to move to larger quarters because of it. In its final years it was located on Basarrate Street, close to the university and the ACU.

In 1956 it was named Medical Studies Center and it was led by Dr. Manuel Artime, because its founder, Dr. Ruiz Leiro became professor in 1953 at the University of Havana's School of Medicine. By that time the single-semester student body had reached 753 and it had a laboratory equipped for the practice of Histology. Its work, by then, was not limited to review and extension of university subjects, but rather to post-graduate courses for professionals that wished to expand their knowledge in a field of specialty. The results were quickly evident: the best grades of graduating students were usually of those who had spent time in the classrooms of the Academy.

Something similar occurred with the birth in 1956 of the Mathematical Studies Center, akin to the other but focused on Engineering, Architecture and Commercial Sciences. It lasted less than the Medical Center, but it became the only institution in Cuba, aside from the University of Havana, that could teach subjects related to technical design at its highest level.

To these we could add, as an example of academic growth, the Catholic Institute of Psychiatry, founded in August 1952, just months after the death of Fr. Rey de Castro, though it was planned prior to it. It aimed to develop the field of Psychiatry within Catholic norms, and was led by young professional, Dr. Carlos Martínez Arango, with an intellectually well-prepared Jesuit, Fr. Fernando Azcárate Freyre de Andrade, the Rector of Calvary Novitiate. They issued various scientific research publications, participated in Congresses and offered an innovative course for Spiritual Directors at the Colegio de Belén, as some congregations had decided to apply psychological evaluations to those aspiring to membership.

The dream of Fr. Rey had been partly fulfilled. The Havana Alma Mater continued as lay bulwark, but in 1957 there were already 28 Agrupados that had reached professorships in the University of Havana, in the newer University of Oriente, in St. Thomas Villanova, as well as in some foreign universities.

Among the most distinguished were Dr. José Ignacio Lasaga, Dean of Psychology at Villanova; Dr. Ruiz Leiro, adjunct professor of Pharmacology at the University of Havana and Engr. José Dust, adjunct professor in Communications at the School of Civil Engineering at the same teaching center. Some were professors at both University Hill and Villanova, as was the case for Doctor in Physicochemical and Physicomathematical Sciences, Marcelo Alonso. The influence of these academic figures on the university environment and on the national scientific movement was indisputable.

By way of example, it is worthwhile to cite the specific case of Dr. Ruiz Leiro, based on a document published by an independent magazine of Cuba's Ministry of Public Health years after that doctor had vacated his position and left the country in opposition to the policies of the government, making the implicit acknowledgment more significant. It refers to the competition for the position of adjunct professor in the School of Pharmacology that took place in 1952:

> Upon the death of Dr. Taboada Boloña and promotion of assistant professor Dr. Radillo García, the latter's newly vacant position had to be filled. It was opened for competition among candidates, the third such competition in the past 5 years, and Doctors Armando Ruiz Leiro and Carlos E. Rojas Fernández applied. Among the members of the tribunal was, as president, Dr. Oscar Jaime Elías; secretary Doctor Rafael Cowley Campodónico; also Doctors

Antonio Valdés-Dapena Victorio, associate professor of Clinical Therapy, Guarino Radillo García and Carlos M. Taboada Millás. Doctor Rojas Fernández retired after the competition. Dr. Ruiz Leiro garnered 3.05 points in the contest and all the members of the tribal awarded him the highest final grade of 73.05. It is worth noting that he received the highest possible score in the four exercises of the contest, 70.0 points. On July 28, 1952 he was properly named adjunct professor, with right of promotion, by Rector's Decree and he filled the position that very day. Professor Ruiz Leiro had one of the most outstanding grade point averages for a Doctor of Medicine of his graduating class on September 24, 1941 at the University of Havana. He was student and resident doctor by contest and resident doctor by contest at "General Calixto García" University Hospital. Due to a deeply rooted vocation for the teaching of medicine he became a magnificent professorial reviewer during the decade of the 1940's, mostly, and his private academy "Simón Ruiz Leiro," founded with Doctor Juan A. Gutiérrez, where they chose to focus on reviews of Biological Chemistry, Normal Histology and Physiology, became the most demanded by students of the School of Medicine. In the University of Havana's 1946 summer school he developed a course on the application of chemistry to medicine that was very highly rated. He was a distinguished leader of the Association of Catholic Doctors of Cuba.[84]

In order to achieve such results, Fr. Rey and the Agrupación had to overcome great difficulties. When it looked like they were well-settled at the Lersundi Palace, the owners reclaimed the facility forcing a hasty exit at the end of 1937. Moreover, in times that were far from a state of economic boom, the rents had risen

---

[84] "School of Pharmacology." History Notebooks... pgs. 7-8. (Spanish)

and available funds did not allow renting a similar or better location, so they had to settle for a smaller house #305 on 25th Street, between L and M, so as to remain near the university.

As the facility was meager for their needs, it was necessary to use donated space elsewhere for the better-attended events. As long as the Agrupación was based there it was not possible to unpack library books and offer services. However, these same difficulties motivated the founder to obtain permanent quarters.

In the files of the Havana Jesuit Vice-Province's offices can be found a handwritten note, addressed by Fr. Rey to the Vice-Provincial, Fr. Ramón Calvo on June 1938, just days after the latter was assigned that position. In it, he highlights the importance of having more time for study in order to prepare and deliver brief courses on Philosophy and Religion, as well as Circles on Social and Legal Studies, monthly retreats and talks, board meetings of the Agrupación that "suffer from inadequate preparation," for "good conduct of the work I have been entrusted." He also needs more time for personal spiritual direction, which implies canceling the "ministry to women," all of this conditioned by the "imperative requirement of an apt house," with the last two words boldly underlined by the author.[85]

His first efforts to acquire funds were fruitful and at the September 11, 1938 Mass he was able to announce the purchase of a lot on San Miguel and Mazón [streets], located diagonally across from the old quarters, where a building worthy of the sodality and designed specifically to meet its ends could be erected.

---

[85] Fr. Felipe Rey de Castro: Note to Rev. Fr. Vice-Provincial, June 1938.

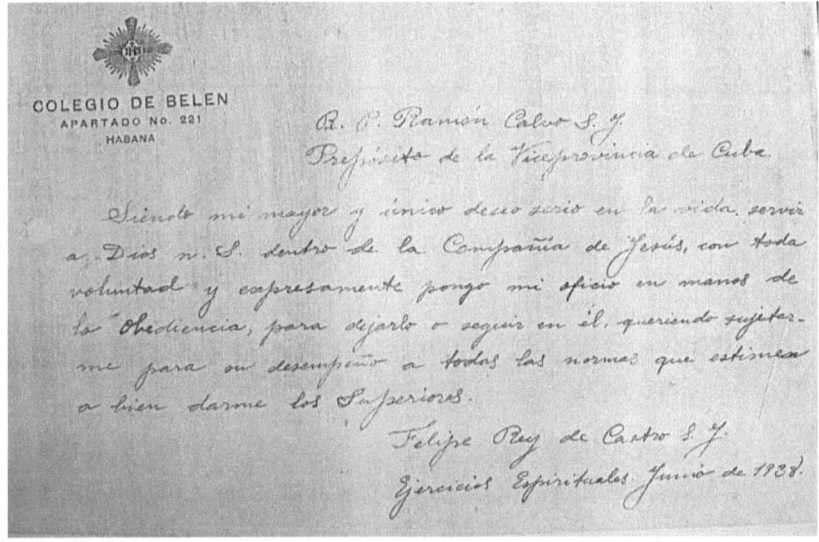

Rev. Fr. Ramón Calvo S.J.,
Head of the Vice-presidency of Cuba,
Being my greatest and only desire in life to serve God, Our Lord, within the Society of Jesus with all my will, and explicitly placing my office in the hands of Obedience, to either leave behind or continue in it, wishing to subject myself in its performance to all the norms Superiors see fit or deign to give me.

Felipe Rey de Castro S.J.
Spiritual Exercises, June 1938

In the above-mentioned files there is a typed copy of the writeup that accompanied the project, written by contractor Enrique Hernández Egea dated November 18, 1938. He describes the construction as "a two-story building strong enough to support a third story on a lot measuring 44 ft. in the front by 118 ft. deep[86] and estimates the total cost of the job at $12,800. There is a footnote written in red pencil indicating: "Leido to the consultants,

---

[86] Enrique Hernández Egea: Note regarding construction of ACU headquarters, pg. 1 (Spanish).

Dec. 1, 1938. Sent plans and my letter to Fr. Assistant in Reina [street] that very day."[87]

Said project had been conceived at least a year earlier, because a 1937 report of the ACU includes a sketch showing attenuated Art Deco lines, particularly in the design of its front-corner door and ten visible windows. It is attributed to architect René Gallardo. It appears that the project did not encounter any obstacles, because that same archive retains a note, dated December 24 of the very year in the General House of the Society of Jesus in Rome, addressed to Fr. Vice-Provincial Ramón Calvo from Fr. Fernando Gutierrez del Muro communicating:

> The project to build your own house for the meritorious Agrupación was fully approved; and the plans were also substantially approved.
>
> [...]
>
> I say that the plans were "substantially" approved, because Fr. Basterra made a few observations that should be taken into account, copy attached.[88]

Thanks to this text we know that the letter in which Fr. Calvo solicited permission from Fr. General had been written in Havana on the second day of that very month, in other words 24 hours after accepting the project. Rarely are approvals of that kind reviewed and approved so expeditiously.

Construction followed a similar pace. The cornerstone was blessed by Msgr. Ruiz, Archbishop of Havana on February 2, 1939, assisted by two priests from the Agrupación, Fr. Richard Chisholm SJ, and diocesan Fr. Eduardo Boza Masvidal. We know that the Agrupación had to move into the first two floors, the ones that were

---

[87] Ibid, p. 1.

[88] Fr. Fernando Gutiérrez: Letter to Rev. Fr. Ramón Calvo, Rome, December 24, 1948. Single page (Spanish).

ready, on the following 8th of August, due to limitations of the house on 25th Street. The first Mass was celebrated in the chapel on Sunday the 27th of that same month, donated by Segundo and Jorge Cateleiro, who also took care to have ready the office and bedroom that would serve as the residence of Fr. Rey. In parallel, Mrs. Rosalía Fernández Quevedo, widow of lawyer Cristóbal Bidegaray Erviti, donated the fittings for the library, to which she had previously donated the collection of law books of her deceased husband. The building was officially inaugurated on December 14, 1939, in a ceremony presided by Nuncio Msgr. Giorgio Carauna.

The work founded by Fr. Felipe appeared to have found its permanent home. It had what he had dreamed of: a house near University Hill, with a chapel, large meeting room, library that was reorganized in 1940, although in the future it would turn into three different ones —Sciences, Liberal Arts and Medicine— that would occupy the third floor of the building, along with classrooms for Study Circles, debates and spaces destined for Agrupados recreation, and would end up housing a residence for those coming from other parts of the island, all of which would facilitate their advanced studies in a Christian environment.

First ACU-owned House, diagonally across from the first rented quarters.

Fr. Rey would live there his remaining years and within its walls would surrender his soul to the Creator. With that work, even if the university had not been "conquered" for Catholicism, there was a strong Christian reference point in that building that was, at once, a witness to piety and a cultural center through which passed, as Agrupados and invitees, many of the most relevant intellectuals of the country and the world.

Historical circumstances did not allow the ACU to develop its work there for much more than twenty years. But these were decisive for its formation, growth and survival and left a trail that will be adequately recognized someday in the history of the Catholic Church in Cuba.

XI
Consecration and surrender

When I started doing the research for this book, I found a note from Fr. Rey de Castro to Vice-Provincial Fr. Calvo, dated June of 1938, written while he was doing Spiritual Exercises. It is brief and surprising:

> My greatest and only serious desire in life is to serve God Our Lord with all my will within the Society of Jesus, and expressly place my assignment in the hands of obedience, to cease or continue it, wanting to rely on all the norms that superiors deem to give me for its performance."[89]

From a purely human point of view this communication seems absurd and inexplicable. On the one hand it appears patently contradictory that the founder of the ACU, who by this time had reaped appreciable fruits, obtained after just seven years of continuous work and loss of sleep raising funds for the longed-for headquarters, would dare to even suggest the possibility of being replaced in his apostolic work by decision of his superior.

On the other hand, we can already tell, based on his life's trajectory, and the character of this Galician religious, that it is impossible to infer, given the difficulties faced to obtain what is needed, that he would intend to create a minor "crisis" in order to call upon himself the attention of the newly appointed Vice-Provincial to facilitate his collaboration, or else, to make him feel

---

[89] Fr. Felipe Rey de Castro: Note to Rev. Fr. Ramón Calvo, Purpose of the Vice- Province of Cuba, June 1937 (Spanish).

responsible for future problems that might befall that work of the Society of Jesus.

He dedicates and will dedicate nearly his entire life to the Agrupación, but a disposition of his superiors would suffice for him to leave it behind to undertake another one decided by them. It is the deepest expression of obedience, the "third degree" called for by Ignatius of Loyola:

> [...] obedience is a holocaust in which the whole man without the slightest reserve is offered in the fire of charity to his Creator and Lord through the hands of His ministers, and since it is a complete surrender of himself by which a man dispossesses himself to be possessed and governed by Divine Providence by means of his superiors —I say that, if this is true, it is certain that it includes in the enjoining of human acts, not merely the execution which carries the command into effect but also the will which acquiesces in the command, and the judgment, which must approve the command of the superior insofar as the judgment by the energy of the will can bring itself to this.[90]

This can be complemented with that passage from the letter of the founder of the Society of Jesus himself to students at the Colegio de Gandía, written in 1547:

> Moreover, in order to know how to lead and direct others it is necessary first of all, to have mastered the lesson of obedience. And as it is most profitable for the Society to have experienced superiors, so it is also in having some method in learning to obey.[91]

---

[90] St. Ignatius of Loyola: Letter to Fr. Andrés de Oviedo, Rector Colegio de Gandía (1548). In: Letters, Book II, CL, p. 125 (Spanish).

[91] SI: Letter to the students of Colegio de Gandía (1547).In: Letters, Book II, CXII, pg. 11 (Spanish).

Hence, in that simple piece of paper Rey de Castro, far from availing himself of tricks of slyness and manipulation of a superior's will, shows he is not a simple activist or businessman, but rather that he has made his own the Ignatian charism. His will is to serve and he has found a novel method of pedagogical and social apostolate, but can only use it if it is the will of his superiors, to which he submits because it is a reflection of divine will. This implies an enormous sacrifice in a man determined and tenacious like him, but also as a great preacher of Exercises he remodels and updates his commitment to the Society of Jesus when he is a practitioner of them.

One should not think that we are dealing here with an isolated expression of fervor. The file already cited has a letter signed by him, dated November 19, 1947, when the ACU is by then a mature and influencing work, in which he continues to be the nucleus and heart of its operation. It would, then, be perfectly understandable for Fr. Rey to consider himself possessor of the right to direct and dedicate to it his full-time until the end of his days. But his surrender surprises us anew when we read:

> Rev. Fr. Vice-Provincial
>
> With the death of Fr. [José] Rivera, Pinar del Rio [Cuba] has been deprived of a missionary Jesuit. I am not so enlightened by Heaven to petition to be his successor, but I am so enough to offer myself sincerely; it could be a very consoling way to prepare myself for eternity, in the last working phase of my life.
>
> If Your Rev. determines to do so, just say the word, further explanation is unnecessary.
>
> From Your Rev., affectionately in Christ,
>
> Felipe Rey de Castro SJ
> Saint Stanislaus, November 13, 1947

How is it possible, one asks, that someone who has for years and through great efforts been confirmed in his mission and even dispensed from living in community in order to devote all his time to the work of the Agrupación, would anticipate a surprising decision from his superior, and accept beforehand his assignment as a simple missionary to Pinar del Rio?

Once again, the reader should reject the idea that the presbyter, self-assured in his institution, is looking, like a courtesan, to display his humility and availability, knowing that no-one could remove him from his vocation for fear of great scandal within and outside the Society of Jesus. Rather it is simply that this priest does not feel himself owner of this charge, that he thinks that he has directed the Agrupación sufficiently so that another may replace him when so decided, moreover, he who has been known and promoted in the Catholic intellectual environment seems to caress the idea of preparing himself for death in a humble task, removed from the limelight of attention.

Fr. Rey, with his humility and obedience, has the wherewithal of those saints that, having completed the work that God inspired in them, do not attempt to retain their charge, nor enjoy their prestige, but rather place it in Christ's hands in order to prepare their soul for the passage to eternal life.

In spite of the sincere offering, the Society of Jesus opted for something else, as Msgr. Antonio Rodríguez explains in his article "Monsignor Evelio Díaz Cía, the martyr Archbishop":

> Pinar del Rio was then [1942, when Msgr. Evelio Díaz is ordained as Bishop], a diocese in which the peasantry showed itself sufficiently prone to religious practice. Many of them went to Sunday Mass habitually in the town's temple. This religious and moral nature of the peasantry from Pinar del Rio had been nurtured since the time of Msgr. Manuel Ruiz by two Jesuit priests: Frs. Saturnino Ibarguren [Servant of God] and José Rivera,

the latter was received by Msgr. Evelio and continued working in the fields of Pinar del Rio until his physical force permitted him. The Society of Jesus replaced him with Fr. Clemente Lombotz [Fr. Clemente Lombó Urbina], who continued to work the territory until tensions between State and Church commenced in the years of the sixties.[92]

Since in previous pages we have made reference on various occasions to Fr. Ramón Calvo Hernández-Agero (Béjar, Spain, 1895 - Haima, Santo Domingo, 1983) it is important to note that the ACU owes much to the understanding and support of this notable Jesuit that was twice Vice-Provincial of Cuba, first from May 17, 1938 to April 30, 1940, when he became Provincial of León, until 1946.

He then returned to the Island and had a second term from March 12, 1947 to September 8, 1952. If Felipe was in debt to the offices of the first of these Vice-Provincials, Fr. Enrique Carvajal, for his return to Cuba as requested by his first disciples, it is not less certain that it was more difficult to work with his successor, Fr. Camilo García, during his mandate between 1931 and 1933.

We have already seen how Fr. Calvo supported extraordinarily the formalities to obtain approval for the building of the headquarters of the Agrupación and granted all dispenses necessary to free the founder in the endeavor of said initiative. Divine Providence often avails itself of human beings as angels or messengers. And the ACU should always thank this religious and teacher that was, additionally, twice rector of Colegio de Belén, the first time during a period of consolidation and growth (1938 - 1940) and the second in a bitter moment that comes to an end with the closure of the center by government authorities (September 23, 1959 - May 3, 1961).

---

[92] Msgr. Antonio Rodríguez: "Monsignor Evelio Díaz Cía, martyr Archbishop". *Palabra Nueva*, Septiembre 19, 2018. (Spanish).

The sad duty of being one of the orators in the burial of Fr. Rey fell on Fr. Calvo. In his moving speech he said:

> For Fr. Castro religion and country would do great work together. We must be forthright in our patriotic and religious duties. We must be Catholic at home, in our marriage, in our profession. We must be true Christians in order to be more like the great priest Fr. Rey was.[93]

After the seizure of Colegio de Belén and following May 13, 1961, Fr. Calvo spent his last days in Cuba at the Pius XII Retreat House in Coronela. On June 27 of that year, he left with Fr. Jesús Nuevo for Miami, where he would start immediately the formalities for the relocation of that centenarian school to that city. He personally obtained authorization from Rome. He died in Haifa, Santo Domingo, on August 15, 1983. The ACU should remember him among its benefactors.

---

[93] Cited by Juan Emilio Friguls: "Contribution of Rev. Fr. Rey de Castro to Cuban Catholicism." *Diario de la Marina*, February 14, 1952, p. 23 (Spanish).

XII
Politics as service

It would not come as a surprise to such a sharp forger of men as Rey de Castro that as his work flourished in Cuba political implications would ensue, reactions both sympathetic and adverse.

In no way did he mean to form "apolitical" men and, in fact, he made sustained efforts to form their thinking around the Social Teachings of the Church, first through his own study circles and later with the collaboration of the Capuchin Salvador Cistierna and Jesuit Manuel Foyaca.

In contrast, what he attained during many years was to avoid implicating his young men in systematic political activity within a party due to the moral risks associated with certain compromises in a Cuban environment where corruption and violence were rampart.

On the other hand, he resisted the creation of a "Catholic Party," most probably because his experience in Spain had persuaded him that to survive it was necessary to ally with politicians very distant from Christianity and in the long run religious affiliation served, at best, as an umbrella under which very diverse elements could find shelter, many of which might discredit the Church.

The fifth decade of the 20th century would be decisive in maturing his criteria about political work by his Agrupados in the public square. Soon after he founded the ACU an important national event took place: the development of a Constituent Assembly in which delegates from traditional parties and others from the armed forces that had pushed Machado out of power participated.

After elections were held to fill seats in the Constituent Assembly, celebrated on November 15, 1939, the struggle between two big alliances was evident: the *Oppositionist Majority* —that included the PRC (*Auténtico/Authentic*), as well as the Republican Democrat, Republican Action and ABC —and the *Socialist Democratic Coalition*— moniker that united the Liberal Party, Nationalist Union, Communist Revolutionary Union, National Democratic Grouping and National Revolutionary Party (*Realista*/Realist). The latter exhibited the apparently unusual alliance of Colonel Fulgencio Batista, now a civilian, and the communists that had been his enemies until very recently.

The publication of the programs of such groupings worried the hierarchy as much as the laity. It was feared, not unfoundedly, that the redaction of the Magna Carta would provide an opportunity to revitalize old tendencies favoring narrow secularism and anticlericalism. But the gravest challenge came from the Communist Revolutionary Union, now in a prominent position within its coalition, that did not hide its wish to harass and restrict religious presence in the public square, particularly with respect to education. That explains the promulgation on February 6, 1940, of the "Exposition of the Cuban Episcopate to gentlemen delegates to the Constituent Assembly," where their position on the matter was expressed.

The prelates directed themselves to the legislative body as "representatives of the Catholic people of the Republic, that constitutes, undoubtedly, the most numerous and important factor, given that they sustain their spiritual interests, the most precious treasure of a community."[94] They immediately address the question of freedom of education: "the parents' right to provide for the healthy education of their children in all forms most adequate according to their own held knowledge and understanding, to-

---

[94]"Exposition of the Cuban Episcopate to gentlemen delegates to the Constituent Assembly, "*The Voice of the Church...p. 26 (Spanish)*

wards the desired end and without any limitations other than those referring to public welfare and tranquility, exclusive domain of the State."[95]

They closed their exhortation demanding authorization for the teaching of Religion in public schools, annulment of the Law of Divorce, recognition of marriage as indissoluble and legal status in the Republic for religious marriage. Finally, they asked that the Magna Carta "work to bring about harmonious understanding of Capital and Work." Their arguments did not hide their rejection of communist ideology:

> We are fervently convinced that a great portion of workers, today part of extremist parties whose objective is a pernicious and inhuman clash of classes, are so because they feel helpless, yet would abandon them, passing from the clash of classes to their cooperation, if they found support for their legitimate aspirations and protection of their rights.[96]

The laity —now much stronger and organized that at the start of the century— also played its part during the proceedings of the Constituent Assembly. Since their concerns were very similar to those of the Bishops, they decided to organize a campaign of "Catholic Affirmation" that developed via radio broadcasted meetings and public events in all of the country's provinces. It was convened by the Knights of Columbus, joined soon thereafter by Caballeros Católicos [Catholic Knights], the Federación de la Juventud Católica [Young Peoples' Catholic Federation] and the Agrupación Católica Universitaria.

The final outcome of this effort was a meeting which took place on February 24, 1940, "Pro-Patria y reafirmación católica [Pro-Homeland and Catholic Reaffirmation]" in the National Theater.

---

[95] Ibid, p. 27.

[96] Ibid, p. 30.

It fell on Agrupado Ángel Fernández Varela to speak for the Agrupación Católica Universitaria. Other speeches were delivered by Oscar Barceló (Anunciata Sodality), Margarita López (Damas Isabelinas/Isabellian Ladies), Julio Morales Gómez (Federación de la Juventud Católica/Catholic Young Peoples' Federation), Luis Bello and Valentín Arenas (Caballeros Católicos) and Mario Pedroso (Agrupación Católica Obrera/Workers' Catholic Association). There were two other speakers not on the program: eminent pedagogue Alfredo Aguayo and José Ignacio Rivero Alonso, director of *Diario de la Marina*, a friend of the Agrupación and father of Agrupado José Ignacio Rivero Hernández.

The closing words were proclaimed by jurist Manuel Dorta Duque, delegate to the Constituent, organizer of the campaign and graduate of Belén, two of whose sons, Juan Manuel and Francisco Manuel, entered the Jesuit novitiate El Calvario two years later. He highlighted the freedom that the Republic had offered Catholic institutions and their patriotic social work until then.

The majority of the country's newspapers noted massive participation at the event that filled the theater and crammed Parque Central and surrounding streets, as well as the thousands of people that listened in from their homes thanks to radial transmissions.

The evolution of the Constituent Assembly where, once again, the cry to invoke God triumphed during the introduction, respected private education, including religious education, and some measures in favor of social benefits for workers tried to find harmony between capital and work. The issues of divorce and the legality of Christian marriage were not considered.

The matter would be underlined by a circular from the Capital's Vicar, future Archbishop and Cardenal of Havana, Manuel Arteaga Betancourt, that highlighted those aspects he judged most relevant in the text of the Constitution:

Noble and animated discussions ensued in which the overwhelming majority of constituents proclaimed the existence of God, from which all authority emanates, and in whose name the Constitution is opened, reasserted freedom of religion with due respect to Christian morality; sustained the need to allow private religious education; prescribed the extinction of perpetual liens on property, thus respecting the right of that sector of the population affected by that measure which will be addressed in future legislation; and left an open door to any reform that experience may dictated in the future.[97]

The remaining text was dedicated to warn about the presidential and legislative elections that would take place the forthcoming July 14. It pointed out that the Church in Havana had no connection with any political party and the freedom of Catholics to vote freely for any party "with the sole exception of any with an anti-religious and atheist program" —which was an overt allusion the communists. It recommended against abstention and in favor of exercising the vote as a civic duty. It closed this way: "Let us all contribute to better outcomes for the Country with faith in God and the sanctity of our ideals."[98]

The outcome of those elections was not what the Church hoped for, the arrival to power of Fulgencio Batista, hand in hand with his communist allies. Schools sustained by religious orders felt uneasiness with norms derived from the Magna Carta, for example the supervision of plans and the education process itself by the Ministry of Education, and the establishment of mandatory subjects such as: Geography, History and Cuban Literature, Civics and Constitution, taught solely by Cuban teachers using official texts, but it was not difficult to put them into practice.

---

[97] "Circular regarding the new Constitution." *The Voice of the Church…*p. 32 (Spanish).
[98] Ibid, p. 33.

It got more complicated in 1941 when communist intellectual Juan Marinello, sworn enemy of religious education, was designated to preside the Commission on Private teaching of the Council on Education. In order to call attention to the danger this implied, another meeting named "Pro Country and School" was held at the National Theater.

The expected aggression toward Catholic schools did not come in this phase, but it was necessary to confront a nationalist campaign that even included some lay Catholics advocating prohibition of foreign cleric teachers and their substitution with Cuban teachers. It did not become law, yet official restrictions previously legislated were kept in force.

These experiences in the public square created an atmosphere at the ACU that led to a cycle of six conferences offered by Fr. Foyaca to Agrupados starting on March 10, 1941 at the Chapel of Las Yaguas on three consecutive nights when he spoke on each of the points of the program. "Points," according to one of the paladins of Christian Social Democracy, capable of attracting with overwhelming force an entire people thirsting for social justice."

Here is how Miguel Figueroa described that initiative's development:

> A small group of professional young men had been planning a campaign that finally kicked-off on October 6, 1941, using Las Yaguas' Chapel as launch venue, where each of the program's twelve points were discussed for three consecutive nights. "Program points", said Francisco Pérez Vich, one of the most enthusiastic champions of Christian Social Democracy, "capable of attracting an entire people, thirsty for social justice, with overwhelming force."
>
> Following this initial success, additional conferences continued at the Anunciata for Catholic laborers and many

from the night schools, and then, better prepared, at Jaruco, Guanajay, Santa Cruz del Norte and Jovellanos

Little by little members of other Catholic institutions of Cuba, Knights of Colombus, Anunciata and Federación de la Juventud Católica [Catholic Youth Federation] joined in. The Agrupación devoted itself completely to this campaign, not only speaking at the meetings, but also leading all the organizational and secretarial work.[99]

The Movement held its first assembly at the Auditorium Theater on November 22, 1942. It was led by Dr. Abel Turbo Tolón, head of the Christian Social Democracy at a national level. It was attended by Bishops of Havana, Santiago de Cuba and Camagüey. The main Catholic congregations of Cuba provided moral support to the effort.

However, this movement, although capable of promoting the Church's Social Teaching publicly, did not turn into an organized political movement, much less into a party that could aspire to claim posts in the Republic's government. Why was it not possible to accomplish in Cuba what was achieved in various European and American nations? Discernment of this matter might be too much for these pages, but it is possible to thresh around some arguments.

Firstly, the 1940 Constitution, although respectful of religious freedom, stressed the laicism of its 1901 precursor. It did not seem viable to form a party with religious affiliation. On the other hand, both the ecclesial hierarchy and Fr. Rey de Castro himself, were reluctant to link the Church with a particular party, as it could generate cumbersome obligations for both sides.

Conditions did not exist in the Cuba of 1941 and ensuing years as they had in the Europe of that time that took Catholics, like Alcide de Gasperi, Robert Schuman and Konrad Adenauer, to

---

[99] Figueroa: *History*...p. 150

relevant political positions. It was not enough for a group of students to study the social encyclicals from Leo XIII to Pius XII and for figures of great intellect like José Ignacio Lasaga to explain individualistic philosophy based on the lectures of Maritain and Mournier. The local environment followed other paths.

Public life in Cuba at the time was a complicated mesh with traditional politicians on one side and younger figures from the anti-Machado revolution on the other. Secularism and anticlericalism predominated and actual politics in the public square drifted between secret compromises and violence. In the majority of parties —with the sole exception of the communist party— one could find a Catholic member, however, only a few could attain relevant positions in the legislature or in government cabinets.

Historian Manuel Fernández Santalices makes reference to some exceptional cases, like the earlier cited Dr. Manuel Dorta Duque, lawyer, professor at University of Havana, and author of an Agrarian Reform project delivered to the House of Representatives but never approved. Another one was Pastor González García, member of the Catholic Youth Federation and the Knights of Columbus, who also militated during his youth in the ABC and got to be sub-secretary of Housing in the short-lived governments of Carlos Manuel de Céspedes and Carlos Mendieta. He joined the Order of Pius Schools, where he was ordained priest in 1954. In 1958, at the request of Cuban Bishops, he was part of the "Comisión de la Concordia [Concord Commission]" that attempted to form a "Gobierno de Unidad Social [Government of National Unity]," that failed.[100]

Among the sodalists of the ACU, Ángel Fernández Varela ran in the midterm elections of 1946 for House of Representatives and won his seat with a great majority of votes. Not so fortunate in subsequent elections of that same body Marino Pérez Durán and

---

[100] Cf. M. Fernández: *Presencia*... ps. 64-65 (Spanish).

Melchor Gastón. Nevertheless, they later achieved important social positions, the first became Dean of the Faculty of Law at the Villanova University and Secretary of the National Federation of Catholic Schools, and engineer Gastón was administrator of "Our Lady of Sorrows" Sugar Mill, owned by his family since 1823, where he continued fecund apostolic work with his workers and neighbors.;[101] in 1957 he was president of the Small Farmers of Cuba and of Catholic Businessmen.

Nevertheless, the most relevant personality of the Agrupación in the political arena was Dr. Juan Antonio Rubio Padilla. As a student in the Directorio Universitario he was opposed to Machado. It should be recalled that one of the first actions of Fr. Rey upon his return to Cuba in 1931 was to visit him in his place of confinement at the Castillo de Principe. He did not forsake his political activism in August of 1933 when the president abandoned his post. He was among the university student leaders that went to Columbia on the eve of September 4 to join the "Sergeants' rebellion." It was he that read the Manifesto del Directorio Estudiantil [Student Directorate Manifesto] that those concurred approved. He moved on to the coup d'etat against provisional president Céspedes and formation of a provisional government known as the Pentarchy.

Some days later, after it was dissolved because of internal contradictions, he differed with some of his comrades —Eduardo Chibás, Justo Carrillo— that proposed Gustavo Cuervo Rubio, Antonio's cousin, as president of the Republic and supported Ramón Grau for the position.

Looked at from a conventional angle, he proved to be a counterproductive figure. Distinguished Belén student, first among Agrupados, the man that kept the Sodality alive during the

---

[101] Cf. Luis Bay Sevilla: "[Sugar] Mill owned for 122 years by the same family." *Diario de la Marina*, January 17, 1946 (Spanish).

founder's absence fortified by the Spiritual Exercises, he was a rebel that was not against violent methods.

One need only recall that he was part of the group that "judged" for treason and had old member of the Directorio, José Soler Lezama,[102] put to death by firing squad and soon thereafter —at the start of November— when he learned that Batista conspired with NorthAmerican envoy Welles to conduct a coup d'etat against Grau, associated himself with Antonio Guiteras, Willy Barrientos and other action-oriented men to kidnap the Colonel, declare him a traitor and put him before a firing squad, though said act was frustrated at the last minute for lack of Grau's collaboration. Spiritual Exercises and firing squads?

Once the national political forces reorganized themselves, Rubio became part of the PRC (Auténtico/Authentic), along with many of his compatriots from the DEU that occupied important position in it. He served as Commercial Adjunct to the Cuban Consulate in Boston. A March 1949 communiqué from the Cuban embassy to the Department of State credits him with these duties and points out that he resides in the emblematic capital of Massachusetts, along with wife Dania Padilla and his children Juan, Ignacio and Elena Rubio Padilla.[103]

During the government of Carlos Prío Socarrás that started on June 1, 1948, Juan Antonio served as Minister without Portfolio

---

[102] Secret Police reports came to light after the fall of Machado that showed that Soler was an informer. He had placed that repressive body on the trail of Ángel Pio Álvarez, engineering student and member of the DEU, implicated in attempts that took the life of Clemente Vázquez Bellos, president of the Senate and of Captain Miguel Calvo, chief the Experts' Section of the police. Due to that Álvarez was detained, tortured and later assassinated. Soler was caught by members of the Directorio, judged and killed by firing squad in a farm on the outskirts of Havana, on the eve of September 4 just before representatives of the organization left for Columbia.

[103] Cf. *Communiqué of the Cuban Embassy to the Department of State of the United States regarding personnel in the Cuban consulates there.* March 5, 1948.

and later as Minister of Health and Social Assistance —position previously held by the eminent neurosurgeon Dr. Carlos Ramírez Corría— from September 28, 1950 to April 3 of the ensuing year. He was replaced by doctor, proprietor and politician of the Democratic Republican Party, Dr. José Raimundo Andreu Martínez.[104]

Dr. Juan A. Rubio Padilla with a group of teachers and colleagues at Belén Jesuit in celebration for his appointment to Minister of Public Health of the Republic of Cuba. To his left (always in the background), the Director of the Agrupación Católica Universitaria, Fr. Felipe Rey de Castro, SJ.

On October 9, 1949, Rubio Padilla held a conference at the Universidad del Aire [University of the Airwaves], "Has there been a revolution in Cuba?," CMQ Network, part of the "Actualidad y destino de Cuba [Current events and destiny of Cuba]" conference cycle. Although the *"Cuadernos* [Notebooks]" of this institution only published it after the end of the cycle, in December 1950, the October 23, 1949 issue of *Bohemia* magazine opened with that text just two weeks after it aired on radio.

---

[104] Cf. *Ministers of Public Health in Cuba.*

That work is of interest, because it is not only an assessment of an agitated and conflicted historical phase, but also a kind of examination of conscience of that Christian politician. In the second paragraph he documents the doubts that grip him and others that contributed to unleash the social violence:

> Painful anguish that of the honest man that has contributed to foment a revolution, to loosen all restraints, to unleash a civil war and only then, in the end, to suspect that he has fallen in the trap of a tragic mirage, and that he not only made a mistake, but that the supposed army of "quijotes [Quixotes]" he happily joined, was just a vulgar sheaf of highwaymen.[105]

Nevertheless, he feels that he was on the right side, not the one of traditional politicians, but rather of the students, whose objectives were: "We wanted a complete and definitive change of the regime that made possible a Machado, and the creation of a new State, rid of foreign guardianship; in service of the basic interests of the nation, social justice and democracy."[106] He also feels that the bloody period was fully justified, for "the revolution brought three changes: national independence, social justice and political democracy."[107]

According to him the previous Republic was fettered by the Platt Amendment and the interventionism of the [United States of] America, which he considers not only superseded —perhaps with certain naivety— but that in matters of political liberty and social justice the gains are nearly absolute. Nevertheless, he feels obliged to make his own the doubts that Jorge Mañach laid out early on about the "unprofessionalism and demoralization" brought by that revolution, for it was followed by exacerbation of

---

[105] J.A.R: "Has there been a revolution in Cuba." *Notebooks of the University of the Airwaves*, p. 31 (Spanish).
[106] Ibid, p. 32
[107] Ibidem.

administrative corruption, pillage of public funds, openly alluded to by him, even though that problem reaches its climax not only after the Constituent Assembly but also during the Auténtico governments, led by his friends and comrades. But the answer comes from the moral field:

> In my judgment, it is necessary to acknowledge a great truth, bitter like gall: the Cuban revolution lacked moral objectives. It was fathered, philosophically, by the secular liberalism of the founders of the Republic, by thirty years of official education, stripped of morality, and by the ideological influence of marxist socialism.[108]

To the surprise of many then and now, seven decades later, the lecturer states that the moral problem was set aside, because the program of the Directorio, as well as that of ABC were hybrids of Rousseau and Marx. This was the reason why: "Morals —and I am referring to a Westerner's morality par excellence, Christian morality— were ignored, theoretically then and practically later."[109] And he adds: "Moral salvation cannot come but paired to a very clear stand in defense of the historic conquests of the revolution, articulated within a new moral ideology."[110]

If thus far we hear the old revolutionary, in the final paragraphs of the conference we hear the voice of the Agrupado looking a different path, not the one of the old republican politicians nor of the conspirators now militating in the Auténtico or other parties of the opposition, but rather in the phenomenon that occurred in Europe following the crisis of democracy and the rise and fall of totalitarianism: "two Christian-Democrat parties. But these parties (here another great lesson for us) did not come about to disown the great conquests of Western civilization but to save them

---

[108] Ibid, p. 34.
[109] Ibidem.
[110] Ibidem.

and thus lift the banner of social justice and political democracy, planting it on the eternal foundation of Christian morals."[111]

His conference ends thusly:

> Here, compass and route. Let us recall the great mottos of the Cuba revolution and deal, with them and with Christian morals, a new and better national flag of service to all, of selfless disinterest and love of neighbor, and then we will truly have conserved our material progress, becoming an instrument of joy, atop a solid foundation of shared morals.[112]

It is perfectly explicable that in a county whose main political undercurrent during the 20th century had been liberal and secular, the apparent shift of the speaker toward a confessional attitude may raise alarm bells, accompanied by a question that Dr. Mañach formulates: Is Padilla suggesting the creation of a religiously hued party? Then Rubio takes the opportunity to further expose his thoughts:

> I will answer Dr. Mañach's question. What a party of that nature would have of religiousness, or of a religious hue, as he has asked, is nothing more than those elements of religion that from the point of view of political action might serve as a solid foundation for said party, because a party of that nature would not be a political party of the Church, that is to say, a political party with a philosophic Catholic foundation; it is not the Catholic Church turned political party; for purely religious ends we have the Catholic Church, uniquely and exclusively. But now, a political party that, from the start, had answers to any number of concerns and questions that we all ask ourselves when a new political party is mentioned (for example:

---

[111] Ibid, p. 36 - 37.
[112] Ibid, pg. 37.

what is moral and what is immoral) would be born with well-known moral precedents and that, in addition, has brilliant moral precedents, because twenty centuries of its application has given rise to Europe.[113]

This was a budding idea, and *Agrupado* #1 has not firmed it up yet, hence his answers to some anonymous young members of the public are not completely clear when "a student" asks him why place a new party under aegis of the Catholic Church went it has generally supported political figures of tainted moral conduct, while a "young lady" makes two signs requesting attention: Why Christian democracy in a country with citizens of diverse religious beliefs or no beliefs at all? And again: Why make reference to Europe when that continent has recently been bereft of good governance?

The intellectual has not reached his destination, but is rather amid his journey on a kind of conversion in his political view. Behind his writings one detects the onus of moral responsibility for having placed himself during his youth in the epicenter of a violent revolution. He has yet to reconcile his political attitude with his Christian convictions. "Why does he insist on Europe? Perhaps because he has been reading Maritain and Mournier and finds in them a Christian spirit with which to renovate democracy, and secondly because he judges the ascent of Christian democracy in Italy, Germany and other nations as providential and useful palliative to the wounds left by fascism and by the very much living influence of communism. Naturally, he lacks personal experience and sufficient historical perspective to judge the doings of politicians like De Gasperi, Schuman and Adenauer. This limitation was not exclusively his as it was shared with very many Christians in the world.

In the context of the ACU of the day those ideas began to lay root with some difficulties. The Apostolic Assembly of 1947 had as

---

[113] Ibid, pg. 38.

its theme "Politics as any apostolate." And the "Acción Cubana [Cuban Action]" movement arose soon thereafter. As Figueroa describes:

> "Acción Cubana" is from that time, the most interesting political movement that arose in our Institution.
>
> It started elsewhere, but was founded by Agrupados intent, at first, to take advantage of opportunities available in any political party, in to order later found their own. Many persons not part of the Sodality, including some hundred women, joined the initial nucleus.
>
> When plans to purchase "El Mundo [The World]" newspaper failed and, hence, Fr. Rey was not able to initiate ACU's apostolic work in the newsprint medium, he decided to place more emphasis in politics and orient the principal efforts of the Agrupación in that direction. With that in mind he formed a Study Circle with *Agrupado* members of "Acción Cubana," personally directed by him, with politics as an apostolate, studying everything and anything that could contribute to form politicians, theoretically and practically, using as the key motivation their answer to St. Ignatius Spiritual Exercises question: "What am I doing for Christ?" To which they answered, "I do politics."
>
> When the Jesuit Hierarchy learned of the existence of "Acción Católica" he was advised that Cuba already had various political parties within which some could lend themselves to the militancy of his group without the need to create a Catholic one.
>
> In the same way, he spoke with Juan Antonio Rubio Padilla after an article signed by him appeared in "Bohemia" magazine in which, including concepts previously expressed by him on "Universidad del Aire" advocating for the formation of a Christian Democratic Party that could

solve Cuba's problems as they were doing in Germany and Italy."[114]

It is clear that, in spite of the enthusiasm of Rubio Padilla, not even that nascent movement could grow into a party. Cardinal Arteaga, as well as the balance of the hierarchy and, therefore, the very same Fr. Rey, were adverse to the birth of a Catholic Party, for fear of contaminating the Church with the corruption of actual politics, and chose not to follow the Christian democratic route, allowing the faithful to militate in those parties that were not expressly anti-Catholic. That was the palliative upheld by the prelates not only then, but still a decade later.

That explains why "Acción Cubana" was moved away from the quarters of the ACU and had to find another place, and forced to grow its base with members that were not Agrupados. When it, once again, posited the possibility of forming the party, the matter was vetoed by the Agrupación, following the guidelines of the ecclesial hierarchy.

Those that were not sodalists at the ACU went their own way and "Acción Cubana" was dissolved in the crucial year of 1952, the one that saw the death of the founder and the coup d'etat that interrupted the constitutional period.

Rubio Padilla served during the government of Prio, as we have already noted, and moved into opposition following March 10, 1952. Starting in 1959 he had another active political period of resistance to the new revolutionary government, initially from Cuba, later from exile in the United States.

The closest thing to a Christian Democrat party was not born directly within the ACU, but rather under the guardianship of the Society of Jesus. It was the Christian Democrat Movement founded by Agrupado Dr. José Ignacio Rasco Bermúdez in Colegio de Belén in 1959. His work was restrained by the heavy

---

[114] Figueroa: *History*...p. 163.

repression of authorities, even to peaceful protest, and he had to suspend activities in the country the summer of 1960. He continued in the United States, where he formed the Frente Revolucionario Democrático [Democratic Revolutionary Front].

A curious detail: Rubio Padilla was not part of that movement in exile. He preferred to found, along with his cousin Gustavo Cuervo Rubio and his successor as Minister of Health, José Raimundo Andreu Martínez, the Frente Institucional Democrático [Democratic Institutional Front].

The First Agrupado died in Miami on September 22, 1989. The bereavement farewell was delivered by Dr. José Ignacio Lasaga who characterized him as a "scandalously honest" man. He was not able to return to Cuba, nor form the Christian party he had dreamt of.

XIII
Catholic Action and Agrupación Católica

It is customary to associate Pope Pius XII with the foundation of Catholic Action, yet careful study shows that its roots are found in the 19th century when certain sectors of the Church developed much needed apostolic activity to counteract the secularism of some States, philosophic materialism, anticlericalism and other hostile currents. Examples of this are the Congress of Malines (Belgium) in 1863 where Catholic Action is born, and the founding by Albert de Mun of the Catholic Youth Association of France. Pope Pius X in his 1905 Encyclical *Il fermo propósito* [The firm purpose... *On Catholic Action*] succeeded in establishing the foundations for organized Catholic Action by lay Catholics looking to "unify its forces in order to place Christ anew in the family, in school, in society," although with a limited vision of the identity of laypeople still seen as an auxiliary of the ecclesial hierarchy. It was Benedict XV who developed this idea more fully and put it into practice when he reorganized Italian Catholic Action and replaced its general directorate with a Board of Directors that granted more autonomy to laypeople.

His successor, Pius XI, in his first Encyclical entitled *Uni arcano Dei* [On the Peace of Christ in His Kingdom], points out the main ills of a society that has come out of the first World War battered and in a Europe where a strong process of dechristianization has arisen, impacted by propagation of philosophic materialism, particularly marxism with its theory of "class struggle" and also widespread growth of concupiscence that distances society from the evangelic message. It is in that context that he pronounces and develops the motto of his pontificate: "The peace of Christ in the kingdom of Christ" and establishes a sort of of program to bring it about, among his points the visible development of the apostolate:

In particular, We refer to the numberless and diverse activities initiated for the education and development, as well as for the sanctification of both the clergy and laity, the organizations of clergy and laity formed to aid the missions in their manifold activities, both physical and moral, of the natural and the supernatural order, by the spreading far and wide of the Kingdom of Christ. We refer to the various organizations of young people which have helped to develop such ardent and true love for the Holy Eucharist and such tender devotion for the Blessed Virgin, virtues which have made certain their faith, their purity, and their union one with another: to the solemn celebrations in honor of the Blessed Sacrament, at which the Divine Prince of Peace is honored by truly royal triumphal processions, for about the Sacred Host, center of peace and love, gather multitudes from every country and the representatives of all peoples and nations, joined together in a union most wonderful by one and the same faith, in adoration, in prayer, and in the enjoyment of all heavenly graces.

The fruits of such piety are manifest, the widespread diffusion and great activity of the apostolate which, by prayer, word of mouth, by the religious press, by personal example, by works of charity seeks in every way possible to lead souls to the Sacred Heart of Jesus and to restore to the same Sacred Heart His sovereign rule over the family and over society. We refer also to the holy battle waged on so many fronts to vindicate for the family and the Church the natural and divinely given rights which they possess over education and the school. Finally, we include among these fruits of piety that whole group of movements, organizations, and works so dear to Our fatherly heart which passes under the name of "Catholic Action," and in which We have been so intensely interested.[115]

Nevertheless, nine years later, a new political issue places Catholic Action in the spotlight again. Thanks to the Lateran Treaty the "Roman question" or dispute over the arbitration of temporal power between the Holy See and the Kingdom of Italy was resolved in 1929, yet the government of Mussolini, in its unceasing effort to impose fascist ideology, begins to remove Catholic orders from educational institutions, including a violent campaign against Catholic Action. This motivates a new Encyclical *Non abbiamo bisogno* [Catholic Action in Italy], promulgated in June 1931. In it, the Pontiff clarifies that Catholic Action was not a political party, was subordinated to the hierarchy and had the right to develop its apostolic work without interference from the State. Even though this caused certain confrontations with the fascist movement it allowed Italian Catholic Action to develop a series of initiatives related to education and cultural affairs like the foundation of movements of Catholic alumni and teachers, the development of social weeks, the celebration of culture weeks and even the foundation in 1936 of a Catholic Movie Center.

The start of "specialized movements" can be dated to around 1924 when José Cardjin founded Young Christian Workers in Belgium. Thanks to this other movements focused on young students or lay adults arose in other European nations.

In the case of Cuba, the creation of Federación de la Juventud Católica Cubana [Young Catholic Federation of Cuba] in 1928 was the precursor of Catholic Action, as mentioned earlier. Msgr. Manuel Arteaga showed interest in founding Catholic Action in 1940 and, with the support of Mexican priest Ricardo de Alba, redacted the first rules in 1941. In fact, a process of consolidation took place that extended to 1944 in which preexisting organizations became branches of it, for example the Association of Caballeros

---

[115] Pius XI: Ubi arcano Dei §53, 54.

Católicos —founded in 1929— became branch A, while Juventud Católica was demarcated among the —male— B and —female— D branches. The League of Damas de Acción would be incorporated in 1942 and immediately became branch C.

The last to come about was Juventud Obrera Católica (JOC) in 1947, whose development was unique for, though it was born from Juventudes de Acción Católica, it gained so much momentum that it became its own autonomous association. The Society of Jesus had a decisive role in that development, particularly in the 1950's when the JOC founded in the new Jesuit community of Villa San José by Fr. Manuel Foyaca de la Concha, the great promoter of the Social Teachings of the Church in Cuba and other countries of the region. The assessor of the JOC was Agrupado Fr. Enrique Oslé Tour SJ.

In those quarters of G Street and 19 were offered brief courses of social awareness with attendance from affiliates from around the Republic. In 1953 they got to have professional propagandists in Ciego de Ávila, Colón and Güira de Selena forming young worker leaders. In 1958 they celebrated their First Social Week in Buen Pastor [Good Shepherd] Seminary, also seat of the Second and Third in subsequent years. In the latter they issued a document in which they condemned "the abuses of exploitative capitalism" but also "communism for positing class struggle and destruction of social economic order in their campaigns and demagogy, under the pretext of false promises made to common people."[116]

ACU's retreat house had hosted the meeting of the Executive Committee of the Juventud Obrera Católica Internacional, with delegates from Europe, Asia, Africa and America, Msgr. Cardjin among them. By 1960 they had their own quarters on Tulipán Street in Cerro. The country's political circumstances that very year were adverse for the organization and it determined to stop its public work.

---

[116] Cited by Sáez: *Presence of the Jesuits*...p. 138 (Spanish).

The widely encompassing and unifying Acción Católica, as well as the presence of various Jesuits as assessors or collaborators of its different branches augured that the Agrupación Católica Universitaria would be a clearly visible part of it. Nevertheless, the ACU's singular characteristics, while not impeding collaboration with Acción Católica on different works and circumstances, did not allow its full and organic integration.

One must not look for an obstacle to such a relationship. Years before, in 1941, when the Bishops announced in a Eucharistic Congress in Camagüey their desire to form Catholic Action, Fr. Felipe followed closely, since 1933, the process of its development in different countries of the world and talked about it to his Agrupados, to the point of including the topic in his Spiritual Exercises' talks. He exhibited a special connection with the thinking of Pius XI on the matter and also, later, with that of his successor Pius XII. By that time the Agrupación, both the rank and file and the hierarchy, was perceived within and without as an inescapable part of the future Catholic Action. Figueroa stated:

> "Even before the latter's official creation, the Agrupación believed and acted since its foundation like it was engaging in Catholic action, while preparing the ground for its future formation. That is how Juan Suárez expressed it on February 23, 1933 to the Uruguayan Catholic Youth Secretariat: "A little more than two years ago we commenced our Catholic Action exclusively within the university, believing that if we did not first shape men apt for such an organization, an enterprise of that magnitude could not completely fulfill the needs of true Catholic Action."

> "Monsignor Ruiz confirmed and encouraged similar convictions repeatedly, one time in writing on January 5, 1938 in a letter to the President of the Agrupación: "I am happy to count among my auxiliaries committed men that

for love of God and neighbor labor assiduously in works of true Catholic Action."117

And as if this were not enough, one could turn for support to the Holy Father's own words:

"Moreover, Pius XII had written to Fr. Daniel Lord in 1940 that the "spirit of fraternal solidarity engaged in the glorious redemptive mission of the Universal Church will best serve to coordinate, as our previous and fondly remembered Predecessor ardently desired and planned, the efforts of various autonomous associations devoted to apostolic works, and thus consecrating, in a manner of speaking, their cordial collaboration in progressing the cause of Jesus Christ."

Furthermore, on September 4 of that very year, in an address to Italian Catholic Action, he went beyond this and said that Marian Sodalities, just as other Catholic Action organizations, were part of the official Cooperation in the Hierarchical Apostolate of the Church without surrendering any of their own spirit or internal organization, but rather coordinating in perfect harmony with other entities of Catholic Action."118

This could be furthered buttressed by the very ideals and norms for Marian Sodalities that Pope Pacelli defined in his address of January 21, 1945:

Consecration to the Mother of God in a Sodality of Our Lady is an entire gift of oneself for one's whole life and for eternity. This gift does not consist merely of a sentimental formula, on the contrary, it is a gift that produces results. It verifies itself in the intensity of a life like

---

[117] Figueroa: *History*...p. 215.
[118] Ibidem.

Christ's and Mary's, an apostolic life, that makes the Sodalist Mary's ambassador and, one might say, her visible hands on earth. This gift proves itself genuine in an interior life that is too great to contain itself and spontaneously overflows into all types of external works of genuine devotion, worship, charity, and zeal.

There you have what is stressed with particular emphasis in your first Rule. Note that in his act of consecration the Sodalist freely and resolutely accepted the commission (a) to apply himself in his particular state of life; (b) to dedicate himself not in a half-hearted way but with great enthusiasm, to the salvation and perfection of others through the kind and amount of action that is in harmony with his particular social condition; (c) to give himself energetically to defending the Church of Christ. This is the magnificent program outlined for the sodalist in his Rules.[119]

In spite of all these fundamentals from the Magisterium that defined the existence and work of the Agrupación clearly as a kind of "Catholic Action," it never managed to integrate itself fully in Cuban Catholic Action. No even appointment of such an imminent Agrupado as José Ignacio Lasaga "National Secretariat organizer and Secretary of the National Board" was able to smooth the differences between both organizations.

Miguel Figueroa Miranda offers some plausible reasons in his *History of the ACU*. Among them, the fact that Cuban Catholic Action followed the Spanish model with a wide presence of secular clergy that managed to centralize its work in parish boards.

I would dare to add to this that in Cuba, as in other parts of the world, there was a given mental distance and even certain

---

[119] Sodality Golden Jubilee Address of Pope Pius XII, January 21, 1945

exclusions between secular clergy and religious congregations, to the point of difficulties toward full cooperation. That explains why the concept that Marian Sodalities were a thing apart quickly took root and though their sodalists were welcomed to Catholic Action as individuals, they were not recognized as working members within them.

This was particularly significant in branch B, that of the youth, because this one brought with it previous experience from the Federación de la Juventud Católica, referenced earlier, much different to what happened with branch A, Caballeros Católicos, inspired by Jesuits and very quick accepters of the ACU as a brotherly entity with whom it had close collaboration throughout the Island.

The decision by Acción Católica, in spite of pontifical norms, that Marian Sodalities were not "catholic action" required that sodalists wishing to be part of it had to enroll in it individually. This was not only surprising, but also rather bitter to Fr. Rey.

The founder of the ACU endeavored to get close to Cuban Catholic Action and made sure that the Board of Directors of the ACU made efforts to maintain cordial relationships with it. These efforts helped the Board of Catholic Action to invite two sodalists of the ACU as delegates of a Parrish Board that held one of its sessions at the Agrupación; likewise, sodalists collaborated on the formation of Acción Católica groups in Varadero and Victoria de las Tunas.

But things did not progress beyond these pleasantries and the letter Rey de Castro sent in 1943 to Msgr. Valentín Zubizarreta, Archbishop of Santiago de Cuba and president of the Conference of Bishops of Cuba, affirmed that the Agrupación "had always been and had engaged in Catholic Action." The letter designed to break the impasse, was not even acknowledged to have been received.

Although His Eminence Manuel Arteaga, guest of the ACU's Apostolic Assembly of 1943, said that the Agrupación "had always been and had engaged in Catholic Action," nothing changed in practice.

Catholic professor and historian Ignacio Uría, in his book *Iglesia y Revolución en Cuba* [Church and Revolution in Cuba] — a very thorough study of the life and work of Msgr. Enrique Pérez Serantes—, delves into this matter with complete clarity. In that very same year of 1943, the prelate, then Bishop of Camagüey, writes to the Society of Jesus asking for assistance to strengthen Acción Católica and receives a prompt response from Fr. Gustavo Amigó, a close collaborator of Fr. Rey in the ACU:

> Fr. Gustavo Amigó replied to your request confirming that the ACU (created by the Society of Jesus) was: "more than willing to cooperate with Catholic Action [...] looking upon it not as humiliating, but rather as a duty in service to the Holy See." Apparently a rumor was circulated that the founder of said association, Jesuit Felipe Rey de Castro, had publicly criticized Catholic Action, something that Fr. Amigó, sub-director of the ACU and friend of Pérez Serantes, denied."

> "I have never heard such a thing, not even in private. Therefore, you may communicate to Msgr. Zubizarreta, on our behalf and officially, that we are absolutely willing and eager to join ranks in Catholic Action according to the norms of the Pope and your conditions [...]. Such cooperation is not abasing, but rather uplifting."[120]

But the diligent historian goes beyond the calming words of the Jesuit, making reference to the "atmosphere" of criticism that enveloped the ACU, no only from the ranks of Acción Católica, but also in certain places of the Church in Havana:

---

[120] Ignacio Uría: *Iglesia y Revolución en Cuba*, p. 85 (Spanish).

Nevertheless, Fr. Rey and the ACU had been criticized by other Catholics. The Jesuit was tagged as "absorbent" and "elitist," while Acción Católica was popular, an initiative for parish Catholics.

The controversy spread to the Franciscan magazine La Quincena [Fornight], which requested that the ACU be part of Catholic Action "immediately." Otherwise:[...] they will continue to be chiefs without soldiers. "Leaders without followers," a weird body that avoided contact with normal Catholics."[121]

These differences did not get in the way of both groups collaborating on the "Mitin Pro Patria y reafirmación Católica [Meeting Pro-Country and Catholic reaffirmation]," nor the following year in a campaign for the defense of private education named "Movimiento Pro-Patria y escuela [Pro-County and schools], nor closely collaborating on the urgent needs of the local Church in different towns and cities of the Country. At a national level certain figures of Catholic Action, like Julio Morales Gómez and Rubén Darío Rumbaut, were close so the Agrupación and attended their public events.

In other cases those "distances" impeded unity on very similar endeavors: it is interesting that sometime around 1949, while Juan Antonio Rubio Padilla progressed in laying foundations for a Christian Democratic party and ACU sodalists met to study the premises of said ideas, Rubén Darío Rumbaut, along with a group of young federados were part of "Movimiento humanista [Humanist Movement]," inspired by the teachings of Jacques Maritain and the example of the Social-Christian group in Chile.

Out of this group, late in the decade of the 1950's, would come "Movimiento de liberación radical [Radical Liberation Movement]," led by federados Andrés Valdespino and Amelia Fiallo,

---

[121] Ibid, p. 86 (Spanish).

which ended up looking for assistance from other revolutionary forces in opposition to the government of Batista, including Movimiento 26 de julio [July 26 Movement], even thought they were not able to come to any agreement. Meanwhile, José Ignacio Rasco prepared the foundations for his ephemeral Partido Demócrata Cristiano [Christian Democratic Party] —later becoming a movement in exile. Why could they not overcome concerns or differences between them to pull together for the good of Cuba?

A study of existing documentation makes it possible to discern that there did not exist a homogeneous relationship between the ACU and the four arms of Catholic Action. Indeed, the nexus with branch A, made up of Caballeros Católicos, an association that as we have noted was born under the guidance of the Society of Jesus, was very close, on both a national and a local level. They collaborated on campaigns in defense of the Church in Cuba and it was common for Agrupados that lived in cities and towns outside of Havana to become distinguished leading figures in base communities of Caballeros Católicos.

Likewise, with Damas Católicas of branch C, as many of them were mothers, sisters or wives of Agrupados and a few of them were also benefactresses of the Marian Sodality. The differences were centered in branches B and D that came about on March 28, 1943 out of the Federación de la Juventud Católica Cubana, founded in 1928 and structured more solidly in 1935. The differences dated from that time and were ingrained by 1943.

During the preparation of this book and previously for many years I have talked in Cuba and elsewhere with members of Federados de la Juventud Católica about their relationship with the ACU and the opinion I have formed is that, in spite of all expressing respectful opinions regarding Fr. Rey and having no doctrinal differences with the Agrupación, at the root of their disagreements was a social concern that influenced their idea about the ecclesial apostolate.

161

The young "federados" came from all social classes, did not, necessarily, attend religious schools and were very rooted in their respective parishes. Catholic Action offered them human and spiritual formation and prepared them for apostolates, but admission was not as rigorous as at the ACU, nor were the daily lives of federados under the type of control exercised within the Agrupación by Fr. Rey and his auxiliaries.

Various persons, even in recent times, have made guarded references to being put off by that "elite" where some of the noted last names of high society predominated; that it functioned as an army whose subjection to the Director did not resemble the more freewheeling freedom of federados. Making use of a "cubanism," many saw them as "esos estirados, que se creían mejor que los demás" [those highbrows, who thought themselves better than others]. Even though no one spoke against accepting them as members of Cuban Catholic Action, they did not want that force of powerful people within their ranks.

The motto "En cada primer puesto un agrupado [An Agrupado in each top position]" was interpreted by some as desire for power and domination before those that felt belittled and even excluded. Nevertheless, it did not keep leaders of both entities from appearing together at certain events nor working together on certain projects, yet organic and satisfactory union was never achieved.

It is sad chapter in the history of the Church in Cuba, because very valuable and well-formed people could have come together for the good of the country to find avenues on behalf of social justice. Sadly, a few years later history would show —when Agrupados and federados were as one in prisons and even in death— the consequences of a lack of unity, but such a matter transcends the aims of this book.

XIV
The female world: toward Mystic Rose

By 1947 the Agrupación Católica Universitaria was already a mature organization, exclusively male. Recall that at the start of his work the founder had even renounced the spiritual direction of women, in order to concentrate on his formed men, from whom he expected rigorous virile behavior, along with dedication to study and piety. Various testimonies show that he was concerned about the courtships of Agrupados and was very reserved about rushed weddings, fearing that the wives might not be up to sharing the spiritual lives of their husbands.

Agrupados had for years attended Sunday Mass and breakfast without their wives or kids, assuming they had any. This does not mean that Fr. Rey was not concerned about families, but rather that he wanted to concentrate on continuous formation of his "young men" and expected them to spend some hours per week with him, free of worries or external "noise." This does not mean, as we have discussed in other sections of this book, that he spurned relationships with parents, wives, sisters, or children of sodalists of the Agrupación or hastened to involve them with the ACU's apostolates.

However, "Maestro" of the Agrupación José Manuel Hernández makes reference in his book, *ACU: The First Fifty Years*, to an "irritating thorn" that Fr. Llorente had to extricate regarding "the participation of wives in the life of the sodality."[122]

---

[122] JMH: ACU: the first fifty years... pg.74 (Spanish)

For this purpose, groups of husbands and wives were formed that met weekly, offering spiritual talks to bring spouses closer to the life of the spirit in the ACU.

The initial model was the "Cana" group, later others sprang up named, "St. Ignatius," "Nazareth," Santa Teresa." Once a month they met at the Agrupación to share with the Director. Once a year the families, including children, go together, first at San Miguel and Mazón, later at Pius XII House of Exercises, to celebrate the Feast of the Holy Family.

In the mid 1950's, Spiritual Exercises were offered for spouses, and the "Corunum (Single heart)" group also arose, made up of the daughters of *Agrupados,* to strengthen their religious formation and cooperate with the apostolic work of the ACU, particularly in catechesis and support of essential tasks in the neighborhood of Las Yaguas.

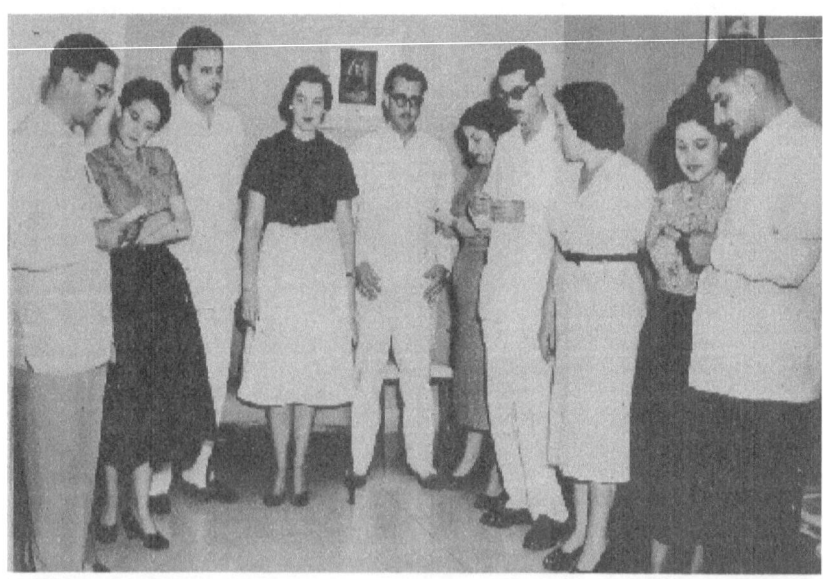

The idea of Fr. Rey de Castro of establishing a new section of the ACU where wives could also participate. This did not take final form until his successor formed Cana Groups.

Someone looking at the ACU from afar and without a spiritual perspective might have thought that the ACU was marked by the habitual Cuban and Spanish "machismo." But it must be kept in mind that the Jesuit wanted to achieve a delicate equilibrium, on the one hand to rebut the common prejudice that questioned the masculinity of devout men and, on the other hand, avoid rumors about the "very liberal" relationships of "pepillos (stylish young men)" with girls their own age, amidst a very permissive society.

We must not judge that attitude as a sign of rejection of women, but rather one of strict discipline. It did not impede excellent relationships with some female religious congregations that actually became collaborators in their apostolic work, such as the lay association "Corte de Maria Reparadoras" —led by Josefina Gelats— that was so helpful in the great project at Las Yaguas.

Once he reaped first fruits from his pedagogy, Fr. Rey de Castro solidified his points of view and got ready for the foundation of an association that would become a sort of "female branch" of the ACU: the Sodality Rosa Mistica (Mystic Rose)." He found an exceptional collaborator: Dr. Rosalba Robert.

Zoila Rosalta Robert Zayas came from a distinguished family of Camagüey. She was born in the home of attorney and cattle rancher Dr. Roberto Robert Guerra and his wife Zoila de Zayas. The air breathed there was not only that of a solid intellectual tradition, but also of rigorous Christian piety. The young woman possessed such intelligence that she was able to obtain two degrees at the University of Havana: Pharmacy and Pedagogy. She met Dr. Armando Ruiz Leiro there, specialist in Internal Medicine and distinguished sodalist at the Agrupación, founder of the Academy of Medicine which we have already mentioned, and practitioner of his specialty at the prestigious Quinta de Salud La Covadonga (La Covadonga Health Clinic).

Unlike many wives of professionals that chose to consecrate themselves to housekeeping responsibilities, Rosalva performed more than one role: she was professor at the School of Pharmacy, University of Havana, and taught Psychology at Santo Tomás de Villanueva University (St. Thomas Villanova University), as well as Religion at Colegio Baldor. Fr. Rey de Castro's interest in her was not only because she was the wife of an Agrupado, but more particularly because of the latter teaching institution.

Rosalba Robert de Ruiz Leiro (front row, holding the medal of consecration to Jesus through Mary).

Baldor had been founded at the start of the decade of the 1940's by attorney and mathematician Aurelio Ángel Baldor de la Vega (1906-1978), erudite, practicing Catholic and known for charity work that included substantial donations for cancer patients and grants for needy children in a center that he himself led during the institution's nearly two decades of existence. He is still remembered today thanks to two outstanding textbooks: *Algebra*, first published in 1941 and reedited many times, and *Arithmetic*, both became required reading in various countries of Latin America.

Although it was a private school, it had a Christian orientation and, unlike other similar schools, its curricula included Religion and participation of professionals and students in many Catholic events around the city. Moreover, it had a significant nexus with the Society of Jesus, for Aurelio's older brother was Daniel Gonzalo Baldor de la Vega (1902-1990), on of Cuba's most notable Jesuits of his generation, twice Rector of Colegio de Belen, first from 1940 to 1947 and later between February and September 1959, when he was sent to Venezuela in what was to be his definitive departure from Cuba — soon thereafter Aurelio would also leave for Mexico with his family. Fr. Daniel had been Vice-Provincial of the Society of Jesus in the Antilles between 1952 and 1958.

We don't know if Fr. Rey met Rosalba while assisting an ACU function with Dr. Ruiz Leiro or if she was recommended by one of the Baldor brothers. Perhaps both things were true. The testimony of Blanca Antón states that Fr. Rey de Castro was her spiritual director around 1947,[123] when she taught Religion to young women in their fourth year of High School, in the facility the school devoted to that use on Línea and 13. He then posited the foundation of Rosa Mística Marian Sodality, independently of the ACU, but founded on like spirituality, designed for young women going to high school and university.

The way the professor attracted the first sodalists was very much like that used by Fr. Felipe in Colegio de Belén. She approached some of her students in the school, those exhibiting greater human qualities and religious motivation. Few at first, but ensuing years brought other candidates. Typically, they were initially invited to participate in three-day sessions of Spiritual Exercises —like those offered by Fr. Feliz Losada in 1949— followed by

---

[123] Cf. Rosa Mística — A Classic ACU Vignette...p. 3.

weekly meetings with Study Circles, where religion and morality topics were discussed.

The first facility of the sodality was a rental property a few blocks from the school, on O Street # 259 in Vedado, close to Havana University and to the home of the ACU. It is interesting that the house was not only the main formation locale for Rosa Mistica, but also the residence for young women coming from the exterior that studied at the University and desired, as did their families, to live according to Christian ethics.

Celebration of Mass at Rosa Mística (Mystic Rose) house in Havana (Fr. Bercedo presiding).

The postulants had to attend Sunday Mass and study circles. After a trial period, they became aspirants. Those that persevered received the medal that identified them as sodalists, then, according to the Marian Sodality Rules they had to do annual Spiritual Exercises, attend Mass daily, pray the Holy Rosary accompanied by a moment of mediation —the residents in the "casita (little house)" on O Street would do so each night with the founder, following all their other obligations. They participated in their chores, whether in Catechesis or others suggested by Fr. Rey, assessor of the Sodality.

The Jesuit Archives at Reina preserves a letter from Vice-Provincial Fr. Calvo to Rey, dated October 15, 1950, regarding a Eucharistic celebration he wanted to convene, in which the University students would meet with those in Congregación de las Hijas de Maria (Congregation on of the Daughters of Mary).

The sender proffers evidence that there are reservations with regard to the religious house, even unease respecting this apparent fusion, and notes that college students that have Eucharistic celebrations and other functions in their sections, are not obligated to attend the Sunday Mass at Reina and points out with discretion that the two separate congregations should not be be confused as being one, but should retain their own particular traits.

Perhaps the founder of the ACU thought that on the female side it was possible to bring together both groups into one stronger and more numerous, but pulled back momentarily in view of the concerns of the superiors, and was not able to take up the matter in the year and a half left of his earthly existence.

We should not look on this document as a hostile act from the always sympathetic and collaborative Fr. Calvo, but as the need to maintain order in matters that might bring unease to the Jesuits in that house and fear of some of them that the new Sodality might try to absorb the older and prestigious Hijas de Maria (Daughters of Mary), a pious and very widely spread association in the country, based in diverse parishes and chapels, looked after by not only Jesuits, but also members of other orders and by secular clergy.

Following the death of the founder, Fr. Teodoro Bercedo García SJ, Chaplain and pastor of Iglesia del Sagrado Corazón (Sacred Heart Church) succeeded him until his expulsion from Cuba aboard the Covandonga ship on September of 1961. That was also the moment that marked the end of Rosa Mística in Cuba.

One of the works of this notable apostolate was the start of a night-school for young women that were not university students nor, on occasion, from Catholic families. Thanks to it, some were able to enroll in the University and some of them became part of the Sodality. One of those students, Rosita Herrera, would later discover a fervent vocation as a Discalced Carmelite of St. Theresa and lived in the San José monastery in San Juan, Puerto Rico.

It is no secret that Rey de Castro looked on this new sodality as a means to form Catholic women professionals, worthy to be spouses of his *Agrupados* and, indeed, there were various marriages among sodalists from one and the other entity, but the most important thing was that out of this fountain flowed excellent mothers of families, highly prepared women among which were Dr. Cibeles Vidaud, psychiatrist in New York, doctors Rita Fojaco and Virginia Miranda, as well as architect Eradia Hurtado.

Following the event of 1959 and particularly during the following two years, a good portion of the sodalists, including Dr. Robert, emigrated to various cities in the United States, Mexico and other nations. They attempted to reorganize in exile. In fact, Eradia Hurtado rented a house on Flagler Street in Miami, to serve as a home base and residence for some young women, just as had been the case in the "casita" on O Street in Vedado that they had left behind. Their assessor was Fr. José María Izquierdo del Rio SJ, who knew the sodalists in Havana. A number of them worked with Cuban immigrants in *South Dade Labor Camp* in Florida City, work that they shared for a time with ACU sodalists, offering spiritual assistance to families recently arrived.

July Alvira deserves special mention. She emigrated to Puerto Rico and carried forth there an intense apostolic work for the balance of her existence, so notable that she has been proposed as a candidate for beatification.

There were various reasons that kept Rosa Mistica from being perfectly restored in exile. First, Eradia Hurtado, as well as others of her collaborators began welcoming members of their families that they needed to assist, and they had to attend to job offers from all over the geography of North America. Secondly, Fr. Izquierdo received a new assignment in Puerto Rico. And to this should be added the significant cultural change brought on by the move to the United States that hindered the selection of new young aspirants with coherent religious beliefs and acceptable vital attitudes.

Even though it seemed that the experience floundered, as sodalists became used to the nations that welcomed them, they were able restore the sodality, not exactly as it functioned in Cuba, but how local circumstances dictated:

> They have opened two social houses in Miami and Puerto Rico, have obtained the blessing of the respective ordinaries and count with 200 sodalists in Miami and 100 in Puerto Rico. Other nations where some of the sodalists have gone to help found or rejuvenate University Marian Sodalities are Panama, Colombia and Venezuela: in all these places the Cuban women offer their experience, acquired in Cuba during university years and in open struggle against communism, and they cooperate according to their personal initiatives and possibilities without imposing ideas, but rather adapting to the circumstances of each country.[124]

From a purely human point of view, the end of Rosalba Robert was very sad.

Following the political events that took place in Cuba starting in 1959, she and Dr. Ruiz Leiro decided to continue developing their habitual work. He continued offering Pharmacology classes

---

[124] Ibid, p. 6.

at the University of Havana and was promoted to Revolutionary Dean of the School of Medicine, though he stepped down just two weeks later and returned to his classroom as a simple professor.

Nevertheless, when the Superior Board of the Government of the University "depuró (depurated)" —euphemism used for firing— 46 professors of the School of Medicine, he was among those that decided to quit, as an ethical act in solidarity with their colleagues. He did so the following July 1 in an open letter published in the newspaper *Información*.

This act, along with the gradual promotion of communists to leadership positions in the government, led to other acts like the siege of the Universidad de Villanueva; the assault on Catholic students in the Havana Alma Mater; the nearly impossible normal functioning of the ACU and Rosa Mistica, forced them to emigrate. On September of 1961 they left the country for Mexico.

They settled in New Orleans, where Dr. Ruiz Leiro was professor at Tulane University, while she completed successfully her studies in Psychology. Together they founded in 1967 and led Hermandad Nazaret, a Catholic congregation, assessed by Jesuit doctor Federico Arvesú Gasset del Castillo. It was conceived as a study and reflexion group based on the teachings of Vatican II Council and destined to serve the human being through Faith and Science. It soon had functioning representation in various cities of North America.

They both received recognition for their academic as well as their apostolic work, among them, Ruiz Leiro received in Tulane the Gloria Walsh Award of 1980 and later became Professor Emeritus, as well as Educator of the Year from the National Association of Cuban American Educators (NACAE) in 1995.

The prestigious doctor died in 2004, his widowed spouse received the rude blow with Christian resignation, but the following year Hurricane Katrina destroyed their home, transformed her apostolic work and left her defenseless. For these reasons, following various decades living in New Orleans, a niece took her to Charlotte, North Carolina, where she spent her final years in an old age home.

Blanca Menéndez, one of her Rosa Mística "young women" visited her there with her Agrupado husband, Manuel Antón, and prayed the Rosary together. Rosalba went to the Father on March 29, 2007 at 91 years of fecund life. Like patriarch Job, God tested her with successive losses, but her faith never wavered. What some might look upon as misfortunes, were for her trials that marked phases on her road to salvation.

XV
Times of consolation

The fifth decade of the 20th century marks the moment of consolidation of the *Agrupación Católica Universitaria*. José Manuel Hernández gives evidence of this in his valuable book, *Agrupación Católica Universitaria. Los primeros cincuenta años.* Thanks to it we know of the visit during those years of American writer Richard Pattee, who visits the institution, talks to its sodalists and directors, participates in its daily life and when he publishes in 1945 his report, *Catholic Life in the West Indies,* affirms that the ACU "was the most solid bastion of Cuban Catholicism at the University."[125]

The sodality, from a symbolic standpoint, made itself very visible in the university environment. At the end of the decade, lots that separated the social building from the corner of San Miguel and Mazón were acquired and the student residence was built there in 1949. The chapel got too small for Agrupado Masses and it was necessary to relocate it to the large meeting room. Adjacent to the University there is now almost a square block, bulwark of the Agrupación. It projects strength, youthful energy, initiative. It is no longer easy to ignore them.

On another front, the journalism classes are yielding fruits. The dream of forming Catholic communicators, idea that Fr. Rey borrowed from Fr. Ángel Ayala, materializes in different publications that are developing. The first and longest lasting of them, *Esto vir*, debuts in 1931 and becomes a workshop for budding journalists. It started simply as a juvenile newsletter,

---

[125] JMH: *Agrupación Católica Universitaria...* p. 53.

light and not too formal, but over the years it developed into an effective communications vehicle not limited to Agrupación, but open to the world, with views on social and political problems.

In his often-cited *History*, Figueroa points out a notable example in the November 1946 issue that includes a brilliant page by Juan Antonio Rubio Padilla in defense of Cardinal Arteaga —who had received the zucchetto that very year in February— when he was attacked by the leftist elements because of a circular he published on the occasion of the inauguration of the school year at Universidad de Santo Tomás de Villanueva. The response was very important because it came, not from any Agrupado, much less one cloistered in a temple and unfamiliar with street life, but by a professional that since his school days was a member of the Directorio Universitario, participated in the revolutionary struggle against Machado and got involved in politics within the Partido Revolucionario Cubano (Auténtico), where he later occupied important official positions.

It is this new life-force, where professionalism goes hand in hand with spirituality and there is a veritable incarnation of apostolic attitude to tackle social problems, that enables the rookie newsletter to continue to be teacher to the ACU. Over time, it changed its tone, its format, its number of pages, it outlived the passing into eternity of its Founder, even conflicts with the new government starting in 1959 that seized their premises and took over its presses, for it was reborn in the United States with another format, another language, other journalists, continuing until today to be one of the most luxuriant emblems of the ACU.

The duration of other periodical publications, born out of one or another social conjuncture, was much more ephemeral, like *Futuro*, a newspaper founded by José Ignacio Lasaga in 1934 and targeted at the student public at that moment in which the

University was shut down, and that disappeared a little later once circumstances returned to normal.

Something similar happened the following year with *Amanecer*, a magazine targeted at schools, likewise with *Sin Trabajo* [Out of Work], that strived to become the press organ of indigent neighborhoods, and the ephemeral *Pa'lante* [Go forth] created by the Literary Academy.

At a given time Fr. Rey dreamed of founding what would be the great Catholic weekly, and *Siempre* was born in 1941. Although it was well received at first, it was circulated for just a few months, because the work was exhausting and required strong financial resources. The experience was repeated in 1944 with *Lumen*, which aspired to scientific content and international circulation. However, its high intellectual level ambitions not only limited the number of readers, but also the supply of writers to sustain it, though it gave birth to *Lumen médico*, of lesser ambition and clearer objective,

In 1944 *Acción Cubana* saw the light of day, a much more modestly formatted publication —just four pages— led by Agrupados, but with the collaboration of members from Federación de Juventud Católica and Caballeros Católicos. Its focus was essentially political and in a certain way it was an organ of the namesake group and thus shared its fate, languished and disappeared when it broke off from the ACU where many were reluctant to engage in practical political activity.

The greatest dream of the founder was not accomplished. He wished for the Agrupación to have a Catholic newspaper of large circulation that, in the name of the Church, could influence society. He thought it was a possibility with the purchase of *El Mundo* newspaper, but it was not possible to amass all the money necessary for its acquisition and some did not support him in the end, because they thought it a problematic responsibility. Everything was left at good intentions.

Today, looking back at history we can judge those times as times of preparation, of trials for times to come in the phase that commences with the death of Rey de Castro, when Fr. Llorente will put in operation the Buró de Información y Propaganda (BIP) [Bureau of Information and Outreach] whose booklets had a quality and controversial presence not only in the Cuba ecclesial space, but also in other areas of society and other locations around the world. This, along with the unyielding *Esto Vir*, were the authentic Catholic press that had been desired for so long.

The consolidation of the Sodality may also be gauged on a symbolic level. On September 15, 1936, during the solemn act of possession of the presidency of the ACU by José Ignacio Lasaga, an inscribed pennant with the monogram of the Agrupación —the acronym of its name ACU, inscribed inside a shield, placed on top of a latin cross— was blessed. It was its identification, emblem of its presence in the public space.

Seven years later, in 1947, in line with the growth and expansion of the sodality, another ceremony served to give final form to its identifying symbols: the pennant became a flag —both had been designed and donated by Dr. Virgilio Lasaga y Castellanos— and the Hymn of the Agrupación was sung for the first time.

The lyrics of the Hymn were composed by José Ignacio Lasaga and succeeded with adroit synthesis to portray the evangelical condition of the Agrupación, its status as Christ's militia in a very Ignatian sense and show the pathway of its apostolate: science, prayer, service and action. The motto of the association: *Esto vir*, closed the stanza that served as the text's refrain:

Uno solo es el Jefe y Maestro	One alone is the Leader and Master
Uno solo el pensar y el sentir	One alone our thinking and will
Uno solo el esfuerzo y la meta	One alone is the goal we strive after
Nuestro lema uno solo: ¡Esto Vir!	Our motto only one: Esto Vir.
Tiene Cristo una Cruz redentora,	Only Christ has a message life-giving
Tiene Cuba una estrella de luz;	For a world that is thirsty for God
Hacia el Cielo elevemos la estrella	Our arms be His arms at forgiving
Y en la Patria sembremos la cruz	Our voices His voice full of love
Nuestra espada invencible la ciencia.	Our shield is the firmness to pray
Nuestro firme broquel la oración	Our science" the invincible sword
El honor más preciado servir	The most valuable honor: to serve
El descanso vivir en acción	Our rest:to live serving our Lord
Uno solo es el Jefe y Maestro	One alone is the Leader and Master
Uno solo el pensar y el sentir	One alone our thinking and will
Uno solo el esfuerzo y la meta	One alone is the goal we strive for
Nuestro lema uno solo: ¡Esto Vir!	Our motto only one: Esto Vir.[126]

It is significant that the music for it was commissioned to professor, pianist, composer and owner of CMBN —brother of the famous composer of danzones Antonio María Romeu— who in his youth led the Banda Municipal de Regla and later Banda del Regimiento de Artillería until 1925, year in which he was named conductor of the Banda del Estado Mayor de la Marina de Guerra, with the grade of Lieutenant and thereafter, in September 1933 promoted to Captain. He was in charge there until 1959. That explains why the composition has a martial flavor, military in the good sense of the term, as it emphasized the vision of the Society of Jesus of unity and discipline under the flag of Christ.

---

[126] Jose Ignacio Lasaga, Hymn of the Agrupación Católica Universitaria Programa de la Velada May 6, 1943 p. 4

The soiree took place in the home of the ACU —San Miguel 1111– on May 6, 1943, at nine in the evening. It was basically a concert by Banda de La Marina led by Romeu that, as usual, started with the National Hymn, followed by the overture to Rossini's opera William *Tell, Scènes pittoresques* by Jules Massanet and *Hungarian Rhapsodies* by Franz Liszt, performed by pianist Mario Orlando Romeu González, son of the director, accompanied by Banda.

After that first part the soiree moved on to the main event: the flag was unfurled and blessed. The new design was rectangular with tree stripes —two in blue with a white one in the center— an allusion to the colors of the Immaculate Conception and the nation's flag, and instead of a triangle, the pennant with shield and cross. The Hymn was then immediately sung for the first time.

The concert continued with pieces for piano with four hands played by Mario Orlando and his sister Zenaida Romeu González: Caprice Viennese by Kreisler, Seville by Albéniz, Invitation to the Waltz by Weber and Russian-American composer Gregory Morris Stone's version of the Russian song Black Eyes.

Then the Banda returned to interpret "Fantasía cubana (Cuban Fantasy)" composed by the director himself and finished the night playing the Hymn anew.

Felipe Rey de Castro and the Agrupación Católica Universitaria

The great number of people that congregated for the event can be judged by five replete double-pages of signatures that, along with the program, are still found in ACU's archives, and only include the names of ACU sodalists present, not family members and guests. The first page starts with the signature of Fr. Rey de Castro and next to his one can identify that of Fr. Gustavo Gonzalo Amigó Jansen SJ (1908-1986), Cuban Jesuit that made his vows in Havana in February of that very year and in spite of his relative youth, given his intellectual capacity and dynamism, Rey had managed to get him to assist with the work of the Agrupación. Adjacent are distinguished Agrupados with the longest and most relevant trajectory: Ángel Fernández Varela, Jorge Casteleiro, Carlos Martínez Arango, Calixto García Rayneri, and on other pages those of Juan Suárez, Eduardo Boza Masvidal, Ignacio Wagner and Sergio Álvarez Mena, among many others.

In October of that very year the first Apostolic Assembly of the Agrupación was convened, presided by Cardinal Manuel Arteaga y Betancourt. It was celebrated to take stock of the work performed by the Sodality, an analysis of its achievements and also of its aspirations and the presence of the prelate spoke of his support for its founder and his sodalists. The Church in Havana and, indeed, the entire Church in Cuba offered their acknowledgment of the apostolic works that radiated out from its beautiful home base.

One example of the maturity and progress of the ACU was the decision, starting with the 1945 Assembly, to award titles of "Maestros" of the Agrupación. This acknowledgment was conferred to Agrupados that had arrived at a kind of zenith in their lives and work. It was not a prize awarded for seniority or for intellectual fame, but rather a distinction for their contribution to form and strengthen that bulwark of the faith. The first to receive them were Ataulfo Fernández Llano and José I. Lasaga. Later on it would be conferred to other notable figures of those ranks like Armando Ruiz Leiro, José Sust, Ángel Fernández Varela, Marino Pérez Durán and René de la Huerta.[127]

Honorary Sodalist H.E. Cardinal Manuel Arteaga Betancourt, Archbishop of Havana and National Director of Catholic Action, performs the dedication of ACU's first Christ the King Apostolic Assembly in 1943: "...I hear vibrant words that are fertile ground for a true apostolate, and I gaze at the splendorous realization of this brilliant and prestigious work that reaches its fulfillment. The Church can be justly proud of this work... for the accomplishment of this great work that makes one conceive hope of a definitive triumph for the Church."

---

[127] Years later, after the ACU had found refuge in the United States it was conferred to Ambrosio González del Valle, José Manuel Hernández Puente, Jesús León Núnez. A question yet unresolved is about the mysterious reasons why Juan Antonio Rubio Padillla did not receive one given his exceptional merits.

Another aspect worth mention in the growth of the Agrupación was the unwillingness to remain constrained to the limits of its Havana home base. The report prepared at the end of 1939 makes known that of the 241 sodalists 31 were absent, six were in other parts of the country and the rest were overseas. The same source document makes known that two small congregations in the United States that took the ACU as role model, one in New Orleans, short-lived, and a longer lasting one in Boston, thanks to the intercession of Cuban sodalist Roberto Arellano, had positive impact on the local Church, primarily based on acceptance of invitations to the group leader and others to give conferences in parishes and other religious organizations.

Agrupados that lived in the interior of Cuba would habitually team up with Caballeros Católicos in their area and some even occupied important positions, as well as in the Society of Jesus apostolate, without losing contact with their home base which they visited on certain occasions for meetings or events or to do the Spiritual Exercises. Nevertheless, the very consolidation of the Sodality gave pause to consider the creation of chapters in other locations of the country, and on November 30, 1947 the Board of the ACU agreed to found the first one in Camagüey, presided by *Agrupado* Rafael Santa María.[128]

Thanks to the testimony of Agrupado Juan Manuel Salvat we also know of the sodality in Sagua, born a few years later:

> In Sagua we had a very small Marian Sodality at the Jesuit Sacred Heart of Jesus School. Schooling there was through sixth grade and we later studied High School at the Institute of Secondary Education, also in Sagua. The Rector of the School was Fr. Benigno Juanes SJ, and we also had Fr. Antonio Altamira SJ as *maestrillo* (novice). They talked about the ACU founded by Fr. Rey de Castro

---

[128] Figueroa: *History...* p. 166.

SJ in Havana and of the importance of the Spiritual Exercises of St. Ignatius. They were both the best teachers we had in those years. Also Fr. Marcial Bedoya SJ who replaced Juanes around 1955.

We pulled together a number of friends: Marcelino García, José Arenas, Aurelio Pérez and others to create a group that would go to Calvario in Havana to do the Exercises. That was in 1952 (possibly in July or August). We started that year and continued doing it until 1956. We traveled to Havana in the school bus. I don't recall who the retreat masters were. One was led by Fr. [René] León Lemus and another by Fr. Francisco [José] Arnáiz [Zarandona].

[…]

In 1952, after our Retreat, we founded the Agrupación Católica of Sagua (ACS), initially with a few graduates of sixth grade. We had weekly meetings on Saturdays and attended Sunday Mass at the School. We then had breakfast in the School and continued, right there, with Catechism classes.

The ACS continued to grow each year with friends we made at the Institute and new graduates from the School. By 1959 we had around 159 sodalists. Sagua had some 36,000 inhabitants at the time.

[…]

One of the most important activities we managed to do was the Radio Program, *Justicia Social* (Social Justice), each Sunday on Sagua's radio station. We explained the Social Teachings of the Church. And we did not stop at the words, for we supported Sagua's sugar workers in a few of their strikes demanding better wages.[129]

Regrettably this process of growth was interrupted, as was the general development of the Agrupación in 1959.

An interesting detail from 1945 was the decision of Fr. Rey to adopt a lay persons originated Cuban celebration: the Cena Martiana (Dinner in honor of José Martí).

The first of these Dinners took place on January 27, 1926 in Manzanillo, an initiative of Juan Francisco Sariol, director of *Orto* magazine and head of a renovating literary group in the area. He requested a record be made explaining its parallel to Christmas Eve:

> The night of January 27, 1926, the undersigned, devoted admirers of the patriotic, immortal works of the Apostle of Cuban Homeland, José Martí, as guests of and in the premises of Revista Literaria Orto, gallant paladin of the old and immortal ideals of liberty and Cuban redemption, agree to proclaim this Act so it may perpetuate, as everlating remembrance, the seventy-third anniversary of the birth of the glorious illuminated of "Dos Ríos (Two Rivers)", in this act, that is akin to the Christian Tradition, due to the considerable similarity the epic independence of Cuba shares with the redemption of the pagan world; we have agreed to pronounce La Noche Buena Mariana [sic]. And in witness thereof, anointed by the ideal and crusaders in the peace of love to the memory of our patriotic legacy, invoking the name of our Teacher.[130]

---

[129] Written testimony of Juan Manuel Salvat.

[130] Eduardo Milián: "La Nochebuena Martiana". Reviewed in Leer and in https://cuba-historia-y-valores-c.webnode.es/news/la-nochebuena-martiana1/ October 25, 2022.

It is curious that on that same date, in such a far off Manzanillo location like Santiago de la Vegas, a similar celebration took place. The most plausible explanation is that in both cases the organizers were linked with Masonic Lodges and that from that date on took over the festivities. These celebrations were not only a shared meal, but also included speeches, recitation of poems, musical numbers and collections or charitable initiatives like the "canastilla martiana" (Martí's layette) that was meant to be gifted to the firstborn of January 28. This kind of civic ritual awakened the suspicion of various Catholic groups that saw it as profane substitution —and even sacrilegious— of Christmas Eve.

With time these celebrations lost their authentic character to the point that the Fifth National History Congress, celebrated in 1946 recommended that it be replaced by other types of events in honor of Martí. Nevertheless, the dinners continued to be held in some places of the country, like Manzanillo itself and Santiago de las Vegas, until 1957. In 1960 the new revolutionary government decided to revitalize it and charged the National Institute of Savings and Housing (INAV in the Spanish acronym), led by Pastorita Núñez, to organize a giant vigil in honor of Martí in Plaza Cívica (Civic Plaza). It is not surprising that the then Auxiliary Bishop of Havana, Msgr. Evelio Díaz attended in good faith and sat next to Prime Minister Fidel Castro. Some of the faithful considered the attendance of the prelate controversial, but perhaps he was recalling ACU's original Christianizing initiative.

According to Figueroa, Fr. Rey had made that decision "with the confidence born from absolute possession of Catholic morals and dogma, and that wholesome character that made him reject repugnant sappiness and unjustified fears, permitting him to act freely on behalf of the greater glory of God.[131] The doctors of

---

[131] Figueroa: *History...p.* 158.

the Agrupación adopted this act at once and it favored the organization of Medical Congresses they planned to propitiate.

Interpreted from our current perspective, Fr. Rey's gesture demonstrated his pastoral maturity. Unlike other non-Cuban religious, he had the capacity to understand and identify with the positive qualities in the place where he was going to develop his apostolic work. Perhaps he lacked deep knowledge of Martí's work, but surely his close collaborators had instructed him on leadership and had shown him its benefits in the world of culture and in the national civic spirit. If Masons and agnostics preferred to emphasize their rejection of the hierarchical Church, their secularism, its liberal character, the ACU —which was a very Cuban organization despite its birth from the endeavors of a Spaniard— would follow the poet of "la rosa blanca (the red rose)," the promoter of "guerra sin odio (war without hate)," he who recognized in the Gospels the foundation of a morality that continued to be the norm in almost the entire world. If the Dinners until then were intended to distance or ignore the Church, this decision was in favor of dialogue with the figure of Martí, from the Faith in reaffirmation of the Cuban nature and work of the Agrupación.

This is not to imply that in that time there were not other illustrious representatives of the Spanish clergy that exhibited a similar attitude toward Cuban inculturation, and at the same time cooperated on civic initiatives in spaces traditionally foreign to the Church, like Galician Bishop Monseñor Enrique Pérez Serantes and the Navarrian poet priest Ángel Gaztelu, however, these figures were exceptional and there were very many members of the Hispanic clergy that ignored the existence of a Cuban culture and even incarnated in their classrooms or pulpits the memory of the national heroes of the 19th century that contributed to the separation of Cuba from the Spanish Crown.

If God had given Rey de Castro a longer existence here on earth he would have been able to multiply gestures like this one.

Through them he presaged conceptions about the relationship of the Church with the world that were only made universal with the Vatican II Council. His evangelizing audacity, like that of Paul, took him to find a new Areopagus.

XVI
Fr. Rey and the Agrupación in the world

Even though upon his return to Cuba in 1931, Fr. Rey de Castro showed the will to consecrate himself to the Agrupación and stay close to it always, the very growth of the sodality, as well as its charism to offer Exercises, he was more than once obliged to nurture a kind of special "foreign relations" apace with his work's reach and prestige abroad.

The first of these trips, after the official foundation of the ACU, took place between June 7 and August 21, 1931. On this trip he offered Exercises in Santiago de Cuba and went from there to Puerto Rico and Santo Domingo for the same purpose. Starting with the first island he commenced to plant the idea of founding a Catholic University Alliance of the Antilles. However, he did not find support in either of the two neighbor islands to realize the endeavor, and gave up towards the end of 1933.

In 1932 two Agrupado students of engineering: Eusebio Azcue and Juan Magraner, participated in a Catholic Student Convention convened in Mexico. In it was established the Ibero-America of Mexico Secretariat and an Agrupado, Armando Reyes, was elected board member for Cuba. This meant that the Agrupación would represent the Catholic students of the country until the future founding of the National Association brought them together.

In that way the ACU started to stand out as a prestigious reference for other nations of the Americas. In May and November 1933 Mexican student members of the Ibero American Secretariat visited the Agrupación. And those that came in the latter month were trusted with representing the Agrupación in the Ibero American Catholic Student Board at the Rome meeting in December.

The appointees approached the Puerto Rico and Santo Domingo representatives anew about the proposed Catholic University Alliance of the Antilles, but without results.

That very year the General Secretariat of Catholic Students of Uruguay asked the ACU for information that would help it coordinate the Catholic student associations in their country's Catholic Action.

When the Ibero-American Secretariat became the Confederation (CIDEC), it held congresses in 1938, 1940 and 1950, and in the latter the ACU was represented by Valentín Arenas Amigó.

In 1940 the ACU also established relations with the Juventud Masculina del Perú (Masculine Youth of Peru). The following year it decided to enroll in the international Catholic movement Pax Romana —after deliberations that started in 1935 and only concluded with negotiations held with Rudy Salat, Secretary General of the same, when he visited Havana in 1941.

This organization had been founded in Freiburg, Germany, in 1921, as an international Catholic student organization. Its original objective was to bring together members of this dynamic social sector in order to help victims of the European War and promote a spirit of peace and amity based on dominant Christian thought, conceived metaphorically as a new "pax romana."

It is likely that initial ACU reservations in favor of affiliation were similar to those of other nations, in so far as relations with other young Catholic organizations of the world were not clearly defined, and it must be kept in mind that the Agrupación in Cuba toiled to be recognized as Catholic Action.

In the Pax Romana Congress held in Washington in September 1939 relations with Catholic Action were officially defined and this, along with the naming of Spaniard Joaquín Ruiz Jiménez Cortés as new president, doctor in Law, neo-Thomist and notable intellectual figure among young Catholic Hispanics —with whom Father Rey most likely sympathized— smoothed the way for the agreement reached with Salat in 1941.

This explains why Rey de Castro decided to attend the 1946 congress personally, held in Spain between June 24 and July 4, 1946. The ACU was not able to send a delegate to the following year's congress, where it was represented by Mexico at the Interfederal Assembly held in Rome, where it assumed the new name of Pax Romana ICMICA/MIIC (The International Catholic Movement for Intellectual and Cultural Affairs/Mouvement International des Intellectuels Catholiques) and established its headquarters in Geneva.

That same decade a number of Agrupados traveled to various international Catholic events, sometimes as representatives of other entities, spreading the work and spirit of the ACU.

That is the case of Marino Pérez Durán, who in 1945, year in which he was President of the Agrupación and Secretary of the Confederation of Catholic Schools of Cuba, attended the Inter-American Congress of Catholic Education. In 1946 Agrupado Claudio Escarpenter led a delegation to the International Marian Congress in Barcelona. In 1949 José Ignacio Lasaga and Marino Perez Durán attended the Second International Week of Catholic Action.

An exceptional Agrupado, Dr. Miguel Figueroa Miranda (1907-1993) deserves special mention in the field of "foreign relations," lawyer and diplomat that during World War II was Charge d'affaires of Cuba before the Holy See, given the absence of Ambassador Conde Nicolás Rivero. For security reasons he had to live within the Vatican enclosure, which allowed him to review the Vatican library and archives for historical research, and also get close to His Holiness Pius XII, which facilitated negotiations and waivers necessary for the development of the ACU, as well as assertion of influence in favor of making Archbishop of Havana, Msgr. Manuel Arteaga, Cardinal in 1946.

Fr. Rey de Castro took his last trip to Rome in 1950. He attended the Congress of Promoters of Marian Sodalities. It was also his last visit to his country of birth and to his family. He left Cuba April 10 and returned June 9.

Thanks to the previously cited letter from Sor Benita Castro we know that on that trip, as on others, he visited his elderly mother in Galicia, and immediately thereafter his aunt and cousin in the Benedict Convent in Cuntis, Pontevedra. Hence, we know:

> On various occasions he gave us retreats, preaching with that unction that you know of: and in 1950, in response to our wishes, he wanted to lead a session of Holy Exercises, but an unexpected request from Rev. Fr. Provincial kept him from doing so. He appreciated this Community very much, where he was sincerely loved and venerated.[132]

The religious did not know that this would be the last time in this world that he would embrace his mother and relatives. The reason why he was called upon by the Provincial in charge of all the Cuban Jesuit communities, Fr. Virgilio Revuelta Fernández, remains an enigma, although it was probably about an amicable exchange concerning the congress in Rome and the progress of the ACU, along with some message for the Jesuit Vice-Provincial in Cuba, Fr. Calvo.

Apparently, upon his return to the home base of the sodality everything was progressing well, thanks to the support of Jesuit Brother Esteban Aguado Barbero (Burgos, 1927 - Villagarcía de Campos, Valladolid, 2020) who was, since 1947, his untiring assistant and in the absence of the Director his substitute in daily matters, while at the same time leaders Carlos Martínez Arango and Alvaro León decided matters of more significant importance to the ACU.

---

[132] Letter from Sor Benita Castro to Jorge Casteleiro, April 2, 1952.

Life at the ACU continued with the drumbeat rhythm of growing achievements. The month of July saw the inauguration and blessing of the new altar and the chapel on the second floor was completely remodeled, thanks to the generous support of Jorge Casteleiro, whom, starting on October 1950 took over the presidency. He could not know that just over a year later he would have to pilot the Agrupación during a critical and painful moment.

The last trip by Fr. Rey out of the Island took place in 1951, but the importance of it is deserving of a separate chapter.

XVII
Crusade of love of Fr. Lombardi and Fr. Rey

An unusual Jesuit arrived in Havana in December 1951, Fr. Riccardo Lombardi (Naples, 1908 - Rome, 1979). By that time he was already a famous preacher for his eloquence and persuasive character, known as "God's microphone." Close to Pope Pius XII, he was charged with a broad campaign in Italy to alert Catholic faithful to vote against communists in the 1948 elections.

The religious priest did not limit himself to this task, as he discovered that the talent he had received should irradiate the rest of the world and be the nucleus of what he called the Work or Crusade of love. Hence, he started an itinerant life from continent to continent preaching in temples, theaters, open venues, congregating multitudes and insisting not only in love of neighbor, but also in the obligation on social justice.

Two exceptional witnesses, Servants of God Chiara Lubich, founder of the Focolares Movement and Fr. Pedro Arrupe, Superior General of the Society of Jesus, left testimonials of their admiration for Lombardi. She asserted: "Fr. Lombardi was a transparent man, an idealist in a certain way, a contemplative. A charism seemed to emanate from him when he spoke. He could be compared to a hermit or to John the Baptist crying out moved by the Spirit. He was in love with the Church...Fr. Lombardi moved you when the used the name of Jesus."[133]

---

[133] "Fr. Lombardi, S.J." *For a better world. Spiritual reanimation service.* Web page accessed November 24, 2022, in http://www.porunmundomejor.com/wordpress/somos/el-padre-Lombardi/ (Spanish).

Arrupe, on his part, who in the last years of his life placed special interest on the preferential option by the Church on behalf of the poor, had been marked by the preaching of his Jesuit brother: "Beyond the impressive dimensions of the "movement" aroused by his public preaching, beyond the things that happened in the Work he founded, Fr. Lombardi has been a man that knew how to communicate the love for Jesus above all things to many persons, the pressing desire to make Him known, to make Him reign."[134]

The Havana of December 1951 was not exactly the ideal setting for Fr. Lombardi. The country lived a moment of economic recovery and, in spite of the defects that the democratic government of Carlos Prío might have, the Capital was a kind of showcase of the country's wellbeing. Upper and middle classes lived a comfortable life and the Church could display the edification of new and imposing temples like: San Antonio, Santa Rita and Jesús de Miramar; there was abundant satisfaction in progress achieved with religious education, as exemplified by Jesuit schools, La Salle Brothers, Marists, French Dominicans, and Mothers of Sacred Heart. The head of the Havana Archdiocese had been a Cardinal since 1946. In that environment it was difficult to point out social inequities and much less to think that days of such well being for that society and Church were counted.

Journalist Juan Emilio Friguls, in charge of the Catholic page of *Diario de la Marina,* dedicated and extensive column to report on the visit of the celebrated preacher, expected approximately between December 6 and 12. It was scheduled to start with his participation, between the 6th and 9th, in the already announced Matanzas Eucharistic Congress, and moving on afterward to Havana.

---

[134] Ibidem.

Following this he inserted some paragraphs taken from a writing of Jesuit Fr. José Antonio Romero[135] that summarizes the work of Lombardi, first as professor and preacher in Italy and then, the extension of his "Crusade of love" to the rest of Europe — Germany, Austria, Holland, Belgium, France— and the United States —New York and Washington. He pointed out his broadcasts from the most important Italian radio stations. He highlighted that the in the center of his exhortations was clarification of history with the presence of Jesus as sole possibility for the future of humanity and concern for the just distribution of wealth among all men.[136]

Even though the family that owned the newspaper was Catholic and he had excellent relations with the hierarchy of the Church, as well as with the main religious congregations present in Cuba, the presence of Lombardi did not enjoy the expected coverage. We have been able to locate just one very brief unsigned review in *7 días en la República* (7 days in the Republic) that was included with the *Diario* in the December 16 issue of that year, though it was probably by Friguls. It does not need much explanation:

> This week Havana Catholicism had a day of popular preaching. A Jesuit famous for his apostolic word, Fr. Riccardo Lombardi, was charged with bringing to us, by way of his "Crusade of love," the message of salvation, of return to the Truth and the Good, that thousands of Havana residents heard first at the Cathedral and later at the modern temple of St. Rita and at the facility of the Anunciata.

---

[135] P. José Antonio Romero SJ (1888-1961). Known in Mexico as Catholic publicist. Founder of Obra Nacional de la Buena Prensa in 1937.

[136] Juan E. Friguls: "Father Lombardi in Cuba." *Sección Actualidad Católica, Diario de la Marina,* November 14, 1951.

Although the auditorium was too small for the preacher —accustomed to crowds of as many as half a million listeners— the sermons of Fr. Lombardi were a success, one more to add to the apostolic journey that the untiring son of St. Ignatius has been realizing in the lands of Europe and America.

Social justice, defeat of sin, conversion, the great return to Christian life, lived and felt in its fullness, were all essential lessons of the preaching of Fr. Lombardi, who on Wednesday, following his sermon at the Cathedral, took a plane for Venezuela, where he should now be, as the new Paul, preaching the message of the Gospels.[137]

We know of the arrival from Mexico of the illustrious guest on the 7th through the very *Diario de la Marina*. The brief bullets point out that he will preach in the Matanzas Eucharitic Congress on Saturday the 8th and Sunday the 9th, while starting on Monday, he will do an additional program in Havana.[138]

The event in Matanzas came about, according to the reports we have read, with all possible splendor. It was inaugurated by Cardinal Arteaga and continued with Masses as public gatherings heard sermons or speeches from some of the Cuban Bishops, as well as lay leaders.

It stands out that we have not found any highlighting of the contributions of Lombardi, perhaps, as happens at many events, these took place at the same time as other activities and the press paid no particular attention to them. As is often the case and very human, perhaps the irritation of the guest, discovering that he was not the center of the event, started here and it would

---

[137] "Fr. Lombardi." *7 days in the Republic*, pg. 6. *Diario de la Marina*, Sunday, December 16, 1951.

[138] "Famous sacred preacher Fr. Lombardi arrives today." *Diario de la Marina*, Friday, December 7, 1951.

explain a bit the tone of the sole fragment of his oratory that we could find, cited by Dr. Ramón Torreira Crespo — historian, not Catholic— in his work: Breve acercamiento a la historia de la Iglesia católica en Cuba (Brief rapprochement to the history of the Catholic Church in Cuba): conquista, colonización y pseudorrepública (Conquest, colonization and pseudo-republic)," who asserts having taken it from the publication *Duc in altum* (row onto deeper water), that appeared in December of that year. The exalted tone of the declaration is surprising as are the opinions poured on a Church with which he had just come into contact hours before:

> Cuba is a country with very hot climate, but very cold and bastard Christianity. Here comfort and riches are loved very much. Authorities blind their eyes to vested interests... The capitalist and reactionary press takes shelter in the Cross of Christ... The Church, doctrine in action, lives on the fence. Lacks unity. The communist campaign attacks God. Hypocritical and overwhelming capitalism makes God into a shield and the Cross into a crook in order to reach the summit of egotism. Catholic Action is disunited and anemic, when not distorted and null.[139]

It was a prophetic tone, but openly provocative and his judgments could hardly sprout from personal experiences, most probably formulated based on comments that someone dropped into his ear. The insults against Catholic Action are absolutely wrong.

A note, also published in Diario de las Americas to Branch C of Catholic Action in Cuba by the Ladies of Catholic Action, has the

---

[139] Cf. Dr. Ramón Torreira Crespo: "Brief rapprochement to the history of the Catholic Church in Cuba: conquest, colonization and pseudorepublica" Read November 3, 2022 in: http:/biblioteca.clacso.edu.ar/ar/libros/cuba/cips/caudales06/fscommand/52T13.pdf

program of the priest in Havana. They especially invite to the session on the "10th of the month at 8:30 a.m. in the Cathedral, dedicated to the rank and file of Catholic Action and affiliated associations. The other sessions to which they also invite are for the 11th, at 8:30 p.m. in St. Rita Church in Miramar, for the people at large, and the 12th at 8:30 p.m. in the Cathedral, also open to all."[140] To this we would have to add the conference in the Anunciata, mentioned by Friguls, that might not have been in the initial plan, but might have been requested by Fr. Esteban Ribas, director of the sodality, or simply by the members of the Jesuit community in Reina.

The stay was too short, perhaps related to the disappointment the orator had over the people's reception, as the journalist indicates and as Lombardi confirmed a while later, in a fragment picked up by Dr. Rubén Darío Rumbaut, a distinguished psychiatrist and leader of Catholic Action, in his article "Una visión profética de Cuba (A prophetic vision of Cuba)" published in *Seminario Católico* in July 1953:

> The nation in which my crusade has resounded the least is Cuba. It abounds in gifts, such riches, such easy living, that the announcement and convocation clarions slide over its people. Other than some select nuclei, and humble and miserable sectors, Cuba lives under the aegis of frivolity. The don't yet understand the plight of the world, and have yet to pay their quota of pain, as nearly all contemporary nations have already paid or are in the process of paying.[141]

It is not hard to imagine that the audience of those sermons, select but not massive, was composed of some members of the

---

[140] Ladies of Catholic Action: "Notice to Branch C of Catholic Action." *Diario de la Marina* Friday, December 7, 1951, p. 22.

[141] Fernández Santalices: *Presence of Catholicism in Cuba*, p. 73 (Spanish).

Hierarchy, members of the Society of Jesus, Belen alumni, a good number of sodalists from ACU and Anunciata, rank and file from the different branches of Catholic Action and some number of interested parishioners.

We know of the attendance to those preachings of lay persons that would soon turn into prestigious intellectuals, among them poets Fina García Marruz and Eliseo Diego and movie critic Walfredo Piñera, that years later left varied testimonials of the profound impression made by the speaker and the influence it had on their appreciation of "Social Christianity."

The attendees were the evangelic yeast not the mass. They represented the living force of the Church, not the majority that declared itself Catholic but was removed from any apostolic commitment. Lombardi, when he made his bitter prophesy, ignored that he had had a select and receptive audience, even if the number did not flatter the self-esteem of one who convened "massive groups."

We know that Fr. Rey attended the conferences and was vividly impressed. This is striking, because the main message was not too novel for him, once we consider that his method of formation of Agrupados placed social teachings side by side with Ignatian spirituality and it was not adventurous to fear that the exalted tone of the preacher —already prejudiced, for whatever reason, against the Cuban Church— might foment rejection or indifference. Just the opposite occurred.

Firstly, according to Figueroa, at that point in time social issues were of increasing interest to the Jesuit. Indeed, the theme of ACU's Apostolic Assembly, held in the earlier month of October, had as a topic "Problems of workerism in Cuba." On various occasions he had manifested to Agrupados that it was necessary to be sensitive to those issues and to exert influence in their social circles about them.

He had seen how some of his young men had reached important political positions —Juan Antonio Rubio Padilla, Ángel Fernández Varela— and they performed their jobs without sacrificing Christian ethics, but perhaps he had encountered and obstacle in his program of "formation of the select." Those born and raised within a comfortable life could be charitable and take on apostolates like Las Yaguas, but it was not easy to "sync" with the roots of social inequity and they might come face to face with the philosophy of comfort and careless enjoyment. It was not a question of political influences, but rather of the need for society's true conversion to Christianity.

That is why the prophetic tone of Lombardi touched him deeply, not only because of Lombardi's charisma, but because —it seemed— of the fact that he acted as an emissary of Pius XII made him into someone that tried to make practical the social teachings of the Pontiff.

We can't rule out the possibility that both sons of St. Ignatius talked privately and that this awakened mutual admiration. In fact, in this instance the prudential reservations that the founder of the ACU had awakened in the process of adherence to Catholic Action or Pax Romana did not come up. He wanted for him and his to be linked to the "Crusade of love."

This would explain his agreement with the preacher to attend a session the latter would convene in Bogota during the first few days of 1952 —right after the visit to Venezuela— with delegates from various countries of Latin America.

Rey de Castro did not travel alone, he brought along *Agrupados* most sensitive to social and political issues, not only the more experienced Juan Antonio Rubio and Ángel Fernández, but also other promising younger men like Ignacio Warner and Manuel Artime. They were accompanied by one of the leaders of Catholic Action, Rubén Darío Rumbaut who later described him as "agile, alert, tireless, surprisingly youthful, conversing with us in the corners about the "New World."[142]

An excellent eyewitness of those days, Miguel Figueroa, describes the surprising reaction of the Director of the Agrupación following his meeting with the Italian priest:

> His encounter with Fr. Lombardi was very impactful and reanimated all his energies, hopes and freshness of his younger years, but the fervor of that enthusiasm, and the exaltation produced in him upon hearing the expansive plans, which he more than anyone else present would comprehend and feel, caused such a commotion in his so logically structured and full of honesty spirit, that it brought him to assess the work achieved at the Agrupación until that time, and conclude that it was necessary to give it a greater social orientation.
>
> "The time has come," he used to repeat in those days, "for the Church's struggle for justice, and we need to start by forming social consciences among our Catholics."
>
> He returned to Havana on January 7 very preoccupied with these ideas and started right away to consider new action plans that he never completed nor shared with anyone.[143]

The very author of the *History of the Agrupación Católica Universitaria* would soon discover in the course of daily activities at the Agrupación in that month of January and the first days of February, the footprints of that encounter in Colombia. He not only recalls that Fr. Rey de Castro mentioned it in the last meeting of the Ascetic Study Circle he attended, but that he also inserted ideas taken from him in his meditations during the January

---

[142] Figueroa: *History*...p. 169 (Spanish).
[143] Ibidem.

retreat, centered on "Fecund apostolates" offered by Fr. Ayala and, very particularly, in his last Sunday talk —Sunday, February 10– where he questioned "a society that boasts of its egotistical materialism and that, scathed by an exploitative liberalism, tramples on social justice, making millions of unhappy beings miserable."[144]

As another Agrupado, Dr. José Manuel Hernández, affirms in his book *Agrupación Católica Universitaria. The first fifty years:* "It is not improbable, then, that upon his return to Havana (January 7, 1952) he would be ruminating the possibility of reviewing the work achieved until then by the Agrupación and imparting on it a more pronounced social orientation. But if this was indeed what he had in mind, he never communicated it to anyone."[145]

Perhaps placing Cuba on the road of Fr. Lombardi was in the inscrutable divine designs, so that, in spite of the indifference of the majority, the founder of the ACU would be able to complete his work and alert his apostles before his departure. He was already a living part of that "Crusade for love."

---

[144] Ibidem

[145] J.M. Hernández: *Agrupación*...p. 63 (Spanish).

XVIII
The road to the Father

Figueroa writes a disturbing and enigmatic passage when he refers to the days following the return from Bogota:

> As if the meeting in Bogota had not caused sufficient anguish, a series of problems awaited his arrival in Havana, all serious and some very complex, that touched his most intimate affectivity and caused him deep concerns and grave fears about the future of some of his dearest illusions; their presence disturbed the calm he needed to serenely assess the positive results of his work to date when trying to redirect it on the course pointed out by Fr. Lombardi.
>
> These setbacks and dissatisfactions were the crown of thorns that topped off the history of his life of constant abnegation and sacrifice.[146]

What were the natures of those "serious" and "complex" concerns? I have shared that doubt with other people personally close to the ACU or acquainted with its history, they all shared my perplexity. The Director had only been absent a few days and had left president Casteleiro and Brother Aguado in charge, both enjoyed his complete confidence and nothing new seemed to have arisen between the walls of the home base of the Agrupación. With regard to the community of Reina, although there were always discordant voices there about the work, Fr. Rey was at the time not only one of the longest serving and distinguished

---
[146] Figueroa: *History*... p. 170.

members of it, but also enjoyed the support of the Vice-Provincial Fr. Calvo.

We have not found anything that shines a light on this matter amidst the documents we have researched. Nevertheless, I dare to conject that the problems found by Fr. Rey upon his return did not differ from those he left behind and in the course of his life he had demonstrated special faith and energy in decision making, never abandoning himself to pessimism or indecision.

Perhaps what happened is that he was looking at his work with new eyes and, anxious of seeing it perfected in light of the ideals of a "Better World," found it lacking. The same had happened to many saints in the history of the Church, feeling that the apostolic congregations or institutions they founded and encouraged were defective in light of evangelical counsels. In the search for perfection they did not tolerate mediocrity and contemplating the grandness of Christ thought little of all they had built.

To this we could add a detail of medical character. Those who travel to Bogota from cities located closer to sea level, suffer the change in atmospheric pressure due to the altitude of that place. That —as experimented some years ago by this book's author— not only produces the effect known as "soroche (mountain sickness)" whose essential symptom is an acute and persistent headache, but also, depending on the constitution of each individual, can provoke and increase in arterial pressure, breathing difficulties and cardiac complications. In order to adequately adapt to those geographic conditions it is necessary to remain there at least two weeks, although some require more time.

Fr. Rey appeared to be healthy and was not a man given to too much time on medical visits. If he had predisposition to arterial hypertension, his stay in Colombia would have aggravated it.

Immersed in the emotions of the session, he ignored it. He most likely ignored it as well upon his return. As is well known, hypertension problems, as well as cardiac ones, can lead to states of depression. Perhaps many of the frustrations of the priest's last few days were not caused by new problems, but rather from his imperious and stubborn character's view of them amidst an unrecognized depressive state mixed with spiritual desolation. It is probable that a physical condition of this type was the material cause of his unexpected death.

In spite of this, we have not found information from those days that Fr. Rey talked with any of his distinguished specialists that were also Agrupados of his complete confidence like doctors Juan Antonio Rubio, Armando Ruiz Leiro or Sergio Álvarez Mena, much less did he avail himself of the psychoanalytic skills of José Ignacio Lasaga. Instead of that, he locked himself in to work feverishly as was his custom and no one gave it much importance. It was not the first time that, preoccupied with some issue, he turned incommunicative and even sullen for a few days and did not tolerate interruptions while meditating or working.

Ángela Domingo, chronicler of the daily *Información* (Information), recalls plans and comments of the Director during those days:

> [...] he talked with Rev. Brother Aguado and other Agrupados about his plans to air-condition the third floor of the Agrupación Católica Universitaria. Some days back we saw him presiding the board of Female Marian Sodalities in which he announced his project to convene a grand Marian congress here in Havana to commemorate the bicentennial of the constitution of Female Marian Sodalities, selecting the month of May for said event to coincide with the arrival at the Capital of the image of Our Lady of Charity at Cobre. He proposed to honor the Virgin with a great procession of floats presenting allegories of the Rosary at which he would invite the various Daughters of

Mary associations established in Havana, as well as the federated of the Young Women of Catholic Action.[147]

And thus arrived the last day of his existence in the world. We choose to turn to Figueroa's book and the transcription he provides from the pages of the diary of the Agrupación that gives account of those bitter hours. Even though we are dealing with a schematic redaction void of adornment, it comes out more veridical and moving than a literary recreation of the circumstances:

> On the morning of the 12th (of February 1952) Fr. Rey celebrated Mass and had breakfast as usual; at 11:30 Brother [Esteban] Aguado called him for lunch at Reina, and he replied he was thinking of staying at the Agrupación that day, which was not uncommon for him.
>
> Upon his return Brother Aguado, accompanied by Brother [Victor] Ibáñez and Fr. Mariano Ruiz, asked about the Father and was told that Fr. Rey did not answer in any of the rooms he used to frequent. It did not draw the attention of Brother Aguado each time Father had the habit of not answering when he was busy on an important matter.
>
> After half an hour, an employee saw the bathroom light on and it raised suspicion that something had happened to Fr. Rey. Brother Aguado was alerted and he climbed in through the window, finding Fr. Rey dead in the bathtub. Based on the hour at which Father took his bath, it is estimated he died two hours afterward, at approximately 11:50 a.m.[148] In the notice published by *Diario de la Marina* the following day, it is reported that doctors Ceferino Catá and Juan Ascanio, Agrupados present at the moment

---

[147] Ángela Domingo: Reverend Fr. Felipe Rey de Castro, S.J." *Vida Católica Información,* February 14, 1952, p. 10 (Spanish).

[148] Figueroa: *History*...ps. 170-171.

the cadaver was found, were the ones that certified he died of "cardiac syncope" and calculated the approximate time of death.

It is not necessary to describe the sense of astonishment at that sudden death, that quickly turned into deep sorrow. The chronicle, however, limits itself to just the facts:

> At first, Dr. Juan Ascanio and other Agrupados at the Agrupación took him out and cushioned him immediately. Brother Aguado sought out Dr. Armando Ruiz Leiro and Fr. Teodoro Bercedo, Reina's Superior. Agrupados were immediately informed, and many came to look upon their beloved Father one last time.[149]

Even before the press could publish funeral obituaries or principal religious communities were alerted, news spread throughout the city. The crowd that paraded before the coffin grew more each remaining hour of that 12th day of February.

The 13th at one in the morning, Fr. [Ceferino] Ruiz, Rector of the Colegio de Belén celebrated the first Mass in the large meeting room, crammed with Agrupados. Fr. [Gustavo] Amigó celebrated at 5 a.m., at 6 a.m. Msgr. Belarmino García Feito, at 7 a.m. Fr. Enrique Oslé, at 8:30 Fr. [Teodoro Bercedo], Superior at Reina, attended by the Calvario community and a few hundred persons.

> A continuous stream of people came to the Agrupación during the day; high ecclesiastical authorities, representatives of religious orders, Catholic Action, etc.[150]

Diario de la Marina placed the news on the front page of its February 13 edition, the headline read "Profound sense of regret due to the death of Rev. Fr. Rey de Castro" and the subtitle said:

---

[149] Figueroa: *History*...p. 171.
[150] Ibidem.

"Founded the Agrupación Católica Universitaria and promoted Retreats" —both endeavors were the recapitulation of an entire life—. Page 6 of that issue welcomed something unusual for a public periodical: five obituaries dedicated to Fr. Rey: from the Society of Jesus, the Agrupación Católica Universitaria, the Association of Medical Studies, one belonging to the Federation of Female Marian Sodalities of Cuba. Such a thing was only normal for certain notable public figures in the fields of politics, science, the arts or the world of business. These were complemented by others published that day or the following one in newspapers of large circulation like *El País*, *Información* and *El Mundo*.

One thing that stands out in these obituaries is that all of them —including the one from the Society of Jesus— point out that he died "after receiving the Holy Sacraments and a Papal blessing. We know his death was sudden, hence Rey de Castro did not receive the Extreme Unction nor Holy Viaticum as the infirm do. But if we recall that he celebrated Mass at the start of day, we know that he consecrated and consumed the Host and, with respect to the "Papal blessing," if it was not received in the final hour, the Holy Father Pius XII, in totally different occasions, had blessed him during the assemblies he attended in Rome, and in episcopal communications. What redactors wrote using a logic that defied historical facts, was strictly correct from a spiritual point of view.

Another important detail is that those obituaries reiterated something traditional in Catholic funerals: "Please don't send floral arrangements. Masses are appreciated." A moving exception was that of residents of Las Yaguas neighborhood, who were ignorant of and chose not to follow the request, sending an offering in the shape of a cross made from white roses. They wished to honor him and show him their gratitude, as they did in funerals of their dearest beloved, through penny-by-penny collections. It was like the small offering of the widow in the Gospels, so pleasing in the eyes of God.

In the gatherings at the funeral could be found, in addition to members of the Society of Jesus and the Agrupación, distinguished laypersons like Dr. Valentín Arenas Armiñan, National President of Catholic Knights of Cuba; Dr. Margarita López, President of Casa Cultural Católicas (Catholic Cultural House); Miguel Suárez, National President of Catholic Action; Dr. Andrés Valdespino, President of the National Board of Juventud Masculina Católica (Catholic Young Men); as well as Coronel Alberto de Carricarte, Dr. Julio Morales Gómez and América Penichet, among many other personalities.

The numerous funeral procession left the Agrupación at five in the afternoon of February 13, destined to Cementerio Colón (Columbus Cemetery). The Catholic journalist Juan Emilio Friguls rated it as "one of the largest religious mourning manifestations seen in Havana in years."[151]

The preserved photos show an impressive number of attendees. There was ample school representation from Baldor, Belén, Electromechanical and from the neighborhood Las Yaguas. *Diario de la Marina* did not just send a journalist, but rather a healthy representation of its personnel, led by its director José Ignacio Rivero Hernández, his brother, administrator Oscar Rivero Hernández and the chief of redaction Gastón Baquero, among others. The Damas Isabelinas (Elizabethan Ladies) sent a delegation, led by Grand Regent, Consuelo Morillo de Govantes.

Naturally, the majority of Agrupados were present, along with the grieving young women from Rosa Mística. Among the clergy present were members of the Society of Jesus, including those

---

[151] Juan Emilio Friguls: Part of the Catholic flourishing in Cuba is due to the work of Fr. Rey de Castro." Diario de la Marina, February 14, 1952 (Spanish).

part of the Agrupación —like Eduardo Boza Masvidal, pastor of La Caridad (Charity parish) and Juan Suárez, pastor of Madruga— and also other members of secular clergy and representatives of religious orders, Franciscans, Capuchins, Passionists, Pauline's, Redemtorists, Claretians, Marians, La Salle and Brothers of San Juan de Dios (St. John of God). Beyond any human differences, Catholic Action was there represented by its President and members of almost all its branches.

Upon arrival at the cemetery the funeral procession stopped before the central Chapel, where Msgr. Alfredo Müller San Martín, Auxiliary Bishop of Havana, representing Archbishop Cardinal Manuel Arteaga y Betancourt. Afterward, the mortal remains of the priest were deposited in the vault belonging to the Society of Jesus.

The funeral prayer in ACU's name was assigned to José Ignacio Lasaga:

> We have just deposited underground the body of one of the greatest men in the history of Cuba. It is just that he was one of those that only appears in the front pages of newspapers on the day of his death. Because the work was always like those great underground currents that rear up here and there in a serpentine brook or the bustle of a fountain, and yet create all the wealth in an area from underground.
>
> [...]
>
> If until today we had only one Director, from now on we will have two: one on Earth, whom we will respect, obey and love, because he will be his successor, and another in Heaven that will continue, as before, looking over our actions and orienting us, now invisibly, with his counsels. Because I am sure that in his royal mansion that was prepared for him in Heaven, there will always be an open

window, and it will be the window that opens toward Cuba[152]

Additionally, the words of Vice-Provincial of the Antilles Rev. Fr. Ramón Calvo, according to *Diario de la Marina*, "were more than a mournful farewell, an allocution to Catholic Cuban youth and particularly to Agrupados —spiritual children of Fr. Rey— to continue the work that with such tenacity the unforgettable son of St. Ignatius founded and is today one of the pillars of Cuban Catholicism." Similarly, "he promised all the support of the Society of Jesus to keep in force the work of Fr. Rey, and demanded a promise from Agrupados before the just sealed tomb of the founder, to remain united in the apostolic work and united under Christ to also keep alive and fresh in each heart our remembrance of Fr. Felipe Rey de Castro as posthumous homage to his unforgettable memory."[153]

During ensuing days, in addition to Masses in suffrage for the soul of the founder celebrated in the parish of Sacred Heart on Reina and in the chapel of the Agrupación, there were others like the one celebrated in the chapel of the Convent of the Madres Reparadoras (Mothers Reparatrix) on Saturday, February 16 at eight thirty in the morning and the one officiated Monday the 18th at seven in the morning in the Jesuit St. Joseph Parish in Camagüey, sponsored not only by ACU sodalists residing there, but also by those who had done the Exercises led by Fr. Rey in that Catholic city on more than one occasion.

---

[152] J.E.F.: "Contribución del R. P. Rey de Castro al catolicismo cubano". ["Contribution of Fr. Rey de Castro to Cuban Catholicism"]. *Diario de la Marina*, February 14, 1952, p. 22 (Spanish).

[153] Ibidem.

The burial services for Fr. Rey de Castro, S.J., a testament to his following.

Felipe Rey de Castro and the Agrupación Católica Universitaria

Celebration in the new Boardroom of the ACU the night of November 3, 1952, following the unveiling of the plaque and the oil painting of the founder of the ACU, Rev. Fr. Felipe Rey de Castro, SJ.

From l. to r., Dr. Jorge S. Casteleiro, President, Rev. Fr. Amando Llorente, SJ, a participant, Mr. José Ignacio Rivero, Director of *Diario de la Marina*, Rev. Fr. Juan Suárez, sodalist and Pastor of Madruga, Rev. Fr. Barbeito, SJ, Sub-Director of the ACU, Dr. Francisco Pérez Vich, Rev. Fr. seated and presiding the ceremony, His Eminence the Nuncio.

XIX
The harvest

Two decades before his transit to eternity, Fr. Rey de Castro had written —on June 12, 1932, from Puerto Rico— to his small group of sodalists:

> I continue to savor that promise that some of you made to me when I departed, namely: that the Agrupación will give proof on this occasion of the profoundly Catholic spirit that animates it, and that hence, neither in punctuality nor number of participants at Sunday Masses, nor in Communions, nor in the incipient Saturday Guard of Honor from which I expect so much for the Agrupación; nor in anything that speaks to the Catholic life of Agrupados, should my absence be missed, moreover, there are some among you, starting with me, which expect that all this should continue to grow progressively. Anything else would mean that the sower and cultivator of the Agrupación is not good, for seed never rests not once it is strewn on the ground.
>
> If I see you persevere and grow during my absence, it would be no small recompense for the little that I have planted and worked among you.[154]

Thirty years later those wishes were completely fulfilled. The founder was no longer physically among his young men, but his work had taken such firm root in a nucleus of his "selects" that they could continue it, centered not only on a set of guiding ideas and disciplined practices, but also with an identity that will allow

---

[154] Figueroa: *History*...p. 172.

them to continue and expand on what had already been accomplished.

It was no simple task to replace the Director. Starting that very 12th of February, Jorge Casteleiro in his duty as President, led successive extraordinary board meetings to ensure the ongoing operation of the Agrupación and discern the name of a possible successor. He convened all his presidential predecessors, as well as the most senior of disciples: Juan Antonio Rubio Padilla. Nevertheless, it was impossible to find a name by consensus.

It was providential that the Board of Directors agreed to assign Dr. Carlos Martínez Arango to lead Agrupados starting with the following Sunday's Mass, the first without the founder. He was capable of delivering remarks that combined his Catholic faith with his broad knowledge of the human mind, in order to enable, amidst the grief, a decision that would allow the work to continue and expand:

> Until now Fr. Rey and the Agrupación, although distinct, were for us the same thing, from now on, even though our understanding be appalled and our heart reluctant we have to begin getting used to disassociating Fr. Rey from the Agrupación, the person from the work.
>
> From his work, personally planned to outlive him.
>
> From his work, conceived by him too grand to last only as long as a man's lifetime.
>
> Hence, in his position as Director of the A.C.U., Fr. Rey must be replaceable.
>
> It is a hard truth that this mortal life runs out. But for us, Agrupados, there must be no doubt in our understanding, that He who in his divine and inscrutable Providence took him from us, will also give us his successor.
>
> One who, like him, will be a bridge, the link to He who Fr. Rey always considered our true Director of the A.C.U.

To Jesus Christ, Our Lord, and to his Most Holy Mother, Immaculate Mary, our Patroness.[155].

The third and decisive extraordinary board meeting took place that very day. Casteleiro gave a briefing on the conversations held with some members of the Society of Jesus. And the consensus born there was to suggest Fr. Amando Llorente SJ as the new director. He was officially named the 24th of February and the next day he met for the first time with the Board of Directors.

Fr. Llorente had met Fr. Rey during his time as "maestrillo (first time teacher)" in Belen and Fr. Rey had offered a session of Exercises there. Years later Fr. Llorente returned to Cuba, where he was assigned to lead the Calvario House of Exercises, where he further developed a relationship with the founder of the ACU.

In fact, when Fr. Llorente made his final vows on February 2, 1952, Fr. Rey not only attended, along with a good number of Agrupados, but before commencement of the ceremony, gave a speech that, unbeknownst even to him, was an acknowledgment of the young man that would succeed him less than a month later.

Fr. Llorente's character was different to that of Fr. Rey de Castro. He was spiritual, but very dynamic, extroverted and often a risk-taker in his apostolic work. He demonstrated a feverish desire for renovation, though always respectful of each and every requirement and tradition of the ACU. To him befell to reap much of what his predecessor had planted, as evidenced by endeavors like the expansion of the home base of the Agrupación; construction of "Pius XII" House of Exercises in La Coronela; celebration of the great Vía Crucis (Stations of the Cross) on Good Fridays at El Calvario, the development of the Buró of Information and Propa-

---

[155] Ibidem, p. 174.

ganda (Bureau of Information and Outreach) which published, systematically, booklets about Social Teaching, Apologetics, Morality, Ecclesiology and Sociology, as well as the execution of two big social research surveys whose results are still referenced: one about the religious sentiment of Cubans and another about the living conditions of the Island's farmers.

Memories of Fr. Rey continued to accompany Agrupados. On the 3rd of November when the new boardroom was inaugurated, it included his framed portrait, painted by the photographer and Cuban artist Félix de Cossío (1913-1999) and a plaque that memorialized his passing to the eternal life in the very place where it occurred, consequence of a remodeling of the building.

In 1953, on the first anniversary of the death of the founder, the cornerstone of what would become Colegio-Dispensario Padre Rey de Castro SJ (School-Dispensary Fr. Felipe Rey de Castro SJ) was placed in Las Yaguas. It was inaugurated on the 8th of February of the ensuing year.

The January 1953 *Esto Vir* issue opens with an editorial written by the director of the publication, Manuel Artime Buesa, entitled Mission Accomplished, and he states:

> The 12th of February will be the first anniversary of your death, Felipe Rey de Castro. We come before you with the same hopeful and faithful outlook with which we entered your Spiritual Director's room. Our heads high, shining, and the dampness that clouds our eyes, will have the pleasant significance of duty fulfilled, because the commemoration of the first anniversary of your death will be a renewal of the vow we took.
>
> [...]
>
> We did not reorganize the Sodality, we did not need a desperate call to unity; everything seemed predetermined, ranks formed instinctively, the Agrupación marched

forward. Indifferent to your death? No, not indifferent, never indifferent, the Lord is our witness that in that pit was buried for ever a bit of our heart. That when your portrait and plaque were hung in the place where you died, and the new Director spoke to us about the responsibility we had to you, there were tears in our eyes and wounds in our hearts.

[...]

We will bring before you new works of apostolate, filled sessions of Spiritual Exercises, progress in the work at Las Yaguas that will carry your name, even greater intensity in the formation of each of us. We will place before you constancy in all you left us and new goals in our walk to Christ. And the pastor that leads us, that has known how to raise the flag that you left flying over your tomb, will also raise his eyes to Heaven, to overflow the joy that fills his heart, and say with us: Felipe Rey de Castro, mission accomplished.[156]

The Agrupación Católica Universitaria had become a true model, not only in the Island, but for the entire Catholic world. This was evidenced in 1954 when, at the First Worldwide Congress of Our Lady's Sodalities, with participation of delegates from seventy countries, Cuban José Ignacio Lasaga was elected by great majority of votes as President of it. The ACU selected Ambrosio González del Valle y Morales as his alternate before the Federation.[157]

---

[156] Manuel Artime Buesa: "Mission Accomplished." *Esto Vir*, Havana, January 1952, p. 1-2 (Spanish).

[157] He was descendant of a prominent family that contributed various distinguished professionals to Cuba's intellectual life. Son of doctor surgeon Ambrosio González del Valle and Dolores Morales. Lawyer. Married Silvia Fonts with whom he had tres sons: Alberto Antonio, Eduardo Antonio and Ignacio. He distinguished himself as an Agrupado, particularly his notable

It is not enough to recall the very important presence of Agrupados with relevant positions at universities, in public political positions and in a wide professional sphere: doctors, lawyers, engineers, nor solely in the unarguable fact that the great majority had formed solidly Christian families, but also in those that thanks to the spiritual formation they received had answered affirmatively the call of the Spirit to be shepherds of the children of Christ in the world. Those vocations by 1956, just four years after the death of Fr. Rey, and according to Manuel Hernández were "27 Jesuit Agrupados and 4 secular priests, among which could be found a canon of Havana Cathedral."[158] With the passage of time these numbers would continue to grow.

The spiritual presence of Fr. Rey was so endearing and vivid that Agrupados wanted his mortal remains reposed in the very heart of his work and they had them transferred to the ACU's chapel, where they were to rest forever at the foot of the altar, under the presence of the Tabernacle and the protective eyes of Immaculate Mary.

---

work diffusing catechetical topics, liturgy and Christian morality, through the Bureau of Information and Outreach (BIP, in is Spanish acronym), co-authored with Luis Valdés Larrauri the booklet *Evito los hijos y quiero comulgar...* and as only author: *El poder de la oración, El don de Dios, la gracia, Siguiendo la misa, Germen de vida eterna, El Cristo total.* He emigrated to the United States after the triumph of the revolutionary process and continued his work in the Sodality. He received the title of "Maestro" of the Agrupación. It appeared as overrepresentation for a small country like Cuba. On the other hand, it is true that Fr. Llorente had by then shown very dynamic work, yet the splendor of the ACU dated from the time of Fr. Rey and the acknowledgment was for work performed over various decades.

[158] Hernández: *ACU: Los primeros cincuenta años*, p. 82 (Spanish).

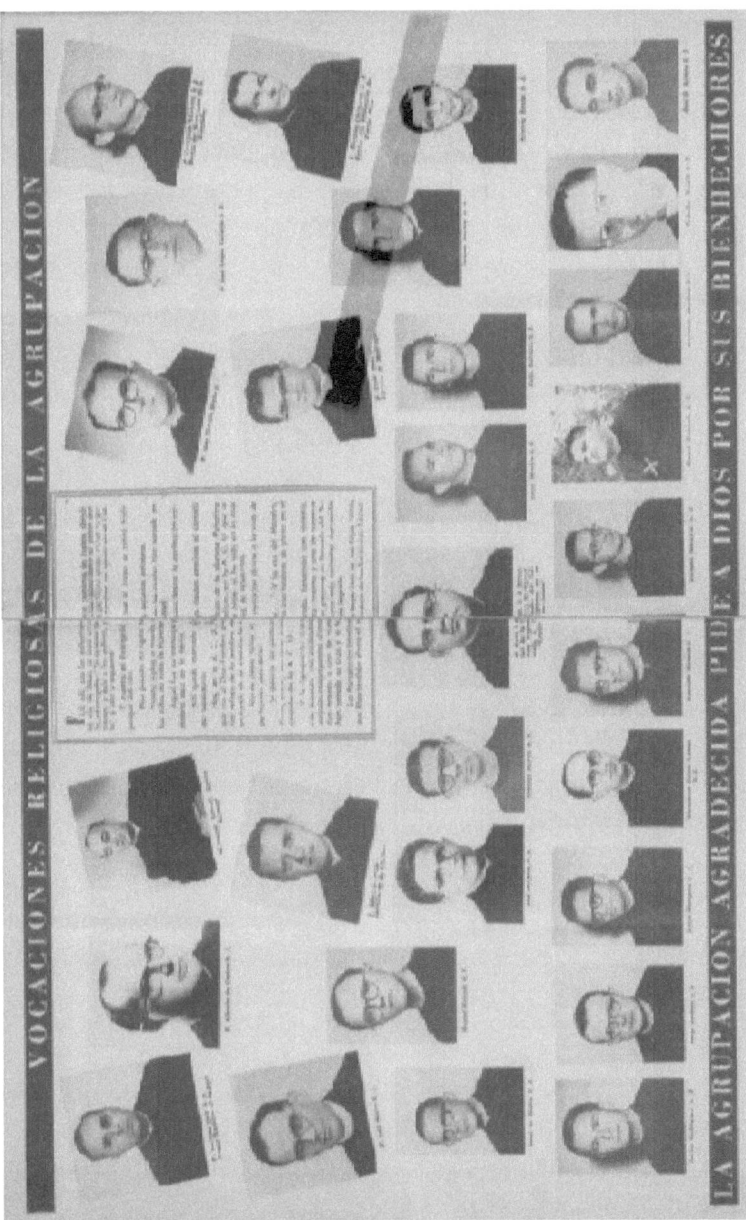

Vocations nurtured at the ACU. Image taken from the *Diario de la Marina* Supplement (1957)

Nevertheless, God works on human history in miraculous ways. Days would come in which the triumphant editorial tone of Artime reflecting the satisfaction of Agrupados, would be converted in just the opposite: persecution, exile, death. Why? The answer could be found in God's warning to the prophet Isaiah: "For my thoughts are not your thoughts, neither are your ways my ways, says the Lord. For as the heavens are higher than the earth, so are my thoughts higher than your ways and my thoughts than your thoughts."[159]

Not the new Director, nor the more experienced *Agrupados* —Rubio Padilla, Fernández Varela— could imagine the events that would transpire with the interruption of democratic rule by a coup d'etat perpetrated on March 10, 1952, less than a month following the death of Rey, that would unleash a political confrontation on the Island whose violence would recall those of the ACU's foundational years. Civil resistance brought on repression and also motivated violent reactions. The fall of the government on the first day of 1959 did not quiet the situation. Those who, like Artime himself, celebrated the occasion and started to collaborate with the new authorities on social endeavors soon discovered that a fragile coalition government began to turn toward a socialism of Stalinist demeanor.

The protests from those in civil society and ecclesiastical hierarchy, from the ends of 1959 until 1961, were answered with draconian measures: expulsion of priests and religious, intervention of private education, prison terms and even life-sentences against opponents.

An epoch came to an end around April 1961. The government had officially declared itself socialist and the Catholic Church, as well as other Christian conferences, were considered enemies to be defeated.

---

[159] Isaiah 55, 8-9.

The ACU was cleansed from official channels. It is symptomatic that amidst the period's agitation, when it was impossible to function normally, the leaders of the Sodality decided to return the remains of the founder to the Jesuit pantheon in Havana's necropolis, to protect them from what would take place days later: the ACU quarters were occupied by governmental milicias and expropriated without explanations. It still stands there today.

The opulent, prestigious, well established ACU had been proscribed in just a few days, the Director and a certain number of Agrupados, emigres to the United States, were like the "rest of Israel" after the captivity. Faith, persistence and undoubtedly the intercession of Fr. Felipe, allowed them to plant roots in exile.

They had lost the building constructed with such sacrifices, their publications, their place in society, yet the spirit of the Agrupación was preserved, acclimated to in another culture and other customs. Cuba awaits God's time to see it reborn on its land, perhaps a little different as to form, but faithful to the charism that the Spirit would breathe into Felipe Rey de Castro in the distant days of 1928.

The interest of sodalists of the ACU in Miami for promoting the process of beatification of Frs. Rey and Llorente, obtained the consent of Cardinal Juan de la Caridad García on January 17, 2019, in the Archdiocese of Havana. What seemed forgotten comes back into the light and a history begun almost one century ago starts to show that like the grain of wheat of the Gospels, seeming to die, yields unsuspected fruit.

Arzobispado de La Habana.
Cancillería.

Yo, Juan de la Caridad García Rodríguez, por la Gracia de Dios y de la Sede Apostólica, Arzobispo de San Cristóbal de La Habana.

Conociendo del interés manifiesto los miembros de la ACU Miami, de tratar de introducir la Causa de Beatificación de los Padres Felipe Rey de Castro y Amando Llorente miembros ejemplares de la Compañía de Jesús, los cuales dedicaron parte de su vida sacerdotal para lograr la participación en la Iglesia de elemento masculino del mundo profesional, procurar su compromiso con el seguimiento de Cristo y la propagación de la Fe católica en el Pueblo Cubano; el primero, realizando con mucho esfuerzo la fundación de la Agrupación Católica Universitaria y, el segundo, continuando la obra emprendida por su antecesor cuando este falleció y, al cesar la obra en Cuba, trasladándose a Miami, continuarla allá.

Vista la necesidad de iniciar este proceso en su primera etapa, sea en Miami, primero y en La Habana después.
Que de iniciarse el proceso de cada caso por separado;

Declaro que NO HAY NINGUNA dificultad de nuestra parte para que se realice en esta Arquidiócesis.

Dado en la ciudad de La Habana, sede del Arzobispado, a los diecisiete días del mes de enero del año del Señor 2 019.

+Juan, Arz. Hab
Juan de la Caridad García Rodríguez
Arzobispo de La Habana

Archbishop of Havana.
Chancellery.

I, Juan de la Caridad García Rodríguez, by the Grace of God and the Apostolic See, Archbishop of San Cristóbal de La Habana [Saint Christopher of Havana].

Cognizant of the expressed interest of members of Miami ACU to explore the Cause of Beatification in favor of Frs. Felipe Rey de Castro and Amando Llorente, exemplary members of the Society of Jesus that dedicated their priestly lives to entice professional men to commit to follow Christ and to propagate the Catholic Faith among the Cuban People; the former, with great effort, via the foundation of the Agrupación Católica Universitaria [University Catholic Association] and the latter through continuation, upon the death of the founder, of the work started by his predecesor in Cuba and translating to Miami and continuing it there.

There is a requirement to start the first phase of the process in Miami and later in Havana.

Each process commencing independently of the other:

I assert that THERE IS NO difficulty whatsoever in our part to carry out the work in this Archdiocese.

Given in the City of Havana, see of the Archdiocese, on the sixteenth day of the month of January of the year of Our Lord 2019.

[Signature]
Juan de la Caridad García Rodríguez
   Archbishop of Havana

Letter of authorization of the Archbishop of Havana to investigate the process of beatification for Fr. Rey de Castro. Editor's English translation of the original.

Bibliography

Minutes of the Immaculate Conception and St. Luis Gonzaga Marian Sodality [*Actas de la Congregación Mariana de la Inmaculada Concepción y de S. Luis Gonzaga*]. Historic Archive of the Society of Jesus in Galicia: Colegio Apóstol Santiago, Vigo, Box 254.

Agrupación Católica Universitaria. Silver Anniversary [*Bodas de plata*]. Special Supplement of *Diario de la Marina*. Havana, Sunday, June 16, 1957.

Marian Year at the [*Año Mariano en el*] Colegio del Apóstol Santiago. Historic Archive of the Society of Jesus in Galicia: Colegio Apóstol Santiago, Vigo.

Argüelles Espinosa, Luis Ángel: «Mexican refugees in Cuba [Los refugiados mexicanos en Cuba]». *The Word and Man* [*La Palabra y el Hombre*], Universidad Veracruzana, Apirl-June 1989, no.70, pp. 117-148.

Ayala & Alarcó SJ, P. Ángel: *Anthology of formation of the selected* [*Antología de formación de selectos*]. Selection and edition by Pablo Gutiérrez Carreras. Madrid, Hazte Oír, 2008. PDF version.

Bay Sevilla, Luis: «A sugar mill that belongs to the same family for 122 years [Un ingenio que pertenece desde hace 122 años a la misma familia]». *Diario de la Marina*, January 17, 1946. PDF version. reproduced by Cuban Genealogy Club, Miami, 2010. Accessed August 19, 2022.

Cabada Castro SJ, P. Manuel: *About Fr. Felipe Rey de Castro. Assorted or complementary information*. [*Sobre el P. Felipe Rey de Castro. Datos sueltos o complementarios*], 2018. Digitized text in ACU's Archives, Miami.

Calvo SJ, P. Ramón: «Words on the burial of Fr. Felipe Rey de Castro [Palabras en el entierro del P. Felipe Rey de Castro]». From the *Diario de la Marina,* February 10, 1952, Catholic Section [Sección Católicas], s/p. Photo of a news clip in ACU's Archive.

Cartas Edificantes de la Provincia de Castilla [Edifying letter from the Province of Castile]. Bilbao, La Editorial Vizcaína, 1919.

Castro, Sor Benita OSB: *Letter to Dr. Jorge Casteleiro* [*Carta al Dr. Jorge Casteleiro*], April 2, 1952. Photocopied text from ACU's Archive, Miami.

Cathedra of Pharmacology HISTORY OF PUBLIC HEALTH NOTEBOOKS 105[*Cátedra de Farmacología*. CUADERNOS DE HISTORIA DE LA SALUD PÚBLICA 105. Accessed at http://scielo.sld.cu/pdf/his/n105/hist06.pdf on September 21, 2022.

Communication from the Cuban Embassy to the Department of State of the United States about personnel in Cuban consulates in said country [*Comunicación de la Embajada de Cuba al Departamento de Estado de Estados Unidos sobre personal en los consulados cubanos en ese país*. March 5, 1948. Typed original in the Archive of the Department of State [Original mecanografiado en los Archivos del Departamento de Estado]. PDF version.

Cuesta, Leonel de la: «Evocation of Villanueva. *Another Monday*, HispanicAmerican Culture Magazine [Evocación de Villanueva». *Otro Lunes,* Revista hispanoamericana de cultura]. Accessed at http://otrolunes.com/archivos/16-20/?sumario/estelunes/evocacion-de-villanueva.html, November 21, 2022.

_____:«I, Fidel, at 65 years of age». *Another Monday,* Hispanic American Culture Magazine [Yo Fidel, a los 65 años». *Otro Lunes,* Revista hispanoamericana de cultura. Accessed at http://otrolunes.com/archivos/16-20/?hemeroteca/numero-18/sumario/este-lunes/yo-fidel-a-los-65-anos.html, November 21, 2022.

Chacón y Calvo, José María: «Death of Fr. Rey de Castro [La muerte del Padre Rey de Castro]». *Diario de la Marina,* February 15, 1952, p.4.

Damas de Acción Católica: «Aviso de la Rama C de Acción Católica Cubana. [Women of Catholic Action: «Notice from Branch C of Cuban Catholic Action]» *Diario de la Marina,* Friday, December 7, 1951, p.22.

Domingo Cuadriello, Jorge: «On the centennial of the Band of Piety». *New Word* [En el centenario del Bando de Piedad». *Palabra Nueva].* Havana, no. 155, September, 2006. Accessed at http://www.palabranueva.net/contens/09/000103-3.htm, November 19, 2022.

«El Padre Lombardi, S.J.». *Por un mundo mejor. Servicio de animación espiritual* [«Fr. Lombardi, S.J.» *For a better world. Spiritual animation service*]. Webpage accessed November 24, 2022 at http://www.porunmundomejor.com/wordpress/somos/el-padre-lombardi/

Fernández Caubí, Luis: *Death is beneficial* [*La muerte es ganancia*], 1971. Typed testimonial in ACU's Archive, Miami.

Fernández Santalices, Manuel: *Catholicism's presence in Cuba. Historical notes from the 20th Century.* [*Presencia en Cuba del Catolicismo. Apuntes históricos del siglo XX*]. Caracas, Fundación Konrad Adenauer, 1998.

Figueroa y Miranda, Dr. Miguel: *History of the Agrupación Católica Universitaria 1931-1956* [*Historia de la Agrupación Católica Universitaria 1931-1956*]. Agrupación Católica Universitaria, Miami, 2020.

_____: *Core ideas of the Agrupación Católica Universitaria* [*Ideario de la Agrupación Católica Universitaria*]. Typed document in ACU's Archive. Digital version.

Friguls, Juan Emilio: «Fr. Lombardi and Cuba [El Padre Lombardi y Cuba]». [*Catholic News* Section [Sección *Actualidad Católica*]. *Diario de la Marina*, November 14, 1951, p.8.

_____: «Arrival today of famous sacred Fr. Lombardi [Llega hoy el famoso predicador sagrado Padre Lombardi]». *Diario de la Marina*, Friday, December 7, 1951, p.1.

_____: «Fr. Lombardi [El Padre Lombardi]». *Diario de la Marina*, Sunday, December 16, 1951.. Suplement *7 days in the Republic* [*7 días en la República*], p.6.

_____: «Contribution of Fr. Rey de Castro to Cuban Catholicism [Contribución del R. P. Rey de Castro al catolicismo cubano]». *Diario de la Marina*, February 14, 1952, pp.1 and 23.

García Sánchez, Ph. D.Sixto: «Karl Rahner and Cuban identity. Reflections on an improbable love [Karl Rahner y la identidad cubana. Reflexiones sobre un amor improbable]». Instituto de Política Internacional UFV, Madrid. Notes 14, October 9, 2020. Accessed at https://ipi-ufv.com/wp-content/uploads/2020/10/ Apunte-2020-14-Karl-Rahner-y-la-identidad-cubana.pdf, September 14, 2022.

García Alonso, Aida: *Manuela the Mexican* [*Manuela la mexicana*]. Mención Ensayo, 1968. Editorial Casa de las Américas, Havana, 1968.

Hernández, Dr. José Manuel: *Agrupación Católica Universitaria. The first 50 years* [*Los primeros cincuenta años*]. Agrupación Católica Universitaria, Miami, 1981.

Hernández Egea, Enrique: Record of the project to erect ACU's headquarters [Memoria del proyecto para la construcción de la sede de la ACU]. Typed issue, November 18, 1938. VPA Archive in Havana.

Himno de la Agrupación Católica Universitaria, partitura con la letra [*Hymn of the Agrupación Católica Universitaria, score with lyrics*]. Includes a five-sheets attachment with signatures of Rey de Castro and agrupados and Evening Program to commemorate the blessing of the flag and first audition of the Hymn of the Agrupación Católica Universitaria, May 6, 1943. Digital version available at https://static1.squarespace.com/static/5cdd76d3523958fe9a568bb f/t/62b1e88c56a658326b38fa8c/1655826634411/Velada+para+ce lebra+la+bendicion+de+la+bandera+e+himno.pdf Accessed September 29, 2022.

Huerta, René de la: «The Fr. Rey I met at the ACU [El P. Rey que conocí dentro de la ACU]». *Esto Vir,* March 1952, pp.14-15.

Ignacio de Loyola, St.: *Spiritual Exercises* [*Ejercicios espirituales*]. Biblioteca Digital Universal, Editorial del Cardo, 2003.

_____: *Letter* [*Cartas*]. Madrid, Press of the widow and son of Aguado, 1875.

_____: *Letter concerning the obedience of students of Coimbra* [*Carta sobre la obediencia a los estudiantes de Coimbra*]. Accessed at http://www.cmasuncion.org/lectura-espiritual/ item/ 12-carta-sobre-la-obediencia-de-san-ignacio-de-loyola, August 11, 2022.

Informe del P. Felipe Rey de Castro sobre la posibilidad de establecer según sus fines la Agrupación Católica Universitaria [*Report of Fr. Felipe Rey de Castro concernir the possibility of properly establishing the Agrupación Católica Universitaria*]. Undated typed document in VPA Archive in Havana.

Lasaga, Dr. José Ignacio: *What is the ACU* [*Qué es la ACU*]. Booklet about the Agrupación Católica Universitaria. Havana, Bureau of Information and Outreach [Buró de Información y Propaganda], s/f [1953]

Leiseca, Juan Martín: *Notes for an ecclesiastical history of Cuba* [*Apuntes para historia eclesiástica de Cuba*]. Havana, Talleres Tipográficos de Carasa y Compañía, 1938.

Los Ministros de Salud Pública en Cuba. [*Cuba's Ministers of Public Health*]*ACIMED.* Havana, September-December, 1998. ISSN 1024-9435.

Milián, Eduardo: «José Martí celebration on Christmas Eve [La Nochebuena Martiana]». Consulted on: https://cuba-historia-y-valores-c.webnode.es/news/la-nochebuena-martiana1/, October 25, 2022.

Pius XII: Apostolic Constitution *Bis saeculari die.* On Marian Sodalities. September 27, 1948. Dicastero per la Comunicazione - Libreria Editrice Vaticana.

_____: *Speech to Marian Sodalities* [*Discurso a las Congregaciones Marianas*]. January 21, 1945. Accessed at https://cupdf.com/document/discurso-pio-xii-a-las-congregaciones-marianas.html on June 27, 2022.

Rey de Castro, P. Felipe: Letter to Rev. Fr. Vice-Provincial, undated. Typed document on Sacred Heart of Jesus Jesuit Residence letterhead. Archive of the Vice-Province of the Antilles, Havana.

_____: Note to Rev. Fr. Vice-Provincial, June 1938. Typed document on Colegio de Belén letterhead. Archive of the Vice-Provincia of the Antilles, Havana.

_____: Note to Rev. Fr. Ramón Calvo, Head of the Vice-Provincia of Cuba, Spiritual Exercises, June 1938. Handwritten document on Colegio de Belén letterhead. Archive of the Vice-Province of the Antilles, Havana.

Rivas Villa S.J, Fr. Ramón & Dr. Roberto Méndez Martínez: *Introduction to the history of the Catholic Church in Cuba* [*Introducción a la historia de la Iglesia Católica en Cuba*]. Historical Background Jesuits in Cuba [Fondo Histórico Jesuitas en Cuba], Havana, 2021.

Rivera Vázquez, Evaristo: *Apostle James School. History of its long pilgrimage [Colegio Apóstol Santiago. Historia de una larga peregrinación].* Vigo, Colegio Apóstol Santiago, 1993.

Rodríguez Díaz, Mons. Antonio: «Monsignor Evelio Díaz Cía, martyred Archbishop [Monseñor Evelio Díaz Cía, el arzobispo mártir]». *New Word [Palabra Nueva],* September 19, 2018. Accessed at https://www.palabranueva.net/mons-evelio-diaz-seguiria-gobernando/ November 22, 2022.

_____: «*The ones that stayed behind* [Los que se quedaron]». *New Word [Palabra Nueva],* Havana, no. 299, April-June, 2022, p.29.

Rosa Mística [Mystic Rose]. A classic vignette of the Agrupación Católica Universitaria. Undadated ACU publicación, Miami [circa 2021]. Digital version.

Rubio Padilla, Juan Antonio: «Has there been a revolution in Cuba? [¿Ha habido una revolución en Cuba?]». *Bohemia,* October 23, 1949, p.3 & 157. Reproduced in *Notebooks of the University of the Airwaves CMQ Network [Cuadernos de la Universidad del Aire del Circuito CMQ].* No.11. Third Course (October 1949-June 1950), «Reality and destiny of Cuba [Actualidad y destino de Cuba]». Havana, Editorial Lex, December 1950, pp. 31-37.

Ruiz Leiro, Dr. Armando: «Remarks of Dr. Armando Ruiz Leiro accepting and thanking the *National Association of Cuban-American Educators*, NACAE, his nomination as Educator of the Year 1995, at the Fourth Annual Conference celebrated in Miami, Florida, October 12-14, 1995» Preceded by a letter from Ricardo Arias Calderón to Dr. A.R.L., January 18, 1996]. Digital version at http://bdigital.binal.ac.pa/iah/PDFRACAL/4.40.5.8.pdf. Accessed on September 19, 2022.

Sáez SJ, P. José Luis: *Presence of the Jesuits in the day-to-day life of Cuba [Presencia de los jesuitas en el quehacer de Cuba].* Two periods and almost four centuries of history. Volume I (1569-1961). Pontificia Universidad Javeriana, Bogotá, 2016.

Santa Cruz y Mallén, Francisco Xavier de: *Histories of Cuban families [Historia de familias cubanas].* Volumes I-VI, Havana, Editorial

Hércules, 1940-1950. Volumes VII-IX, Miami, Ediciones Universal, 1985-1988.

Testimony of Juan Ramón Salvat [*Testimonio de Juan Ramón Salvat*]. Received via email. Miami, January 23, 2023. Author's archive.

Testimony of Fr. Sergio Figueredo SJ on behalf of Fr. Felipe Rey de Castro SJ. [*Testimonio del P. Sergio Figueredo SJ a favor del P. Felipe Rey de Castro SJ.* Gesú Church, Miami, January 2021. Digital transcription by Efraín Zabala. ACU Archive, Miami.

Testimonio oral [Oral testimony] *#1* (Edited). Frs. Felipe Rey de Castro (1889-1952) & Amando Llorente Villa, SJ (1918-2010). Jorge Betancourt, Frank Salas & Pablo López – May 8, 2018. Digital Archive PDF format.

Torreira Crespo, Dr. Ramón: «Brief rapprochement to the History of the Catholic Church in Cuba; conquest, colonization and pseudo-republic [Breve acercamiento a la historia de la Iglesia católica en Cuba: conquista, colonización y pseudorrepública]». Accessed on November 3, 2022 at: http://biblioteca.clacso.edu.ar/ar/libros/cuba/cips/caudales06/fscommand/52T13.pdf

Uría, Ignacio: *Church and Revolution in Cuba* [*Iglesia y Revolución en Cuba*]. Ediciones Encuentro, Madrid, 2011.

Various: *The Voice of the Church in Cuba. One-hundred Episcopal documents* [*La Voz de la Iglesia en Cuba. Cien documentos episcopales*]. Obra Nacional de la Buena Prensa, México, D.F., 1995.

Zardoya Loureda, María Victoria: «Amidst chronicles and critiques. The indigent neighborhoods of Havana as seen by the press [Entre crónicas y críticas. Los barrios de indigentes de La Habana vistos por la prensa»]. *1930-1959. Arquitectura y Urbanismo*, vol. XLI, no. 1, pp. 6-20, 2020. Accessed at https://www.redalyc.org/journal/3768/376862818002/html/, July 15, 2022.

Index

A

Adenauer, Konrad, 139, 147
Aguado, Esteban, Brother, 194, 207, 209, 210
Aguayo, Alfredo, 136
Alba, Ricardo de, 153
Albarrán Domínguez, Joaquín, 15
Albarrán Domínguez, Pedro, 15
Alcalá Zamora, Niceto, 71
Alonso, Bonifacio, Fr., 17
Alonso, Marcelo, 120
Alpízar, Félix, 101
Altamira, Antonio, SJ, 184
Álvarez Mena, Sergio, 182, 209
Alvira, July, 170
Amigó, Gustavo, Fr., 159, 182, 211
Andino, Julio, 58
Andreu Martínez, José Raimundo, 143, 150
Antón, Blanca, 167
Antón, Manuel, 173
Apráiz, Cástor, Fr, 19
Arellano, Roberto, 184
Arenas Amigó, Valentín, 192
Arenas Armiñan, Valentín, 213
Arenas, José, 185
Arenas, Valentín, 19, 136
Arias, Antonio, Fr., 76
Armiñán, Valentín, 73
Armisén, Modesto, Fr., 31
Arnáiz, Francisco [José], 185
Arrupe, Pedro, Fr., 197
Arteaga Betancourt, Manuel, Cardinal, 136, 149, 153, 158, 176, 182, 183, 193, 200, 214
Artime, Manuel, 119, 204, 222

Arvesú Gasset del Castillo, Federico, SJ, 172
Ascanio, Juan, 210
Ascanio, Manuela, [the Mexican], 107
Asensio, Francisco Javier. SJ, 64
Ayala, Ángel, Fr., 45, 47, 71, 175, 206
Azcárate Freyre de Andrade, Fernando, Fr., 46, 53, 55, 95, 119
Azcue, Eusebio, 191

B

Baldor de la Vega, Aurelio Ángel, 166
Baldor de la Vega, Daniel Gonzalo, Fr., 167
Baquero, Gastón, 213
Barbeito Ramos, Francisco, 17
Barbeito, Fr., 217
Barceló, Oscar, 136
Barrientos, Willy, 142
Basterra, Fr., 124
Batista, Fulgencio, 75, 103, 134, 142
Bea, Agustín, Fr., 33
Bedoya, Marcial, SJ, 185
Bedriñaga, Francisco, 98
Bello, Luis, 136
Beltrán Cuesta, Esteban, 58
Beltrán, Esteban, 68
Benedict XIV, 57
Benedict XV, 151
Bercedo, Fr., 168
Bercedo, Teodoro, Fr., 169, 211
Bernal del Riesgo, Alfonso, 19
Betancourt Cisneros, Gaspar, 65

239

Bidegaray Erviti, Cristóbal, 125
Blanco, Luis, 54
Bouso, Antonio, 102
Boza Masvidal, Eduardo, Fr., 95, 124, 182, 214
Buigas, Rafael, 57

C

Calvo, Fr., 169, 194, 208
Calvo, Ramón, Fr., 122, 123, 124, 127, 131, 132, 215
Carauna, Giorgio, Msgr., 125
Cardjin, José, 153
Cardjin, Msgr., 154
Carricarte, Alberto de, 213
Carrillo, Justo, 141
Carvajal, Enrique, Fr., 39, 69, 131
Casal de la Lastra, Julián del, 15
Casteleiro, Jorge, 35, 182, 194, 207, 217, 220
Castro Ruz, Fidel, 15, 187
Castro, Benita, 26, 29, 34, 194
Castro, Gerardo de, 25
Castro, José María de, Fr., 25
Castro, Juana de, 25
Castro, María Ventura, 25
Castro, Maturino de, SJ, 106
Catá, Ceferino, 210
Cataleiro, Segundo, 125
Cateleiro, Jorge, 125
Céspedes y Quesada, Carlos Manuel de, 75, 76, 140
Céspedes y Quesada, Carlos Manuel de,, 141
Chaurrondo, Hilario, Fr., 94
Chibás, Eduardo, 141
Chisholm, Ricardo, 54, 57, 68, 69, 95
Chisholm, Richard, SJ, 124
Cistierna, Salvador, Fr., 100, 133
Coro del Pozo, Angelberto, 54, 58
Cossío, Félix de, 222
Cowley Campodónico, Rafael, 120

Cuervo Rubio, Gustavo, 141, 150
Cuesta, Leonel de la, 115

D

Díaz Cía, Evelio, Msgr., 130
Díaz, Evelio, Msgr., 130, 187
Diego, Eliseo, 203
Domingo, Ángela, 209
Dorta Duque, Manuel, 136, 140
Dorta, Francisco Manuel, 136
Dorta, Juan Manuel, 136
Dust, José, 120

E

Escarpenter, Claudio, 193
Espadas, Román, SJ, 14

F

Farra, Manuel, 98
Fernández Caubí, Luis, 68, 86
Fernández Gayol y Lobato, Fr., 73
Fernández Llano, Ataulfo, 54, 55, 65, 182
Fernández Quevedo, Rosalía, 82, 125
Fernández Santalices, Manuel, 140, 202
Fernández Varela, Ángel, 136, 140, 182, 183, 204, 226
Fiallo, Amelia, 160
Figueredo, Sergio, Fr., 87
Figueroa, Miguel, 40, 43, 52, 62, 65, 100, 138, 157, 176, 193, 205, 207
Fojaco, Rita, 170
Foyaca, Manuel, SJ, 64, 74, 133, 138, 154
Franco, Francisco, 73
Franganillo Balboa, Pelegrín, Fr., 17
Freyre de Andrade, [Hermanos/Brothers], 101

Friguls, Juan Emilio, 132, 198, 199, 202, 213
Fröbes, Joseph, 33

G

Galán Arias, Antonio, Fr., 15
Galán, Román, SJ, 64
Gallardo, René, 124
García Alonso, Aida, 106
García Feito, Belarmino, Msgr., 211
García Marruz, Fina, 203
García Rayneri, Calixto, 95, 182
García Rodríguez, Juan de la Caridad, Cardinal, 227, 229
García, Camilo, Fr., 15, 30, 42, 43, 69, 74, 131
García, Marcelino, 185
García, Sixto, 33
Gasperi, Alcide de, 139, 147
Gastón, Melchor, 141
Gaztelu, Ángel, 188
Gelats, Josefina, 165
Goberna Costas, Rafael, Fr., 17
Gómez Arias, Miguel Mariano, 15
Gómez, José Miguel, 15
Gómez, Miguel Mariano, 79
González del Valle y Morales, Ambrosio, 223
González del Valle, Ambrosio, 183
González García, Pastor, 140
Grau San Martín, Ramón, 75, 79, 98, 115, 141, 142
Gregory XIII, 56
Guarino, Radillo García, 120
Gubianas, Alfonso María, Fr., 62
Guiteras, Antonio, 75, 142
Gundlach, Gustav, 33
Gutierrez del Muro, Fernando, 124
Gutiérrez, Juan A., 121

H

Hernández Egea, Enrique, 123
Hernández Puente, José Manuel, 183
Hernández, José Manuel, 51, 163, 175, 206
Herrera Oria, Ángel, 47, 71
Herrera, Rosita, 170
Huerta, René de la, 89, 183
Hurtado Ruiz, Emilio, 17
Hurtado, Eradia, 170

I

Ibáñez, Víctor, Brother, 210
Ibarguren, Saturnino, Fr., 130
Incera Soriano, César, 54
Injera Soriano, Roberto, 54
Izquierdo del Rio, José María, SJ, 170
Izquierdo, José, 102

J

Jaime Elías, Oscar, 120
John Paul II, 33
Juanes, Benigno, SJ, 184

L

Laredo Bru, Federico, 79
Lasaga y Castellanos, Virgilio, 178
Lasaga, José Ignacio, 46, 53, 55, 56, 58, 64, 100, 105, 120, 140, 150, 157, 176, 178, 182, 193, 209, 214, 223, 245
Lázaro, José M., 65
Leclere, Rosa Pastora, 102
Ledón, Álvaro, 93, 108
Leo XIII, 140
León Lemus, [René], Fr., 185
León Núñez, Jesús, 183
León, Alvaro, 194
Leunis, Jean, Fr., 56

Llorente, Amando, SJ, 88, 163, 178, 217, 221, 227, 229
Lombardi, Riccardo, Fr., 197, 198, 199, 200, 203, 204, 205, 206
Lombotz, Clemente, Fr., 131
López, Antonio, 33
López, Margarita, 136, 213
López, Pablo, 88, 108
Lord, Daniel, 156
Lorraine, Charles of, 49
Losada, Feliz, Fr., 167
Lubich, Chiara, 197

M

Machado, Gerardo, 30, 41, 64, 74, 79, 115, 133, 141, 144, 176
Magraner, Juan, 191
Mañach, Jorge, 144, 146
Manuela, Ascanio, 106
Mariñas, José M., 58
Marinello, Juan, 102, 138
Maritain, Jacques, 147
Martí, José, 187, 188
Martínez Arango, Carlos, 119, 182, 194, 220
Marx, Carlos, 145
Masferrer, Rolando, 116
Maura, Miguel, 71
Mella, Julio Antonio, 19, 76
Méndez Martínez, Roberto, 3, 4, 11, 12, 235
Mendieta Montefur, Carlos, 15, 79
Mendieta, Carlos, 140
Menéndez, Blanca, 173
Merk, Agustín, 33
Milián, Eduardo, 186
Miranda, Virginia, 170
Morales Gómez, Julio, 136, 160, 213
Morillo de Govantes, Consuelo, 213
Mournier, Emmanuel, 147
Moynihan, Edward, Fr., 18

Müller San Martín, Alfredo, Msgr, 214
Mun, Albert de, 151

N

Nuevo, Jesús, Fr., 132
Núñez, Pastorita, 187

O

Oslé Tour, Enrique, 55, 68, 95
Oslé Tour, Enrique, Fr., 154, 211
Ozanam, Federico, 99

P

Pattee, Richard, 175
Pedroso, Mario, 136
Peñalver y Peñalver, Narciso José de, 99
Penichet, América, 213
Pérez Cisneros, Guy, 81
Pérez Durán, Marino, 140, 183, 193
Pérez Serantes, Enrique, Msgr., 69, 88, 159, 188
Pérez Vich, Francisco, 217
Pérez, Aurelio, 185
Piñán, Manuel, SJ, 19
Piñera, Walfredo, 203
Pius X, 151
Pius XI, 56, 64, 151, 155
Pius XII, 48, 49, 57, 64, 132, 140, 151, 155, 156, 157, 164, 193, 197, 204, 212, 221, 235
Portocarrero, René, 94
Primo de Rivera, José Antonio, 73
Prío Socarrás, Carlos, 15, 115, 142, 198
Przywara, Erich, 33

R

Radillo García, Guarino, 121

Rahner, Karl, 33, 34
Ramírez Corría, Carlos, 143
Rasco Bermúdez, José Ignacio, 149, 161
Revuelta Fernández, Virgilio, 194
Rey de Castro, Felipe, SJ, 4, 11, 13, 16, 22, 25, 27, 28, 30, 31, 34, 36, 43, 44, 46, 47, 48, 50, 63, 66, 68, 69, 73, 76, 85, 87, 88, 92, 95, 105, 108, 110, 117, 119, 122, 123, 125, 127, 129, 132, 133, 139, 143, 158, 159, 164, 165, 166, 167, 170, 178, 182, 184, 188, 191, 193, 194,204, 205, 210, 211, 212, 213, 215, 216, 217, 219, 221, 222, 223, 227, 229, 231, 232, 233, 234, 235, 237, *See also* Rey, Fr.
Rey Rodríguez, César, 54
Rey, Apolinar, 25, 26
Rey, Fr., 22, 23, 34, 36, 39, 40, 45, 51, 54, 55, 56, 58, 59, 61, 62, 65, 67, 68, 69, 73, 78, 82, 87, 88, 89, 91, 92, 93, 94, 95, 100, 105, 106, 109, 115, 120, 121, 122, 125, 126, 129, 130, 132, 141, 148, 149, 158, 159, 160, 161, 162, 163, 167, 169, 175, 177, 186,187, 188, 195, 197, 203, 207, 208, 209, 210, 212, 215, 220, 221, 222, 224, 232, 233, 234
Reyes, Armando, 191
Ribas, Esteban, Fr., 202
Ribas, Estevan, Fr., 51
Rivas Serna, Esteban, SJ, 20
Rivas, Esteban, SJ, 19
Rivera, Evaristo, 27
Rivera, José, Fr., 129, 130
Rivero Alonso, José Ignacio, 136
Rivero Hernández, José Ignacio, 136, 213
Rivero Hernández, Oscar, 213
Rivero, José Ignacio, 217
Robert Guerra, Roberto, 165

Robert, Rosalba, 165, 166, 167, 171, 173
Rodales, Antonio, 99
Rodríguez Pérez, José, SJ, 105
Rodríguez, Antonio, Msgr., 130
Rodríguez, Antonio, Msgr.., 70
Rodríguez, Enrique, 58
Rodríguez, Mariano, 94
Rojas Fernández, Carlos E., 120
Romero, José Antonio, Fr., 199
Romeu González, Mario Orlando, 180
Romeu González, Zenaida, 180
Romeu, Antonio María, 179
Rouco, José, 22
Rousseau, Jean Jacques, 145
Rubinos, Fr., 81
Rubio Padilla, Juan Antonio, 16, 17, 20, 21, 22, 23, 24, 39, 41, 42, 43, 53, 54, 75, 94, 106, 141, 142, 143, 148, 149, 150, 160, 176, 204, 209, 220, 226, 236, 245
Rubio Padillla, Juan Antonio, 183
Ruiz Jiménez, Joaquín, 192
Ruiz Leiro, Armando, 55, 118, 119, 120, 121, 165, 183, 209, 211
Ruiz Leiro, Dr., 171, 172
Ruiz, Ceferino, Fr., 211
Ruiz, Manuel, Msgr., 100, 130
Ruiz, Mariano, Fr., 210
Ruiz, Msgr., 42, 80, 99, 124, 155
Rumbaut, Rubén Darío, 160, 202, 204
Ryder, Jeannette, 107

S

Saco, José Antonio, 65
Sáez, Fr., 30, 43
Sáez, José Luis, SJ, 12
Salat, Rudy, 192
Salvat, Juan Manuel, 184, 186
Sanmartín, Maximiliano, Fr., 27
Santa María, Rafael, 184

Sariol, Juan Francisco, 186
Savoy, Eugene of, 49
Schuman, Robert, 139, 147
Simón Gutiérrez, Juan A., 118
Sixtus V, 56
Sobieski, 49
Soler Lezama, José, 142
Suárez Pérez, Juan, 55
Suárez, Juan, 58, 69, 95, 155, 182, 214
Suárez, Juan, Fr., 217
Suárez, Miguel, 213
Sust, Jose, 183

T

Taboada Boloña, 120
Taboada Millás, Carlos M., 121
Torreira Crespo, Ramón, 201
Torriente, Ricardo de la, 102
Tro, Emilio, 116
Tudela, Andrea, 102
Turbo Tolón, Abel, 139

V

Valdés Daussá, Ramiro, 101
Valdés-Dapena Victorio, Antonio, 121
Valdespino, Andrés, 160, 213
Varela, Félix, 65
Victorino, Brother, 19
Vidal y Balaguer, Francisco, 71
Vidaud, Cibeles, 170

W

Wagner, Ignacio, 182
Warner, Ignacio, 204
Welles, Ambassador, 76, 142

Z

Zabala, Efraín, 4, 14, 237
Zardoya, María Victoria, 98, 99
Zayas, Zoila de, 165
Zubizarreta, Valentín, Msgr., 158, 159

Appendix

Book of Life

"... Holy City, Jerusalem, coming down from Heaven...
only those whose names are written in the Lamb's book of life will enter [into it]."
— Rev 21: 10, 27

Consecrated to Jesus through Mary in the Agrupación Católica Universitaria

1931-1939

1. Juan Antonio Rubio Padilla
2. P. Ricardo Chisholm Fernández, SJ
3. Ataulfo Fernández Llano
4. Angelberto de Coro del Pozo
5. César Incera Soriano
6. Roberto Incera Soriano
7. César Rey Rodríguez
8. Julio Andino Pella
9. Eduardo Chilsholm Fernández
10. Rafael Díaz Masvidal
11. Cecilio González Vallejo
12. Alfonso Gutiérrez Sanabria
13. Ernesto Gutiérrez Sanabria
14. Ovidio de Laosa Capote
15. José Ignacio Lasaga Travieso
16. Padre René León Lemus
17. Oscar Lombardo Valladares
17A. Alberto Petit Hernández
18. José Mario Mariña Esquirol
19. Carlos Martínez Arango
20. Ismael Orta Lemus
21. Enrique Oslé Tur, SJ
22. Hno. Miguel Pichardo Peñalver
23. Juan Simón Gutiérrez
24. Padre Juan Suárez Pérez
25. Armando Trelles Reyes
26. Pedro H. Cruz Nogués
27. Mario Alcoz Gómez
28. Enrique Amorín de Armas
29. Debuit deleri
30. Mons. Calixto García Raineri
31. Alfonso Ledo Rodriguez
32. Aurelio Montez Medina
33. Luis Morse Delgado
34. Manuel Otero Ruisánchez
35. Antonio Solinde Gómez
36. P. Juan Suárez Pino
37. Pompirio de la Vega Gander
38. Alfredo Vidal Pérez
39. Julio Alfara Cárdenas
40. José Alvarez Díaz
41. Sergio Alvarez Mena
42. Padre Alberto de Castro Rojas
43. Francisco Cuadra Aguirre

245

44. René Font Canto
45. Francisco Gómez Hernández
46. Juan José Gómez Hernández
47. Eugenio Jiménez Fumagalli
48. José M. Lázaro García
49. Manuel Meza Santo Domingo
50. Francisco Pérez Vich
51. Andrés del Pino Santua
52. Aníbal de los Reyes Noreña
53. Osvaldo Rodríguez Rodríguez
54. José María Rouco Ajá
55. Luis Felipe Salazar
56. Manuel Suárez Carreño
57. Andrés Triny Rodés
58. Juan José Varela Alvarez
59. Luis de Velasco Castellanos
60. Ramón Barcia Conejo
61. Emilio Fernández García
62. Antonio de Goicoechea Cosculluela
63. Manuel Maza Páez
64. José Ramón Miquel Franca
65. Marino Pérez Durán
66. Aureliano Rodríguez Hernández
67. Rafael Talavera Gastón
68. Alfredo Alexander Riva
69. P. Fernando Azcárate Freyre de Andrade
70. Debuit deleri
71. Félix Chediak Ahuayda
72. Santiago Choca Garganta
73. Armando Ruiz Leiro
74. Hector Trelles Reyes
75. Miguel Figueroa Miranda
76. Virgilio Lasaga Castellanos
77. Eladio Armengol Alonso
78. Celso Bilbao Paz
79. Obispo Eduardo Boza Masvidal
80. Guillermo Bravo Viña
81. Enrique Capote Trespalacios
82. Víctor Carriba Rodríguez
83. Guillermo A. Cowley Morales
84. Antonio Chaves Figueredo
85. Felipe España Bárcena
86. Ángel Fernández Varela
87. Alfredo Gasell Díaz
88. Gabriel González Regalado
89. Braulio López Martiarsu
90. José Mieres Cuartas
91. Antonio Pereira Naveira
92. Baldomero Pichardo Peñalver
93. Manuel Luis del Riego González Mata
94. Esteban Rodríguez
95. Oscar Antonio Sala Marrero
96. José Sust Mendez
97. Félix Temes Montenegro
98. Manuel de la Torre Rosell
99. Debuit deleri
100. Debuit deleri
101. Arnaldo Aponte Frau
102. Alberto Armengol Alonso
103. Francisco Barrera Cañedo
104. Gabriel Cuadra Aguirre
105. Francisco Ferrán Rivero
106. Francisco García Bengoechea
107. Luis Homero de la Osa Capote
108. Manuel López Pérez
109. Miguel Luis Morera
110. Abelardo Martínez Escoto
111. Alfonso Matas Larrañeta
112. Octavio Morán Freire
113. Manuel Otero Oliva
114. Gonzalo Pérez Durán
115. Eugenio Revilla García
116. P. Luis Ripol Galán
117. Manolo Vega Penichet
118. Emilio Azcárate Freyre de Andrade
119. Alberto Borges
120. Leopoldo Cancio
121. Jorge Casteleiro Colmenares

Felipe Rey de Castro and the Agrupación Católica Universitaria

122. Alfredo Cortés
123. Orlando Chils Cruz
124. Andrés Delgado Sánchez
125. Víctor Durán
126. José J. Estraviz Sueiras
127. Enrique Ferrer
128. Enrique Fiol Villageliú
129. Juan Fiol Villageliú
130. Carlos Iduarte Andux
131. Agustín Irulegui Soto
132. José Antonio López García
133. Orlando López García
134. José López García de Villalta
135. Bartolomé Monserrat Cardell
136. Jorge Morejón Curiel
137. Alfredo Pereira Naveira
138. Enrique Salabert Toscano
139. Roberto R. Arellano Cano
140. Marcelo Alonso Roca
141. Ángel Alvarez García
142. José R. Agüero Gastón
143. Jorge Betancourt Manrara
144. Leonardo Bravo Viña
145. Alberto Córdova Cordovés
146. Luis María Cowley Morales
147. Luis Cuza Ramírez
148. Juan Chaves Figueredo

149. Luis Fernández Urtiaga
150. Rafael Ferrándiz Zaratiegui
151. Pedro Figueredo Claréns
152. José Alonso García Otero
153. Luciano de Goicoechea Cosculluela
154. Máximo Gómez Vilá
155. Virgilio Lasaga Travieso
156. Álvaro Ledón Ferrán
157. Nivio López Pellón
158. Renán A. Lorenz Navarro
159. Jorge Miquel Franca
160. Jaime Montserrat Cardell
161. Raúl Olivera Borges
162. Aquilino Ordoñez Carceller
163. Jaime Ordoñez Carceller
164. Raúl Ricardo Piñeiro Pujol
165. Juan Plasencia Cosculluela
166. Néstor Porto Jorrín
167. Leandro Rueda Morales
168. Rafael Sánchez Pérez Uría
169. Guillermo Schulz Obadín
170. Octavio Smith Foyo
171. Ignacio Suárez Carreño
172. Fernando J. Subirats Rubio
173. Debut deleri
174. Francisco de la Torre Madraza
175. Benigno Villadóniga Rodríguez

Pase 1940-1949

176. Federico Arvesú Gasset del Castillo
177. Manuel Carreña Camps
178. Efrén Córdova Cordovés
179. Gerardo Coterillo Serna
180. Ramón Choca Garganta
181. Luis Cowan Fernández
182. Andrés Domínguez Mausset
183. Juan Domínguez Mousset
184. Fernando Figueredo Clárens

185. Antonio Fojo Bujosa
186. Debuit deleri
187. Francisco Irañeta Irañeta
188. Manuel Jiménez Figueredo
189. Agustín Jover Tristá
190. Rigoberto Amado León Díaz
191. Carlos Maruri González
192. Felipe Mencía Gutiérrez
193. Roberto Ortiz Crabb

194. Debit deleri
195. Jorge Peón Pérez
196. Pablo Pérez Baquedano
197. José Luis Ripol Galán
198. Enrique Rubio Rubio
199. Serafín Sáenz Basarrate
200. Pedro Santa Cruz Goicoechea
201. Rafael Santa María Martínez
202. Luis Valdés Larralde
203. Manuel Vilaret Aguiar
204. Guido Ascanio de los Santos
205. Alberto Camacho Lagomasino
206. Manuel Carbonell López
207. Pedro Carrillo González
208. José Coutin Monne
209. José Albino Currais Fernández
210. Juan Manuel Dorta-Duque Ortiz, SJ
211. Luis Echevarría Capó
212. Luis P. Garrigó Fernández Valle
213. Melchor Gastón Segrera
214. Manuel Gutiérrez Ortíz
215. Octavio A. Hernández Ortíz
216. Fermín Iduate Andux
217. Ángel Lamela López
218. José Antonio López Naranjo
219. Guillermo Martínez Díaz
220. Ricardo Martínez Ferrer
221. Fernando Martínez Izquierdo
222. José Menéndez Vallejo
223. José Antonio Mestre Sirvén
224. Domingo Nazabal Alvarez
225. Juan O'Nagshen Arango
226. Alfonso Ortega Lanza
227. Juan Ortega Lanza
228. Debuit deleri
229. Victoriano Pardo Menéndez
230. Jesús Pardo Viadero
231. Rafael Portuondo Bello
232. Manuel Prado Rodríguez
233. Benito H. Pratts Respalls
234. Fernándo Quintana Arias
235. Carlos Ripoll Galán
236. Alberto Roque Fernández
237. Orlando Ruiz Leiro
238. Francisco Sala Parera
239. José Antonio Sánchez Martínez
240. Luis Santamarina Muriño
241. Luis Sixto Guerra
242. Evelio Tabío Roig
243. Claudio Ramírez Arellano
244. Antonio Alonso Avila
245. Manuel Alonso Fernández
246. Rafael Andino Ovies
247. Rafael Bedia Pérez
248. Armando Bermúdez López
249. Rubén Bush Santos
250. Carlos Carrillo González de Méndez
251. Francisco Carrillo González
252. Nicolás Colás Velázquez
253. Fernando Costales Sáenz
254. José Luis Espiniella Álvarez
255. Manuel Fariñas Díaz
256. Eduardo Fernández Canal
257. Ángel Figueredo Clarens
258. Enrique Ganzedo Ruíz
259. Guillermo García Tuñón
260. Ambrosio González del Valle
261. Julio Luis Hernández Ortiz
262. René de la Huerta Aguiar
263. José Manuel Miyares Rodríguez
263A Ramiro Rencurrell Ceballos
264. Rafael Malina Sabucedo
265. Miguel Palmer
266. Emilio Perea Michelena
267. Javier Puig García
268. Ramón Rasco Bermúdez
269. Ángel Radón Badell
270. Carlos Rubí Malavez

271. Efrén Surís Ramírez
272. Carlos Zaboada Millás
273. Ignacio Tamayo Mesa
274. Juan Tapia Tamayo
275. Jorge Alberto Valdés
276. Jaime Valhey Arias
277. Joaquín Viadera Wyatt
278. Ignacio Warner Landa
279. José Eduardo Acosta Martínez
280. José D. Acosta Sotolongo
281. Juan F. Aguilar León
282. Ramón Arias Arias
283. José Arruza Cristino
284. Antonio Arvesú Gasset del Castillo
285. Luis Bango Giroud
286. Antonio Barquet Chediak
287. Lorenzo Barquín y Ruiz
288. Pablo Carreño y Camps
289. Alejandro Carrió y Caballero
290. José Orestes Castellanos Averasturi
291. Joaquín Clavería Ferrer
292. Pedro Coll Llach
293. Francisco Contijock Yanci
294. Rodolfo Díaz Pons
295. José Antonio Fernández Bacallao
296. Raúl Fernández Llorca
297. Otto Francesch Renzola
298. Nicolás B. García de Celis
299. Pedro Manuel González Fernández
300. José Luis González Portal
301. Agustín de Goytisolo Recio
302. José Manuel Hernández Puentes
303. Gonzalo Lage Ranzola
304. Gustavo Lage Ranzola
305. Antonio Lasaga Travieso
306. Eduardo Madan Alfonso
307. Emilio Arturo Maril Rivero
308. Antonio Martínez Izquierdo
309. Alberto Oteiza Arjona

310. José Padilla Lagomasino
311. Álvaro Pérez López
312. Raúl Pino Arango
313. Pedro Pablo Pujals Hernández
314. Ramiro Rodríguez Queral
315. Ernesto Rojas Castro
316. Héctor Romeu González
317. Antonio Rubio Rubio
318. César Sabucedo Sabucedo
319. Jorge Salazar Dobarganes
320. Debuit deleri
321. Joaquín Nin Cullmell
322. Manuel Estrada Santaya
323. Debuit deleri
324. Oscar Aizcorbe de la Presa
325. Ismael Angulo Cuellar
326. Genaro Cal Pujol
327. José F. Martínez Piedra
328. Antonio Silva Ferrer
329. Francisco L. del Valle Goicoechea
330. Fernando Andino Ovies
331. Perfecto Arango Arenas
332. Roberto Fernández Morrell Batista
333. Antonio Pérez Alonso
334. Francisco L. Pérez SJ Lerena
335. Marco Ant. Suárez González del Burgo
336. Jorge Echarte Romero
337. Jorge Sardiña García Menocal, SJ
338. Antonio González Mora Ferrer
339. Enrique Hernández Miyares Chávez
340. Antonio Marrero Gutiérrez
341. Ricardo Arellano Suárez
342. Valentín Arenas Amigó
343. Virgilio Acosta Martínez
344. José Ignacio García Bengoechea
345. Ceferino Catá Lage
346. Luis Parajón Díaz
347. José Ignacio Rasco Bermúdez

348. Virgilio E. Beltrán Allen
349. Ignacio Fernández Díaz
350. Benjamín Fernández Menéndez
351. Oscar de Castro Sarría
352. P. Fernando Martínez Caula, SJ
353. José Zayas Rodríguez
354. Roberto Pons Candis
355. Francisco Barroso Machín
356. Raúl Rogés Suárez
357. Luis Fernández Caubí
358. Adolfo Tomás Morales de la Concepción
359. Andrés Raúl Arango Mestre
360. Luis Arias León
361. Juan F. Ascanio Sampera
362. Manuel Díaz Suárez
363. Claudio Escarpenter y Fargas
364. Luis Martínez Iribarren
365. Rolando Rodríguez Fernández
366. Frank Salas Henríquez
367 Roberto Salomón Rugarcía
368. Emilio San Martín San Martín
369. Ricardo Moreira Bandini
370. Basilio del Real Cuervo
371. Otto Díaz Díaz
372. Miguel Kohly de la Torre
373. José R. Adán Espinosa
374. Mario Ambrós López
375. Eugenio González de Méndez
376. Carlos Bujosa Vázquez
377. Antonio Domínguez Mousset
378. Mariano Dumás y del Portillo
379. Eugenio Erquiaga Urquía
380. José Escarpenter Fargas
381. Luis Figueroa Miranda
382. Juan Agustín Gómez Gallet Duplessis
383. Alberto Iglesias Núñez
384. Emilio López González
385. Francisco López Macías
386. Radamés Martínez Alvarado
387. Emiliano Machado Pardo
388. Raúl Morffi Iglesias
389. Debuit deleri
390. José Luis Pérez de Grande
391. Ramón Rodríguez Aguirre
392. Manuel Sanjurjo Paz
393. José Ramón de la Vega Falcón
394. Alberto de la Vega Falcón
395. Luis Vals Angulo
396. Luis Suárez Carreño
397. Alberto Arango Mestre
398. Jorge Arango Mestre
399. Eduardo Arango Varona
400. Roberto Bandín Cruz
401. Antonio Curbelo Leonard
402. Armando Diego Gallo
403. Raúl Echenique González
404. Salvador Juncadella Gama
405. Elpidio Lapinel Escalante
406. Rafael F. Madan Heydrick
407. Mario Martínez Delgado
408. Alberto Martínez Piedra
409. José Maseda Menéndez
410. Carlos Moreira Bandini
411. Felipe Ortíz Gómez
412. Francisco Ortíz Muñoz
413. Lino Pérez Gómez
414. Rafael Portuondo Arnaz
415. Reinaldo Poveda Iñiguez
416. Esteban V. Prellezo del Barrio
417. Vicente Rangel Rivera
418. Eugenio Salomón Rugarcía
419. Miguel Ángel Tomé Biosca
420. José Antonio Cubeñas Peluzzo
421. Pedro Achaval Dávila
422. Adrián Alcoz Cándano
423. Adolfo Arenas Amigó
424. Enrique Arenas Amigó

Felipe Rey de Castro and the Agrupación Católica Universitaria

425. Aurelio Barreta López
426. Jerónimo Boza Boza
427. José Carlos Domínguez del Rosal
428. Otto Fernández Reyes
429. Fabián Lacret Subirats
430. Rinaldo Lago Carbonell
431. José Martínez Delgado
432. José Manuel Meredic de la Campa
433. Debuit Deleri
434. Miguel Ángel Orue Delgado
435. Roberto Oteiza Carricarle
436. Raúl Blanco Quintana
437. Pedro Rafael Faraj
438. Antonio Ravelo Nariño
439. Luis Ros del Castillo
440. Carlos de la Torre Alcoz
441. Antonio del Valle Goicoechea
442. Plinio Villanueva Armentero

Pase 1950-1951

443. Carlos Acosta Martínez
444. Alberto Andino Bolívar
445. Alberto Armas Pérez
446. Felipe Aróstegui Ubernaga
447. Manuel Artime Buesa
448. José Luis Balbona Menéndez
449. Raúl Betancour Ramos
450. César Baró Esteva
451. Rolando Bernal Méndez
452. Julio Bordas Alonso
453. Roberto Burgaleta Fernández
454. Andrés Cao Mendiguren
455. Roberto Diego Gallo
456. José Enrique Echemendía Pérez
457. Alfredo Fernández González
458. Lino B. Fernández Martínez
459. José Manuel Fernández Pérez
460. Julio García Oliveras
461. Julián Gómez Rodríguez
462. Juan Ignacio Gutiérrez Regil
463. Manuel Hernández Acosta
464. Jorge Hernández Miyares
465. José Ignacio Marqués Lancís
466. Ricardo Martínez Vascos
467. Emilio Montero Machado
468. Rodolfo Ortiz Sánchez
469. Francisco Pérez Blanco
470. Rafael Pina Gali
471. Aníbal Porta Bolaños
472. José Rubio Barrios
473. Alexánder Saker Sr. Hani
474. Félix Solaún Zabala
475. Guillermo Antón Romero
475. Jorge Suárez Marrill
476. Manuel Vigil Rodríguez
477. Rafael Yaniz Pérez
478. Arnaldo Abreu Rivas
479. Manuel Antón Zapatero
480. Antonio Arruza Man
481. José Báez Mujar
482. José Joaquín Balerdi Oyarbide
483. Carlos M. Barba García
484. Celestino Borrón Carreras
485. Joaquín Bosque Cárdenas
486. Luis de Jesús Caballero Valdés
487. Joaquín Camella Anclada
488. Pedro Entenza Escobar
489. José Raúl Corujo Blanco
490. José Antonio Esnard Lacorbe
491. Jorge Fernández Montejo
492. Luis Gómez Sainz-Terrones
493. Orlando González Betancourt
494. Augusto Gutiérrez Gutiérrez
495. Alfredo Hernández Díaz de Acevedo

496. Francisco Javier Márquez Arechabala
497. Sergio Miguel Martí Martínez
498. Ernest Martín Fuste
499. José Mela Pérez
500. Jorge Menéndez Arenas
501. Vicente Nonell Espiniella
502. Ernesto Núñez de Villavicencio Chacón
503. Santiago Núñez de Villavicencio Chacón
504. Manuel Alberto Pedrozo Pelegrín
505. Fernando Pérez Montes
506. Antonio Pérez Rodríguez
507. Joel Raurell Vidal
508. Rafael Rodríguez Fernández
509. Juan José Sotus Romero
510. Pedro Luis Tamayo de la Torre
511. Juan José Tetzeli Deym
512. Rev. Carlos García-Carreras Seís
512. Carlos de la Uz y Arenal
513. Carlos del Valle González de Méndez
514. Luis López Álvarez

Editor's translation of the original Spanish letter included in November 1952 issue of *Esto-Vir* [latin for "be a man"]

Rome, Sep-24-1952

Mr. President of the Agrupación Católica Universitaria:

I learned that the Agrupación Católica Universitaria, which you so aptly preside, is going to celebrate its traditional annual Assembly next October and that, following an in depth look at a timely theme, will cover remaining activities carried out in various apostolic fields: poor neighborhoods, hospitals, secular schools, prisons, leprosarium, etc.

The mere listing of these well known works and, even more, their continuance over time in face of no small sacrifices, brings clearly to light that most solid foundation from which they are erected, which can be no other than a vigorous interior spirit acquired at the Marian Sodality by means of Spiritual Exercises, a rich sacramental life and spiritual direction.

Back in 1950, when the International Congress of Directors of Marian Sodalities led by the Society of Jesus was held here in Rome, I had the good fortune of meeting your founder, Father Felipe Rey de Castro; I admired his initiatives at the time, his knowledge of men, his adaptation to modern times and the fruits of blessings obtained thanks to your generous and constant collaboration. Later, I had the opportunity to propose your Sodality as model for other nations. I can now see that time has not affected the opinion which I held of it, but rather that

---

Dr. Jorge S. Casteleiro
President, Agrupación Católica Universitaria
Havana (Cuba)

now, as then, it follows an identical trajectory, solidly forming members, 230 professionals and a similar number of university students, able to powerfully influence the nation's public square.

Last February, when God chose to suddenly call your dearest Founder and Director to Himself, some might have feared that with his disappearance your Work would suffer a setback. But no. The good Father knew to build on living rock — Christ, Holy Spirit, devotion to Virgin Mary, Sacraments, Spiritual Exercises. Thus, your Agrupación, far from dying with its Founder, feels even more strengthened and protected from on High to fertilize the good seeds deposited in your generous hearts so they might bloom into new apostolic endeavors.

During these coming days you will be unveiling the portrait bust of Fr. Rey de Castro. May this bust bring to mind the wise counsel received from him; may it animate and comfort you in the struggle for God and for the Church; the bust will continue to speak to you and counsel you through the new Director that God has given you who, sparing no work or sacrifice, will lead the Agrupación to conquests of new laurels of eternal glory, always following the norms of your much admired Cardinal Archbishop. Continue, then, fervently cultivating an intense spiritual life. Continue to carry out the same university, professional, catechistic, social and missionary apostolate.

I beseech Most Holy Virgin Mary, your celestial Patroness, to always continue lavishing her maternal blessing; to which is now added the intercession of Father Rey de Castro and the vigor of your own prayers, without overlooking that of those in your own ranks that have passed on to complete service to the Holy Church.

Servant in Christ to you all

[Signature]

(John B. Janssens, S.J.)

Felipe Rey de Castro and the Agrupación Católica Universitaria

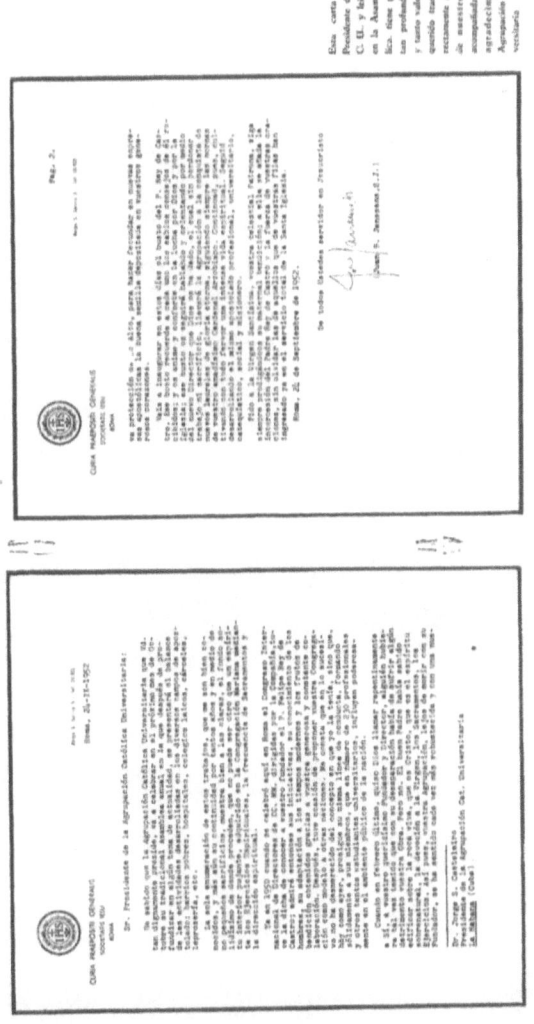

REPRODUCTION OF ORIGINAL LETTER INCLUDED IN NOVEMBER 1952 ISSUE OF *ESTO-VIR* [LATIN FOR "BE A MAN"], THE AGRUPACIÓN CATÓLICA UNIVERSITARIA'S INTERNAL NEWSLETTER \

Prayer
to Fr. Felipe Rey de Castro S.J.

Thank you, God Our Father, for gifting us Felipe Rey de Castro, priest, prophet, teacher and pastor.

Thank you, Jesus, for selecting him and forging him into a Teacher.

Thank you, Holy Spirit, for anointing him thus sanctifying him and sanctifying our people.

Our Lady of Charity, intercede for he who prayed to you 50 times per day and present his immense charitable work to Our Father.

St. Ignatius, intercede for the beatification of your disciple.

(Implore for the favor you desire to beatify Fr. Felipe and to live each of his teachings).

Amen

Author: Archbishop of Havana Juan de la Caridad Cardinal García
Editor's translation from the original Spanish

ORACIÓN
A P. FELIPE REY DE CASTRO S.J.

Gracias, Dios Padre, por regalarnos a Felipe Rey de Castro, sacerdote, profeta, maestro y pastor.

Gracias, Jesucristo, por elegirlo y convertirlo en Maestro.

Gracias, Espíritu Santo, por ungirlo para santificarlo y santificar al pueblo.

Santa María de la Caridad, ruega por quien te rezaba 50 veces al día y presenta a Dios Padre su inmensa obra caritativa.

San Ignacio, intercede para la beatificación de tu discípulo.

(Pídase la gracia que desea para la beatificación del Padre Felipe y vivir cada uno sus enseñanzas).

Amén

Autor: Arzobispo de La Habana Juan de la Caridad Cardenal García

www.ingramcontent.com/pod-product-compliance
Lightning Source LLC
Chambersburg PA
CBHW030515080526
44586CB00011B/199